THIRD EDITION

Practical Handbook to

Elementary Foreign Language Programs

(FLES*)

Including *Sequential FLES, FLEX,* and *Immersion* Programs

Gladys C. Lipton

National Textbook Company
a division of NTC/CONTEMPORARY PUBLISHING COMPANY
Lincolnwood, Illinois USA

DEDICATION

This book is dedicated to children all over the world who have known the joy of learning another language in the elementary or middle school, and to four very special children: Lorrie, Jeremy, Seth, and Rachel.

This book is also dedicated to **FLES*** practitioners all over the country; the members of the National **FLES*** Commission of AATF and the National **FLES*** Committee of AATSP; the many, many teachers from kindergarten through university levels who have attended the National **FLES*** Institute at the University of Maryland, Baltimore County; and all the members of the Advisory Board of the National **FLES*** Institute.

MORE ABOUT THE AUTHOR

As a prominent educator and leader in her field, Dr. Lipton (often referred to as the guru of **FLES***), has published widely in professional journals, and serves as Associate Editor of the **FLES*** section of *Hispania*. She is the Chair of the National **FLES*** Commission of AATF and the former Chair and founder of the National **FLES*** Committee of AATSP. She is the President of the National American Association of Teachers of French (AATF), 1998–2000. Winner of ACTFL's prestigious Florence Steiner Award for outstanding K–12 Foreign Language Leadership, Dr. Lipton serves as a consultant on K–12 Foreign Language Programs, nationally and internationally, and has presented keynote addresses at numerous conferences for foreign language teachers and supervisors as well as for non-foreign language generalist administrators and supervisors.

Editorial Director: Cindy Krejcsi
Executive Editor: Mary Jane Maples
Editor: Elizabeth Millán
Director, World Languages Publishing: Keith Fry
Design Manager: Ophelia M. Chambliss
Cover and Interior Design: Karen Christoffersen
Production Manager: Margo Goia
Production Coordinator: Denise M. Duffy

ISBN: 0-8442-9330-X

Published by National Textbook Company,
a division of NTC/Contemporary Publishing Company,
4255 West Touhy Avenue,
Lincolnwood (Chicago), Illinois 60646-1975 U.S.A.

Library of Congress Catalog Card Number: 97-69971

7 8 9 VP 0 9 8 7 6 5 4 3 2 1

ACKNOWLEDGMENTS

I should like to express appreciation to the hundreds of **FLES*** and secondary school foreign language teachers with whom I have worked over the years. I am grateful for the intellectual stimulation they have provided as well as the warm friendships that have developed.

I am particularly thankful to my husband, Robert Lipton, for his patience, his encouragement, and his tremendous support of this project as well as the many other endeavors I have undertaken.

I am indebted to Keith Fry, Director/World Languages Publishing at NTC/Contemporary Publishing Company, for so many things: for his expertise, assistance, and encouragement of the writing of this third edition of the book.

Finally, I would like to thank my first foreign language methods teacher at Brooklyn College (New York City), who introduced me to the attractions of **FLES*** by scheduling a visit to a grade 4 French *FLES* class in a nearby elementary school. Little did I know then that that visit would be the initial thrust in my exciting career as a **FLES*** teacher for more than seven years, secondary school foreign language teacher, coordinator, and supervisor (K–12), doctoral student, author, director, teacher-trainer in **FLES*** and secondary school methods, workshop presenter, keynote speaker, editor, consultant—who knows what else!

GLADYS C. LIPTON
Director, National **FLES*** Institute
University of Maryland, Baltimore County

Contents

CHAPTER VII

RECRUITMENT, PREPARATION, AND SELECTION OF **FLES*** TEACHERS   65

CHAPTER VIII

NATIONAL STANDARDS FOR FOREIGN LANGUAGE LEARNING AND **FLES*** CURRICULUM DEVELOPMENT   85

CHAPTER IX

WHAT APPROACHES ARE USED IN ALL TYPES OF FLES* PROGRAMS? 123

Cʜᴀᴘᴛᴇʀ X

FLES* Mᴇᴛʜᴏᴅᴏʟᴏɢʏ: Iɴsɪᴅᴇ ᴛʜᴇ FLES* Cʟᴀssʀᴏᴏᴍ 157

CHAPTER XI
NATIONAL STANDARDS FOR FOREIGN LANGUAGE LEARNING AND THE CONTEXTUALIZED FOCUS OF **FLES***   197

CHAPTER XIV

PR FOR FLES*—HOW TO GET PUBLICITY FOR YOUR PROGRAM 273

CHAPTER XV

SELECTED STRATEGIES, GAMES, AND ACTIVITIES FOR FLES* 301

Introduction

WHAT IS **FLES***?

The world is changing. Technology is changing. Educational programs are also changing—and **FLES*** programs are changing, too. But the basic premise of introducing children to one or more foreign languages (and cultures) has been with us a long time. And yet, each new generation of parents and teachers rediscovers the enormous educational and intercultural value of an early start in the study of foreign languages.

In the 1950s and 1960s, **FLES*** programs dealt with dialogues and songs about candy, crayons, and colors. These simple topics are not sufficiently interesting to today's generation of children, who have become blasé about intergalactic travel and interstellar communication. Not surprisingly, though, **FLES*** programs have endured, have been revived and reinstated, have developed new approaches and styles, have become important as an interdisciplinary approach to elementary school education, and have branched out to offer new and exciting options.

Definitions at a Glance

FLES* (say "flestar") is the overall term for all types of foreign language instruction in the elementary and middle schools (kindergarten through grade 8). It encompasses the three major program models: *Sequential FLES, FLEX,* and *Immersion.*

Sequential FLES is an introduction to one foreign language for two or more years, with a systematic and sequential development of integrated language abilities (listening, speaking, reading, and writing) and culture, within the parameters of themes, topics, or content areas. Good fluency is expected if scheduled five times a week (thirty minutes a day) for four or more years (approximately 49 percent of all elementary foreign language programs).

FLEX is an introduction to one or more foreign languages, with few language skills expected. Little fluency (but sufficient language and culture to motivate students to continue) is expected with a once- or twice-a-week program that emphasizes limited language acquisition and extensive cultural awareness (approximately 49 percent of all elementary foreign language programs).

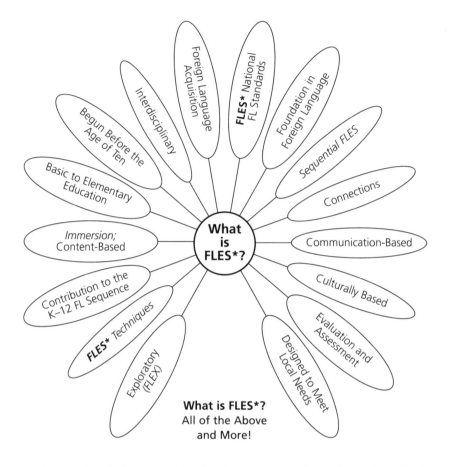

What is FLES*?
All of the Above
and More!

Immersion is the use of the foreign language throughout the school day by teachers and students for teaching the various subjects of the elementary school curriculum. Good fluency in the foreign language is expected after four or more years in the program (approximately 2 to 3 percent of all elementary foreign language programs). NOTE: There may be all kinds of variations in each program model as to goals, expectations, schedules, and student outcomes.

FOR REFLECTION

A **FLES*** teacher who walks into an elementary school classroom of 25 children is confronted with a veritable salad of different learning styles—at least 25 varieties.

ELIZABETH MILLER (1995, 1)

Why **FLES***?

WHAT IS THE IMPORTANCE OF **FLES*** PROGRAMS?

Many people find it difficult to understand that the question "Why **FLES***?" is still being asked. In the 1950s and 1960s, the heyday for elementary school foreign language programs in the past, parents and administrators were easily convinced that an early introduction to a foreign language for young children was worthwhile, interesting, important, and even chic! Toward the end of the 1960s, taxpayers began to look for ways to cut budgets, and all kinds of questions were asked all over again. Some of the contemporary reasons for implementing **FLES*** programs today are:

- Children enjoy learning a foreign language.
- Children are curious about strange sounds and secret codes.
- Children are curious about customs in other countries.
- Children are excellent mimics and are less self-conscious about using authentic pronunciation than are adolescents or adults.
- Children do not generally object to repetition and drill, particularly if used in the context of games and activities.
- Children, because of their ability to imitate so well, are capable of developing good habits of listening and correct pronunciation.
- Children, by starting second language study early, advance in the development of an intelligent understanding of language concepts, which will help in learning additional languages.
- Children enjoy correlating the study of a foreign language with other areas of the school curriculum.
- Children begin to master the sound system of the foreign language and develop a feeling of "at-homeness" with the language.
- Children's foreign language exposure helps them develop an openness to other people and other ways of life and helps them understand that English is not the only language in the world.
- In their study of a foreign language, children begin to comprehend that knowing a foreign language may help them in their future careers.

RESEARCH FINDINGS—A RATIONALE FOR **FLES***

Over the years, parents, educators, researchers, early childhood specialists, and others have endorsed the concept that the best time to introduce foreign languages is when the child is young, before language and speech patterns are fixed, probably before the age of eleven, based to a large extent on the recommendations of Dr. Wilder Penfield, a Canadian neuropsychologist (1959).

Research studies yield the following significant information concerning the implementation of foreign languages in elementary schools (K–8):

1. Children have the ability to learn and excel in the pronunciation of a foreign language. (See Dulay, Burt, and Krashen 1982; Fathman 1981; Krashen 1983; Krashen, Long, et al., 1982; Krashen and Terrell 1983.)

2. Children who have studied a foreign language in elementary school achieve expected gains and have even higher scores on standardized tests in reading, language arts, and mathematics than those who have not. (See Lipton 1979; Masciantonio 1977; Rafferty 1986; McCaig 1988.)

3. Children who have studied a foreign language show greater cognitive development in such areas as mental flexibility, creativity, divergent thinking, and higher-order thinking skills. (See Foster and Reeves 1989; Landry 1973, 1974; Rafferty 1986.)

4. Children who have studied a foreign language develop a sense of cultural pluralism (openness to and appreciation of other cultures). (See Carpenter and Torney 1973; Hancock, Lipton, et al., 1976; Lambert and Tucker 1972; Lambert and Klineberg 1967.)

5. Children studying a foreign language have an improved self-concept and sense of achievement in school. (See Genesee 1987; Masciantonio 1977.)

6. Elementary-school foreign language study has had a favorable effect on subsequent foreign language study in high school and college. (See Brega and Newell 1967; Carroll 1967; Dunkel and Pillet 1962; Sommerville Board of Education 1962; Vocolo 1967; Lipton, Morgan, and Reed 1996.)

7. Harold Chugani, brain neurologist at the Children's Hospital at Wayne State University in Michigan, by examining glucose metabolization, has observed a timetable under which various regions of the brain develop. The brain continues to consume glucose through age ten, and then slows down (Nadia 1993).

8. Boyer (1995), in his recommendations for the elementary school of the future, gives strong support for elementary school foreign language programs.

9. Lipton, Morgan, and Reed (1996) report that on the 1995 Advanced Placement French Language Examination, the group who performed best were the 917 candidates who indicated that they had French in grades 1–3.

Children as Language Learners

We have all heard that "children are like sponges—they just soak up foreign languages." Families traveling abroad often report that the children learn to speak the foreign language much faster than the adults. There are many, many testimonials to this effect, particularly with regard to children before puberty. But, in addition to the testimonials, we have solid research studies that weigh the scales in favor of starting the study of a foreign language before the age of ten.

Some research studies confirming this ability in children have been available for years. For example, Penfield (1959), a neurosurgeon, encouraged the study of foreign languages before the age of ten or eleven, before the language and speech patterns of the brain lose their plasticity. Lenneberg (1967, 179) hypothesized that the "development of specialization of functions in the left and right sides of the brain begins in childhood and is completed at puberty."

Sylwester (1995, 20) summarizes some of the biological brain research. He indicates that the "networks for sounds that aren't in the local language may atrophy over time, due to lack of use. We can see its results in the difficulty that most older Japanese adults have with the English 'l' and 'r' sounds, which aren't in the Japanese language. A Japanese adult who learned English as a child would have no trouble with the two sounds." Asher (1988, 256) concurs when he indicates that "if students start their second language learning before puberty, they have the greatest chance of acquiring a near-native pronunciation." Others also agree: Dulay, Burt, and Krashen (1982, 78) state that "children under ten who experience enough natural communication in the target language nearly always succeed in attaining native-like proficiency, while those over fifteen rarely do."

Some of the most convincing biological evidence of the child's ability to learn languages has been presented by several brain researchers (see Nadia 1993). As mentioned earlier, Harold Chugani has used PET scans "to observe which brain structures were metabolizing the most glucose, and therefore were the most active" (PET, or positron emission tomography, is a recent brain imaging technique). Michael Phelps, a biophysicist and chair of the Department of Molecular and Medical Pharmacology at the University of California, Los Angeles, advocates great use of the potential of children's brainpower: "If we teach our children early enough, it will affect the organization or 'wiring' of their brains." He also says that "foreign language instruction is often deferred until high school, despite the fact that youngsters can learn to speak like natives—that is, to think in the language without having to translate—whereas teenagers or adults usually cannot. When small children learn a new language, the ability to use that language is wired in the brain." Both researchers agree that "connections are strengthened by repeated use."

Susan Curtiss, a professor of linguistics at the University of California, Los Angeles, has been researching the way children learn languages. Curtiss states that "we now know that when it comes to learning language, an immature (young child's) brain offers a huge advantage" (Wisconsin Public Radio Association 1995, 5). (For more information on brain research, see Begley 1996 and Nadia 1993.)

In an article devoted to research on the functions of a child's brain, Begley (1996, 56–57) indicates some preliminary information about the "language brain." The "learning window" of opportunity for language learning is indicated "from birth to 10 years." This has tremendous support for the introduction of foreign language to young children before the age of ten, because in that period, the circuits of the brain are wired. According to Begley, Chugani says "it's far easier for an elementary-school child to hear and process a second language and even speak it without an accent." Begley notes that still another researcher, Patricia Kuhl, of the University of Washington, has developed the concept of a "perceptual map" of the brain. Based on the wiring of the circuits of the brain, such a map helps to explain why "a child taught a second language after the age of 10 or so is unlikely ever to speak it like a native."

Language acquisition researchers are in agreement that "preteen children are more successful at learning the phonology of a new language" (Fathman 1982, 120). Thus, near-native pronunciation is one of the outstanding benefits of an early start.

School reformers such as Postman (1995, 150) think that "if it is important that our young value diversity of point of view, there is no better way to achieve it than to have them learn a foreign language, and, it should go without saying, to begin to learn it as early as possible." Boyer (1995, 73) urges that "foreign language instruction begin early, certainly by the third grade, that it be offered daily, and be continued through all the grades."

The long-range benefits of starting a foreign language before the age of ten are cited by Krashen and Terrell (1983, 45) when they indicate that "children are 'better' with respect to ultimate attainment over the long run. Those who start second languages as children will usually reach higher levels of competence than those who start as adults." The results on the 1995 Advanced Placement French Language Exam demonstrated that students who started French in grades 1–3 and 4–6 outperformed students who started French at grade 7 and later. (Also see "What Research Do We Have About **FLES*** Programs?" at the end of this chapter.)

More Research Studies Are Needed

Although we have a considerable amount of research indicating that the early study of a foreign language is useful, worthwhile, and highly beneficial to children, more research studies are needed on the following questions:

- What are the short-term and longitudinal results of studying a foreign language in elementary school and the effect on English language skills and achievement in the different subject areas?

- What are the short-term and longitudinal results of studying a foreign language in elementary school and the formal achievement in the foreign language from the point of view of all four abilities and culture?

Suggested Criteria for Research on FLES* Programs

1. Does the research have a solid research design?
2. Have all the major variables been controlled? (Apples and oranges should *not* be compared.)
3. Do the researchers have research backgrounds?
4. Is the research being conducted in the United States? What kind of population is involved? How does the research compare with research conducted elsewhere in the United States?
5. Is the research replicable?
6. Have the researchers included a large enough sample?
7. Is the research being conducted in an objective fashion, without bias?
8. Do the data support the conclusions?
9. Are the conclusions being drawn *solely* from anecdotal evidence?
10. Are programs formally evaluated every five to seven years and reviewed annually? Have modifications been made in the programs, based upon evaluation and review?

FLES* appeals to many different people. For example, a superintendent of schools of a large school district said:

> I believe that the earlier we can have youngsters come in contact with a second language, the more they will learn, the more retention they will have.

A principal of an elementary school said:

> I have always been an advocate and strong supporter of having foreign languages in the elementary schools as a supplement to the curriculum.

I have always felt that learning a foreign language increases the students' understanding of a country and its culture.

A parent of a fourth-grade child expressed great enthusiasm for a program in her child's school:

The elementary school-age children have an enthusiasm to learn that will not always be with them. While learning colors, foods, and numbers, children are made aware of the customs, family lifestyles, history, art, and culture of other children in the world at a time when they need to know there are many other ways, besides their own, in which to live and work.

In response to the suggestion to leave foreign languages to the high schools, it is usually too late, once they have become teenagers, to convince them that they should be interested in something else besides their school social life and career goals. It is common knowledge that older students have far more difficulty learning a second language than elementary school-age children. The difficulty could be lessened quite a bit if the student had a basic understanding and interest implanted in elementary school.

Students are made to realize the importance of other ways of doing things. This may well be one of the best ways to teach the new generation not to discriminate against, belittle, or be unwilling to accept people simply because they are "foreign." If students have not had exposure to, or appreciation of, foreign languages and lifestyles, or do not understand that people can be different, they will have no understanding, respect, or interest in foreign concerns and people.

FLES* is not just fun and games to the exclusion of the sequential development of language skills in *FLES* and *FLEX,* or to the exclusion of content in *Immersion* programs. A **FLES*** program is not a frill when it is carefully designed; when there is a competent, trained teacher; when it implements a valid curriculum; and when the goals of the program are clearly understood by the educational community, parents, administrators, teachers, and students. When effectively taught, the learning process in **FLES*** is joyful for students and teachers. This is the not-so-secret "secret" component of **FLES***!

The National Standards in Foreign Language Education Project (1996, 98) stresses the importance of starting foreign languages early: "Just as mathematical reasoning skills should be learned and applied in many contexts and operations according to the age and developmental level of the child, so too should the elements of another language and culture be learned and applied."

Other support for starting foreign languages as early as possible has come from the following sources:

1. The National Association of Elementary School Principals passed a resolution in support (1987).

2. The U.S. Secretary of Education's *James Madison Elementary School Report* recommended an early start in foreign language study (Bennett 1988).

3. The National Council of State Supervisors of Foreign Languages (NCSSFL) and the American Council on the Teaching of Foreign Languages (ACTFL) issued a joint statement in support of **FLES*** programs (1990). The text of this joint statement follows.[1]

NCSSFL/ACTFL Statement on the Study of Foreign Languages in Elementary Schools

Education studies and reports over the last fifteen years have caused educators, legislators, and policymakers to reaffirm the priority of foreign language instruction in our nation. New goals and objectives of proficiency in languages demand longer, well-articulated programs to meet critical needs of literacy, national defense, and international economics.

There are a number of national, regional, and local policy bodies ready with resources to assist language educators in reaching their goals. Educators must recognize and use this assistance. Citizens are demanding that more Americans become proficient in other languages and that they understand other cultures.

The National Council of State Supervisors of Foreign Languages (NCSSFL) endorses beginning foreign language instruction in the elementary grades for all students. We recognize the prevalence of three different types of elementary school programs. They are *FLEX*, *FLES*, and *Immersion*. On a continuum, these programs vary in levels of language proficiency to be reached, amount of cultural knowledge to be gained, and time required to reach the programs' goals.

FLEX (foreign language experience or exploratory) is designed to provide limited foreign language experience to presecondary students. *FLES* (foreign language in the elementary school) seeks to afford students sequential language learning experience which works toward proficiency in the four abilities. *Immersion* programs deliver all or a large part of content learning through means of the foreign language.

In an effort to ensure high quality instruction, elementary school foreign language teachers should complete training which encompasses appropriate methods and materials for elementary school foreign language instruction, the nature of the elementary school learner, and the nature of the elementary school curriculum. It is highly recommended that modern foreign language teachers possess a minimum oral proficiency level of Advanced on the ACTFL/ETS proficiency scale.

---

[1] Reprinted by permission of ACTFL and NCSSFL.

Articulation and integration with middle school or junior high school curriculum are integral components of a foreign language sequence that leads to usable foreign language proficiency. All skill-building programs which start in the elementary grades must have continuity between elementary and secondary levels. In addition, a process for program evaluation is essential when implementing these foreign language models.

NCSSFL believes that the best foreign language programs in the elementary schools will result from a careful study of the outcomes desired by each local district and its citizens. It is hoped that this statement clearly indicates that we, as foreign language program specialists, desire quality instruction and carefully planned programs to assure success in elementary school foreign language programs.

DOES FLES* HELP AP FRENCH STUDENTS PERFORM BETTER?

In data released about the 1995 Advanced Placement French Language Examination, Lipton (University of Maryland, Baltimore County), Morgan, and Reed (both from the Educational Testing Service) provide strong evidence of support for **FLES*** (1996). The researchers asked several questions of candidates for the 1995 AP Exam to determine the possible effects of the length of French study on AP grades. When only the students who identified themselves as learning French in an academic setting rather than abroad or at home were considered, the group who performed best on the AP French Language Exam were the 917 candidates who indicated that they had French in grades 1–3. The AP grade scale goes from a high of 5 to a low of 1. Overall results were as follows:

WHEN FL STUDY BEGAN	AVERAGE AP GRADE
Grades 1–3	3.25
Grades 4–6	2.95
Grades 7–9	2.84
Grades 10–12	2.32

The performance differences were greater for the listening and speaking sections of the exam than for the writing and reading sections. However, advantages from an early start in language learning are discernible in each of the skills.

What Research Do We Have About FLES* Programs? A Summary

1. Children have the ability to learn and excel in the pronunciation of a foreign language.

2. Children who have studied a foreign language in elementary school achieve expected gains and have even higher scores on standardized tests in reading, language arts, and mathematics than those who have not.

3. Children who have studied a foreign language show greater cognitive development in such areas as mental flexibility, creativity, divergent thinking, and higher-order thinking skills.

4. Children who have studied a foreign language develop a sense of cultural pluralism (openness to and appreciation of other cultures).

5. Children studying a foreign language have an improved self-concept and sense of achievement in school.

6. Elementary-school foreign language study has a favorable effect on subsequent foreign language study in high school and college.

7. Brain researchers question why foreign language is deferred until high school. When small children learn a new language, "the ability to use that language is wired in the brain." By examining glucose metabolization, Chugani has observed a timetable under which various regions of the brain develop. The brain continues to consume glucose rapidly through age ten and then slows down (Nadia 1993).

8. Boyer (1995), in his recommendations for the elementary school of the future, urges that "foreign language instruction begin early, certainly by third grade, that it be offered daily, and be continued through all the grades."

9. Lipton, Morgan, and Reed (1996) report that on the 1995 Advanced Placement French Language Examination, students who began their study of French in grades 1–3 and 4–6 outperformed those who began in grade 7 or later.

FOR REFLECTION

If it is important that our young value diversity of point of view, there is no better way to achieve it than to have them learn a foreign language as early as possible.

Neil Postman (1995, 50)

The Current Status of All Types of **FLES*** Programs

Many parents, administrators, and teachers are interested in starting some kind of foreign language program in elementary and middle schools (K–8). There are several states with some type of "mandated" or "semi-mandated" program: Arizona, Louisiana, Oklahoma, New Jersey, Montana, Pennsylvania, Massachusetts, Florida, Colorado, Oregon, New Mexico, Georgia, North Carolina, and others; along with priorities for Texas, Hawaii, and others. Kansas City, Missouri, has had a court-mandated program.

Many school districts have successful programs without a mandate. Approximately one-tenth of all elementary schools in the country have some kind of foreign language program in both public and private schools. Even though there is high interest in this topic in various segments of the educational community, there are many questions about which kind of program is best. One thing is certain—we want the *best*—we want a *quality* program for our children! This guide is dedicated to helping parents, school board members, administrators, and teachers in school communities in making wise decisions at the local level. The author has had contact with a large number of policymakers, school administrators, and teachers across the country who are involved with all types of **FLES*** programs, and many of their experiences, ideas, successes, and concerns are reflected in this guide.

In these days of budget crises on the national, state, and local levels, some misguided policymakers say, "They can always take foreign language when they get to high school!" Foreign languages and the study of foreign cultures for children are *too important* to postpone until the high school years. Besides, there is a great deal of research indicating the benefits of foreign language study for children. (For a rationale for teaching foreign languages to children, see Chapter Two.) It would seem that budget crises are going to be with us for many years (see Chapter Six), so we need to explore the most cost-effective means to deliver the kind of **FLES*** program that is best for our children. Some of the new issues in education involve site-based management, school choice, and restructuring of schools. The inclusion of foreign language programs in the elementary school appears to be an increasingly popular choice with the new teams of parents and school administrators as decision makers.

FLES* programs focus on different directions, according to the needs and interests of the school community. For example, some emphasize the importance of global and multicultural education, some become part of the holistic elementary school curriculum, some are related to bilingual programs, and some work toward long sequences leading to foreign language proficiency.

DESCRIPTION OF THE PROGRAM MODELS

The three **FLES*** program models *(Sequential FLES, FLEX,* and *Immersion)* have a great deal in common. They provide foreign language instruction to children, they sensitize children to different ways of life, they help children develop an openness to people from other cultures, they encourage students to continue FL study at upper levels, and they are valuable FL programs that enrich children's lives. Each contributes, in different ways, to a K–12 FL sequence.

Sequential FLES

This type of program permits a wide variety of formats and time and scheduling patterns, and has as its major focus the teaching of one language for two or more school years. The goal is to provide instruction in the four abilities: listening (understanding), speaking, reading, and writing, as well as cultural awareness. The *Sequential FLES* program attempts to provide long exposure to one foreign language, with the expectation of good foreign language proficiency, depending on the goals, the budget, the schedule, the frequency of the classes, the language ability of the teacher, and other factors. *Sequential FLES* is sometimes called "revitalized" or "intensive."

Some of the general characteristics of the *Sequential FLES* program model are:

- Foreign language in grades K–8
- One language taught for two or more school years
- Foundation language learning that includes the four abilities and culture
- Outcomes resulting in good proficiency within the parameters of the program, if scheduled five times a week for a minimum of thirty minutes for each session
- Promotion of interest in future foreign language study
- Promotion of interest in the target language and culture

- High correlation of foreign language study with social studies, language arts, and other areas of the elementary school curriculum through thematic units and situations
- Integral part of the elementary school curriculum
- Use of either classroom or itinerant teachers (other delivery models are possible)
- Worthwhile program for *all* students in grades K–8
- Wide variety of materials to support the content of the program and the interests of the students
- Wide range of time devoted to foreign language based on local needs, finances, and grade levels, spanning from 5 to 20 percent of the school schedule
- Contributes to a K–12 foreign language sequence

FLEX

FLEX provides an introduction to one or more foreign languages. A *FLEX* program can be designed in a variety of formats, but the two basic models that have emerged are the *Exploratory* and the *Limited Exposure*. In the *FLEX-Exploratory* model, students explore two or more languages, with the emphasis being on the nature of language and how it relates to culture. Some language skills are acquired. In this model, classes may be scheduled in a two-, six-, or nine-week program.

In the *Limited Exposure* model, students are introduced to *one* language in a six- or nine-week program, or in classes that meet once or twice a week for the school year. Some language and cultural skills are acquired, but they vary in proportion to the amount of time and intensity devoted to the program.

A *FLEX* program, which may also be called "language awareness," permits a wide variety of formats and time and scheduling patterns. It has as its major focus the exposure of students to one or more languages or cultures for one or more school years. It emphasizes cross-cultural appreciation and contrasts. It is considered a minimal foundation in language learning, with limited goals in foreign language proficiency. It is primarily a language/culture/motivational program.

Some of the general characteristics of the *FLEX* program model are:

- One or more foreign languages taught for one or more school years
- Minimal foundation in language learning dealing with the integration of the four abilities and culture, although sometimes only the oral abilities are included in the program, depending on the grade level
- Expectation of limited foreign language proficiency
- Promotion of interest in future foreign language study and in the choice of future foreign language classes

- Promotion of interest in the target language and culture
- High correlation of foreign language study with social studies, language arts, art, music, and other areas of the elementary school curriculum
- Can be an integral part of the elementary school curriculum
- Use of either classroom or itinerant teachers (other delivery models are possible)
- Worthwhile program for *all* students in grades K–8
- Variety of materials available to support content and interest of the students
- Content usually consists of *brief* thematic, linguistic, and cultural units
- Schedules depends on goals, local needs, budget, and grade levels, with a range of from 2 to 5 percent of the school schedule
- Contributes to a K–12 foreign language sequence

Immersion and *Partial Immersion*

This model provides instruction in the foreign language for at least 50 percent of the school day—and in *Total Immersion*, close to 100 percent. The goal for students who stay with the program is to achieve functional proficiency in the foreign language while achieving normally in all subjects taught in the foreign language. The foreign language is an integral part of the elementary school day because it is the language of communication and instruction. There is some variety of formats (depending on the degree of immersion in the model), and English may be introduced in differing grades (usually in grade 3). The amount of English is increased, so that by grade 6, the day is usually 50 percent in English and 50 percent in the foreign language, although the ratio will vary from program to program. In many ways, the *Immersion* model follows the bilingual model developed in the 1960s in the United States and Canada.

Some of the general characteristics of the *Immersion* program model are:

- Focus on one language
- Subject areas of the elementary school curriculum taught in the foreign language
- Outcomes resulting in good foreign language proficiency
- Promotion of interest in future foreign language study
- Promotion of interest in the target language and culture
- Very high correlation with subjects in elementary school curriculum

- Current interest in two-way (dual) *Immersion/Bilingual* programs
- Use of classroom teachers who must have a high level of foreign language proficiency and be trained in teaching the elementary school curriculum
- Worthwhile program for *all* students in grades K–8, although not all students can cope with the challenges
- Limited materials available; most materials must be either translated or imported from other countries, whose programs may differ from those in the United States
- Content consists of topics in the elementary school curriculum
- Time may vary from 50 to 100 percent of the school schedule
- Contributes to K–12 foreign language sequence

Comparison of the Different Types of FLES* Programs

Sequential FLES	FLEX (Exploratory, Language Awareness)	Immersion and Partial Immersion
One foreign language taught for two school years or more	One or more foreign languages taught for one school year or more	One foreign language taught in K–6
Grades K–6	*Grades K–6*	*Grades K–6*
Foundation language learning in four abilities and cultures†	Minimal foundation; language learning in four abilities and culture† (sometimes only oral skills)	Subject matter of elementary school curriculum taught in the FL
Outcomes	*Outcomes*	*Outcomes*
Good proficiency, depending on the time (standards orientation)	Limited FL proficiency (standards orientation)	Good proficiency in the foreign language (standards orientation)
Interest in language and culture(s)	Interest in language(s) and culture(s)	Interest in language and culture(s)
Interest in future FL study	Interest in future FL study	Interest in study of other FLs
Correlation of FL with social studies, language arts, and other subjects	Correlation of FL with social studies, language arts, and other subjects	High correlation with social studies, language arts, and other subjects
Integral part of elementary school curriculum	Integral part of elementary school curriculum	Integral part of elementary school curriculum

(continues on next page)

†NOTE: Four abilities—listening, speaking, reading, and writing—plus culture, with a major focus on the five "Cs" goals orientation of the National Standards for Foreign Language Learning.

Comparison of the Different Types of FLES* Programs (Continued)

Sequential FLES	FLEX (Exploratory, Language Awareness)	Immersion and Partial Immersion
Teachers	*Teachers*	*Teachers*
Specialist or classroom teacher	Specialist, classroom teacher, or volunteers	Classroom teacher who is a specialist in FL and elementary school teaching
Students	*Students*	*Students*
Available to all students; some selections due to budget	Available to all students the first year	Available to limited number of students who can cope with the challenge
Materials	*Materials*	*Materials*
Wide variety to support content and interests	Wide variety to support content and interests	Some variety to support content and interests, but generally available only from foreign countries
Content	*Content*	*Content*
Thematic units such as greetings, health, sports, food, etc.; cultural themes and others	Thematic units with limited vocabulary and structure; cultural themes and others	Content of social studies, science, mathematics, etc.
Time	*Time*	*Time*
Wide range of time based on local needs, finances, and grade levels (range from 5% to 20%)	Wide range of time based on local needs, finances, and grade levels (range from 2% to 5%)	50% to 100%

Although it is difficult to gather accurate statistics on all types of **FLES*** programs nationwide, we have information from the results of two national surveys. The first (Rhodes and Oxford 1988) found that approximately 17 percent of elementary schools in this country offer foreign language instruction. Further, concerning the different program models, approximately 98 percent of the respondents reported *Sequential FLES* and *FLEX*, while approximately 2 percent were involved in *Immersion* programs.

The second survey was conducted by the Joint National Committee on Languages (1995). The results of this survey found that an estimated 5 percent of U.S. elementary schools offer foreign language instruction. However, this study collected data solely from public schools and did not survey the private-independent schools sector. In this author's opinion, one can reasonably extrapolate the result to double the amount, which would bring the total of both public and private elementary schools offering foreign languages to approximately 10 percent.

At this writing, a new national survey of K–12 is under way, conducted by the Center for Applied Linguistics, Washington, DC.

In collecting data on the extent of **FLES*** in the United States, it is important to remember several important factors:

1. There is a growing tendency for school districts to observe the "equity principle." This means that regardless of the size of a school district, all students must have access to all programs in the district. It also implies that all schools in a school district will have parallel offerings. The equity principle may contribute to the expansion and growth of **FLES*** programs, but it may also prevent some school districts from offering foreign languages in elementary schools because of lack of funds, shortage of instructional materials, or other reasons.

2. When gathering data for national surveys, merely collecting information about the *number* of schools offering **FLES*** programs is insufficient. Student enrollment figures are extremely important for both *public* and *private* schools.

3. It is difficult to collect data on a state-by-state basis because many states have reduced their staffs of foreign language specialists and no longer collect data of this kind.

- **FLES*** is the overall term for foreign language in the elementary school.
- *Sequential FLES* attempts to provide long-term exposure to one foreign language in elementary school.
- *FLEX* is a limited language experience (exploratory) program (language and culture) in one or more than one language.
- *Immersion* or *Partial Immersion* is a program in which the foreign language *is* the language of the elementary school program.

🖑 FOR REFLECTION

Critical reflection can trigger a deeper understanding of teaching.

JACK RICHARDS AND CHARLES LOCKHART (1994, 4)

Options in **FLES***
Program Models

GOALS AND OBJECTIVES

Before embarking on the establishment of one specific type of **FLES***
program, it is important (and necessary) for the various persons responsible for making decisions to raise a number of questions and try to get
some answers from the group and from experts outside the group.

It is the goal of this section to serve as a guide for planning committees considering the options for their schools. For each program
type, a number of questions are indicated. These questions ideally will
trigger additional questions that may be pertinent to the local needs.

Before any decision is made about the type of program to be developed in a school or school district, policymakers, educators, school
board members, parents, and other community members need to
explore the options and the outcomes they want for their children. They
need to ask such questions as:

- What do we expect the children to achieve in a foreign language
  program?

- Which program model or models are most appropriate for our
  school community?

- Who wants **FLES***? Who is opposed to it? What are their reasons?

- How much of a financial commitment can be made in both short-
  range and long-range planning?

- What is the most cost-effective program that will achieve realistic
  and doable goals?

- When should it be determined that the program is ready to be
  implemented?

- What nuts-and-bolts decisions must be made?

- When should it be said that a **FLES*** program is not worth the effort
  because all the groundwork has not been done?

As we have seen earlier, there are three basic program model options.
A school district may opt for just one program model or may consider

Which Program Model is Best?
FLES*
(approximate percentage of existing programs)

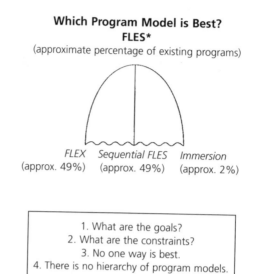

FLEX   Sequential FLES   Immersion
(approx. 49%)   (approx. 49%)   (approx. 2%)

1. What are the goals?
2. What are the constraints?
3. No one way is best.
4. There is no hierarchy of program models.

more than one program model, starting one in the next year or two and another later on. It should be noted that without adequate coordination and supervision, more than one program model is not realistic.

Which Program Model Is Best?

This is a question that administrators frequently ask, but realistically, it is one that can be answered only in terms of the wishes and the needs of the local school district. The decision about which program model (or models) is best should be made locally, preferably by an advisory committee made up of administrators, parents, teachers on all school levels, supervisors, guidance counselors, school board members, university representatives, business representatives, and others. For guiding principles, see Chapter Six.

What Nuts-and-Bolts Decisions Must Be Made?

- Specific needs of the school community
- Program design and goals setting: What is expected by parents, administrators, and members of the community? Are the goals realistic? What degree of foreign language proficiency is expected?

What do we want the children to be able to do? Do we want the children to develop cultural understanding? Are there factors in the community that might impel us to select one language over another? What are the options in delivery models? Can the program be implemented in a number of different ways?

- Selection (if any) of students: Will there be a selection, or will all students be included?

- Entry grade level: Which beginning grade level is best? Will this program be articulated with higher levels of foreign language? Will all students on this grade level be included?

- Selection of language(s): Which language or languages are to be taught in the elementary and middle schools (K–8)? Should less commonly taught languages such as Russian or Japanese be considered for a long sequence? Are other languages spoken in the local area? Which language(s) will meet the students' needs? Which languages can be continued at the secondary school level? Does the school community have a preference for any given language(s)? Which languages provide the greatest capability for interdisciplinary activities related to social studies, science, and language arts? Which languages provide the greatest capability for teaching youngsters about cultural and linguistic diversity in our country? What are the specific language needs of the school/school community?

- Coordination and supervision: Will there be someone responsible for the coordination and supervision of the program? Will this person be knowledgeable about foreign language instruction at this level? Will this person be an advocate for the program?

- Articulation: Will students complete their **FLES*** program and go on to more advanced levels? How and when will articulation procedures be planned?

- Time and schedule of classes: Will classes be scheduled so that optimum conditions will prevail for the accomplishment of the goals of the program model selected? What kind of time is available? Is this sufficient to accomplish the goals of the program? How long will each class session be? How many times a week will classes meet? What has to be modified in the current school schedule?

- Recruitment and selection of foreign language teachers: Are teachers available who are fluent in the foreign language they will teach, who are familiar with **FLES*** methods, and who are cognizant of the rest of the elementary school curriculum? Will there be a steady supply of qualified teachers? Are the local and state colleges and universities supporting this program?

- Training of foreign language teachers: Are plans being made for pre-service training and for in-service training? Will there be support for teachers' attendance at conferences and summer institutes?

- Training of the classroom teacher: In many cases, in all three program models, the **FLES*** teacher *is* the classroom teacher. In those cases where there is an itinerant **FLES*** teacher, the regular classroom teacher needs in-service training in how to incorporate the foreign language program into the rest of the elementary school curriculum.

- Budget estimation, source(s) of funding, length of funding: Is there money for teachers, curriculum development, preservice and in-service training, and materials? Is funding for education very limited? What are the sources of funding? Is the funding for one year only, or is it fairly certain for a ten-year period? What budgetary and other constraints must be taken into consideration?

- Content of instruction: Who will be responsible for developing the appropriate curriculum? Is there a plan for dovetailing the **FLES*** curriculum with the rest of the elementary and middle school curriculum? Is there a plan for articulating the **FLES*** curriculum with the secondary school foreign language curriculum?

- Methodology: Will the curriculum fit the new trends in **FLES*** methodology, such as TPR (Total Physical Response), higher-order thinking skills, and interdisciplinary and content-based instruction? Will the two cornerstones of **FLES*** programs—*communication* and *culture*—be stressed?

- Materials of instruction: Are materials available for the type of program model and outcomes desired? Are they appropriate for elementary and middle school youngsters? Are they varied? Are they culturally authentic? Are they available for one or more years? What will be done if few appropriate materials are available?

- Review of existing research: Has the advisory committee collected information about research findings and the rationale for teaching foreign languages at this level? (See Chapter Two.)

- Review of programs in other areas of the country: Has the advisory committee collected information about successful programs in different parts of the country? Will on-site visits be made?

- If *Immersion* is chosen, which subjects will be taught in the foreign language? Will it be *Total Immersion* or *Partial Immersion? Dual-Language Immersion?*

- If *Immersion* is chosen, when will English be started? Who will teach it? Will all aspects of language arts be covered?

- Procedures for the evaluation of the program: How will it be determined whether the goals of the program have been accomplished? (For *Immersion* students, have they covered the elementary school curriculum?) Will there be both informal and formal evaluation of the program? Will there be evaluation of student performance *in* the foreign language? Will there be evaluation of student performance in the rest of the elementary school curriculum? Will there be evaluation of student performance in English? Will there be periodic evaluation of the program—for example, every five years? Will there be ongoing procedures for feedback and modification of the program? Will the evaluation plan document whether or not the program is achieving its stated goals?

- What other pertinent data relate to the local situation, such as ethnic populations and foreign languages spoken in the community and the number of ESOL students?

- Is there a long-term commitment to the program from an educational point of view and from a financial capability point of view? How will the program fit into the long-range overall educational plans?

- Development of plans for publicizing the program: Will there be an ongoing process of informing the public about the accomplishments of the program? Who will be responsible for doing this? Will publicity about the program also invite feedback? Will regular notices be sent to the media: newspapers, radio and TV, computer networks, etc.?

- Status of **FLES*** in the elementary and middle schools: Does foreign language study have an important status in the overall elementary and middle school plans? How does it fit into the rest of the school curriculum?

- Resources: Have all the resources in the community been identified? Which people, inside and outside the school system, can be of assistance? Are there plans for parental involvement in the program? Which businesses in the community could assist the program? Which governmental agencies and universities could support the program? Which international agencies (such as embassies) might provide support, materials, or services?

In each school community, there are specific needs and constraints, and that is why each school community must go through the rather arduous and lengthy task of examining needs, anticipating problems, and planning both short- and long-term goals. **THERE ARE NO SHORTCUTS!**

Summary of FLES* "Must-Have's"

- **FLES*** advisory council
- Parent involvement
- Long-range planning and goals
- Long-range funding
- Broad base of support
- Solutions about beginning grade(s), students, schedule, etc.
- Basis for languages selected
- Plans for modification and feedback
- Curriculum
- Materials of instruction
- Plans for articulation
- Fluent, well-trained teachers
- Plans for in-service and professional development of teachers
- Evaluation design
- Plans for publicity and public awareness
- Ongoing program for obtaining feedback

🔅 FOR REFLECTION

Unless **FLES*** teachers take the lead by encouraging others to explore and read the world via books, magazines, cassettes, videos, in both the target language and in English, we are missing valuable opportunities.

KATHERINE KURK (1993, 15)

Questions and Answers About **FLES***

Why start a foreign language program in the elementary and/or middle schools?

It is true that given the proper motivation, anyone at any age can learn a foreign language. Research studies indicate that before the age of ten is the optimum time to achieve an excellent, near-native pronunciation and intonation of a foreign language. We know that learning how to pronounce a foreign language for an adult can be quite difficult—almost as if we are "tripping over our tongues." Children up to the age of ten or eleven do not seem to have this difficulty. Furthermore, research has indicated that from the long-range point of view, those who start foreign languages as children can reach higher levels of proficiency than those who start later. (See Chapters Two and Five for references on research.)

Which **FLES*** issues are highly important?

The issues of *access* and *equity* are considered foremost by many **FLES*** advocates (teachers, supervisors, parents, and administrators on school and university levels across the country). It follows that *no* child should be denied access to FL study. While support for equity and access is widespread, implementing **FLES*** programs that reflect these tenets requires a great deal of resourcefulness in view of our continuing fiscal crises in education.

Will studying a foreign language interfere with children's expected progress in basic subjects, such as reading and mathematics?

Research studies show that for *Sequential FLES* and *FLEX* programs, there is no interference with expected gains in such basic subjects as reading and mathematics. (See Chapter Two on research.) In *Immersion* programs, there is a lag in English reading and language arts skills for several years, since the study of English is delayed, but Canadian studies show that children make up this lag after several years of studying English in school (Genesee 1987). Studies on a statewide population in Louisiana (Rafferty 1986) indicate that children in *Sequential FLES* not only continue to make progress in the "basics," but in some cases, those studying a foreign language show greater gains than those not studying a foreign language. The author obtained similar results (Lipton 1979):

A Comparison of IOWA TESTS of Basic Skills Results for LEX[†]
Participants and Nonparticipants

		Participants in Languages Experience Program		Nonparticipants in Languages ExperienceProgram	
		Number	*Mean*	*Number*	*Mean*
Grade 3	Ability	276	110	587	106
	Vocabulary	279	4.3	587	4.1
	Reading Comprehension	279	4.5	587	4.1
	Language Total	275	5.0	587	4.6
Grade 5	Ability	349	111	308	108
	Vocabulary	347	6.1	308	5.8
	Reading Comprehension	347	6.1	308	5.8
	Language Total	348	6.6	308	6.1

[†]LEX = *FLEX*.

WHERE ARE SCHOOL DISTRICTS GOING TO GET TEACHERS WHO ARE QUALIFIED AND TRAINED TO TEACH IN **FLES*** PROGRAMS?

At the present time, it is not easy to find qualified, trained teachers of **FLES***, whether it is for *Sequential FLES, FLEX,* or *Immersion.* Many teachers currently teaching in the secondary schools might be interested, but while they may be fluent in the foreign language, they lack the extra training needed to teach younger teachers. *Immersion* teachers, too, if they are fluent in the foreign language, need to take many courses in the rest of the elementary school curriculum, as well as in how to teach and reach young children. Some school districts have hired foreign teachers, but they need training in how to teach in American schools. Although there are still very few **FLES*** teacher-training institutions, there are several colleges and universities, such as Teachers' College, New York City; Concordia College in Minnesota; and the University of Maryland, Baltimore County, Baltimore, Maryland, that offer summer institutes for **FLES*** teachers.

THE ELEMENTARY-SCHOOL CURRICULUM IS OVERCROWDED WITH MANY SUBJECTS. HOW CAN WE ADD STILL ANOTHER SUBJECT?

If a community selects an *Immersion, Partial Immersion,* or content-based program, the required content in all or some of the subjects will be taught in the foreign language. In *Sequential FLES* and *FLEX* programs, the curriculum and content can be developed to use everyday communicative language to integrate various components from social studies, mathematics, music, drug abuse education, etc., as reinforcement or enrichment of the regular curriculum in an interdisciplinary approach.

SHOULD ALL FLES* PROGRAMS DELIVER A HIGH LEVEL OF FL FLUENCY?

No one can argue against the delivery of a high level of FL fluency whenever possible. However, all types of **FLES*** programs represent *initial* steps in FL study that go beyond linguistic accomplishments (as do the *Standards for Foreign Language Learning* [National Standards in Foreign Language Education Project 1996]), such as foreign language and cultural knowledge, a better understanding of one's own language and culture, practical applications of the FL in real-life situations, a sense of the *power* of the FL through interdisciplinary activities, and others. Furthermore, all types of effective **FLES*** programs motivate students to want to *continue* their FL studies. Ernest Boyer, the president of the Carnegie Foundation, in his book *The Basic School: A Community for Learning* (1995, 73–74) urges "that foreign language instruction begin early, certainly by third grade, that it be offered daily, and be continued through all the grades." But, he also recommends some *FLEX-Exploratory* activities, urging that "words and phrases from many languages" be introduced so that students will understand "the wonderfully diverse ways people communicate with each other."

WHAT CAN CHILDREN REALLY LEARN IN A FEW MINUTES A DAY IN A *SEQUENTIAL FLES* OR *FLEX* PROGRAM? IS IT REALLY WORTH THE EFFORT, TIME, AND MONEY?

Unless a school community has agreed upon specific goals and outcomes of the program, it may not really be worth the effort. An elementary school/middle school program is only viable if the goals are clearly stated and accepted by the entire school community, and if there is provision for demonstrating that the goals have been achieved. If parents, for example, expect that their children will be "fluent" after one year's study of a foreign language (for twenty minutes, two times a week), then they have set very unrealistic goals for the program! Members of the community and parents must understand that it takes a *long time* to become fluent in a foreign language. An early start enables students to begin when pronunciation skills are easily learned, and a longer sequence is likely to lead to higher levels of foreign language proficiency .

WHICH TYPE OF **FLES*** PROGRAM IS BEST?

One cannot say which program model is best without identifying the context of the educational community. Constraints such as the expectations of the school/school community, fiscal resources, language choices, and ongoing supply of fluent, well-prepared **FLES*** teachers often preclude an idealistic "lockstep, cradle-to-grave" approach.

This is a question that the members of the school community have to answer at the local level. Each school community must make the decision based on the kinds of outcomes that are indicated locally.

No one program model is best for all children and for all school districts. Each program model has its merits. Each can be developed to meet local needs. Each can be implemented successfully, provided that everyone is aware of the outcomes expected from the model selected. The key factor is that if a **FLES*** program is to be successful, *it must be a significant part of the total school educational program.*

WHAT DO THE THREE **FLES*** PROGRAM MODELS (*SEQUENTIAL FLES, FLEX-EXPLORATORY,* AND *IMMERSION*) HAVE IN COMMON?

They provide foreign language instruction to children, they sensitize children to different ways of life, they help children develop an openness to people from other cultures, they encourage students to continue FL study at upper levels, and they are valuable FL programs that enrich children's lives.

WHAT IS THE OPTIMUM AGE LEVEL TO INTRODUCE A FOREIGN LANGUAGE?

Penfield (1959), a well-known Canadian neuropsychologist, wrote that because the "uncommitted cortex must be conditioned for speech in the first decade," the study of a foreign language is best introduced before the age of ten in order to capitalize upon children's physical and psychological abilities. This does not mean that it is not possible to learn a foreign language after the age of ten, but it indicates the special reasons why beginning earlier might be better. (For recent brain research studies, see Begley 1996 and Nadia 1993.)

DOES IT COST A LOT TO START A FLES* PROGRAM?

Cost is certainly a factor in establishing a **FLES*** program, no matter which program model is considered. However, a number of options are available, both in program models and in delivery models. School communities should first determine the outcomes of the proposed program and then design the type of program that is in consonance with their goals, their budget, and their local situation. Certainly a more sophisticated program might have a more costly budget. Using classroom teachers, whether the program is *Sequential FLES, FLEX,* or *Immersion,* would be the least expensive type of program, although *Immersion* start-up costs are high for materials. If a school community is interested in a quality program, costs involved, such as start-up, materials, teachers, and coordination, must be included in the estimated budget. Even when there are budget problems in the school community, children should not be deprived of the benefits of starting a foreign language early.

WHO SHOULD STUDY A FOREIGN LANGUAGE— JUST GIFTED STUDENTS?

Experience and research have shown that *all* children can learn some foreign language skills if taught with patience and effective pedagogy for their level. This is especially true when the objectives of the program are language and cultural awareness and exploration. Teachers within the class situation can make provision for more able students by providing more challenging experiences in the four abilities (listening, speaking, reading, and writing) and culture.

DOES THE STUDY OF A FOREIGN LANGUAGE IN THE EARLY YEARS CHANGE ATTITUDES TOWARD OTHER PEOPLE?

Studies have shown that the early introduction of a foreign language tends to break down the "monocultural" outlook of children in all types of programs. This was observed to be true during the early days of **FLES*** in the 1960s (Sommerville Board of Education 1962; Brega and Newell 1967; Vocolo 1967) and confirmed by more recent research on bilingual education and *Immersion* programs in Canada (Lambert and Tucker 1992).

IF A CHILD STUDIES A FOREIGN LANGUAGE IN ELEMENTARY SCHOOL AND CONTINUES THE SAME LANGUAGE, WILL RESULTS IN HIGH SCHOOL AND COLLEGE SHOW GREATER LANGUAGE PROFICIENCY?

There is a body of research concerning the effects of **FLES** * upon later foreign language achievements. In the 1960s, in the Sommerville, New Jersey, schools, foreign language achievements of high school students with and without prior **FLES** * study were compared (Sommerville Board of Education 1962). The results showed that former **FLES** * students achieved scores approximately 10 percent higher than those of students who had not had previous **FLES** * experience. In another study conducted in Lexington, Massachusetts (Brega and Newell 1967), results indicated that those students who had had **FLES** * outperformed those who had not had **FLES** *. While these studies took place in the 1960s, the results are still valid, but obviously, much more updated longitudinal research is needed. A strong argument for **FLES** * appears in the data of an ETS study on the 1995 Advanced Placement French Examination: Students who began French before grade 7 (in academic settings) outperformed those who began French in grade 7 or later (Lipton, Morgan, and Reed 1996).

IS IT TRUE THAT CHILDREN WHO HAVE BEEN EXPOSED TO A FOREIGN LANGUAGE IN THE EARLY YEARS OFTEN FIND IT EASIER TO LEARN OTHER LANGUAGES THROUGHOUT THEIR LIVES?

Many teachers have observed this to be true, although there has been little research to confirm it. Teachers find that those students who have studied another foreign language find it much easier to adjust to a different sound and structure system. They probably have acquired good study habits for learning another language and have internalized the various ways of studying another language.

SINCE THE GOAL OF LEARNING LANGUAGES IS PERFORMANCE OR PROFICIENCY, CAN'T THIS BE ACHIEVED IN A SHORT PERIOD OF TIME, AS THE COMMERCIAL LANGUAGE SCHOOLS CLAIM?

It would appear that the amount of time and the quality and intensity of that time are important in helping students achieve language proficiency. Adults can accomplish this in a short time when they are highly motivated and can devote their time intensively toward language learning, particularly if they have language ability. For most people, however, effective instructional programs, as well as an early beginning, would help to ensure greater language control and achievement.

WHICH LANGUAGE(S) ARE MOST IMPORTANT FOR ELEMENTARY-SCHOOL CHILDREN TO LEARN?

The choice of language should be decided at the local school (county or district) level with input from parents, as should the specific goals of the program. Some school districts even believe that it is valuable to introduce one language one year and another language the next year, but this is valid only when the goals are language awareness or exploration. Generally, it is most effective when a school community starts a **FLES*** program that can articulate with the languages being taught in the junior and senior high schools. Some districts select languages of the minority groups in the community to assist in better intercultural understanding. The choice of which language or languages will be offered is a highly emotional issue. Some administrators have made decisions, for example, that this year's grade 4 will study Russian and that next year's grade 4 will study Japanese. This approach works only when administrators take into account the wishes of the majority of the parents and every effort is made to obtain parental input into the decision.

WHAT IS THE BEST WAY TO TEACH FOREIGN LANGUAGES IN THE ELEMENTARY AND MIDDLE SCHOOLS?

Effective pedagogical procedures will be discussed in more detail in Chapters Nine, Ten, Eleven, and Twelve. In general, the best approach is to teach pupils how to listen carefully, how to pronounce accurately, how to read and write limited amounts of foreign language material, and how to role-play cultural experiences by "being in foreign shoes," so to speak. Thus, it is recommended that children in **FLES*** programs be taught integrated listening, speaking, reading, writing, and cultural abilities appropriate to the goals of the program and the grade level of the students in real-life situations, with the major focus on the five C's of the *Standards for Foreign Language Learning*.

WHO SHOULD TEACH FOREIGN LANGUAGES IN ELEMENTARY AND MIDDLE SCHOOLS?

The type of teacher selected for the program depends on the goals of the program and the available funds, but the teacher should have the competencies listed in Appendix F. (See Chapter Seven for some of the competencies needed by **FLES*** teachers.)

FLES* PROGRAMS WERE WIDESPREAD IN THE 1960s, BUT BEGAN TO LOSE COMMUNITY SUPPORT IN THE 1970s. WHY DID THIS HAPPEN? IS IT LIKELY TO HAPPEN AGAIN?

That **FLES*** is a "good thing" is widely accepted by educators, administrators, parents, and others concerned with quality programs in the schools. The reasons for failure in the 1960s are many and complex, and it is important to examine them. Perhaps it is an oversimplification to state that funding was the primary cause. Another basic reason was the fact that programs failed to deliver the foreign language proficiency promised at that time. Also, many of the people teaching in the 1960s programs were not certified foreign language teachers, and very few had received specialized training. Still another reason was the lack of acceptance of the programs in the junior and senior high schools, which required countless numbers of youngsters to start their language study anew, as if they had gained nothing in the elementary years.

WE HAVE BEEN HEARING THAT *IMMERSION* PROGRAMS OFFER THE BEST RESULTS. IS THIS TRUE? WHICH TYPE OF PROGRAM IS BEST?

The results obtained by some *Immersion* programs are very good, but it would be inaccurate to state that this type of program is the only viable program for elementary schools. Many parents, for example, are still wary about having the basic skills of elementary school taught in a foreign language. Although Canadian studies indicate that *Immersion* programs show good results (Lambert and Tucker 1972; Genesee 1987), we need more research on *Immersion* programs in the United States. Some of the Canadian reports even show dissatisfaction with the level and accuracy of foreign language achievement by the students (Hammerly 1971; Pawley 1985). Some educators and parents think that this type of program is not for all students. The best answer to this question is that there is no best type of program because each program selected should be tailor-made to the needs of the students, the school, and the community, based on the goals established for the program. In some instances, the best program will be a *Sequential FLES* program. In others, it will be an *Immersion* program. In still others, it will be a language/culture awareness *FLEX* program. The best type of program is one that states its objectives and then is able to deliver the results delineated by these objectives.

SHOULD ALL **FLES*** PROGRAMS BEGIN A LONG SEQUENCE IN ELEMENTARY SCHOOL THAT CONTINUES IN SECONDARY SCHOOL?

A long sequence can strongly contribute to greater language proficiency. However, different school communities may have different goals and certainly have different budgets. The goals of the school community determine the length of the program. As long as the objectives have been clearly stated, understood, and accepted by all of the people concerned, the length of the program can be tailored to meet those goals and fit the budgetary constraints.

WHY BOTHER TEACHING A FOREIGN LANGUAGE IN ELEMENTARY SCHOOL FOR ONLY A YEAR OR TWO?

It is true that a longer period of time would be more worthwhile. However, if the goals a school district can afford and wishes to implement are limited, then even a short exposure to foreign language and culture in the form of *FLEX* as an introductory taste will have beneficial results.

WITH ALL THE SUBJECTS STUDIED IN ELEMENTARY SCHOOL, ISN'T FOREIGN LANGUAGE SOMETHING THAT DOESN'T FIT THE CURRICULUM?

The study of a foreign language fits very well in the elementary and middle school curriculum. Children are naturally curious about codes and different forms of communication. They are also very interested in different people's customs, and they study some of those in social studies. They enjoy singing songs from other countries in the foreign language, which also enriches the music program. They learn how to perform folk dances to add an international flavor to their physical education program. They learn about famous mathematicians and scientists as well as famous artists, composers, etc., from other countries. The study of a foreign language adds a broad new dimension to the rest of the school curriculum. Furthermore, by including some of the content from other curriculum areas, the foreign language class reinforces many of the concepts in other areas. An interdisciplinary approach in **FLES*** yields an integrated, holistic curriculum for children.

I HAVE HEARD THAT MANY CHILDREN DROP OUT OF *IMMERSION* PROGRAMS BECAUSE THEY ARE TOO DEMANDING. IS THAT TRUE?

There are no statistics as yet on the number of dropouts from *Immersion* programs (although Trites [1981] conducted some research in Canada). We know that some children get fatigued or overstimulated during the first year or so because of the challenge of learning in the foreign language. Some *Immersion* schools send letters home to parents indicating that the children may exhibit nervous behavior during the first year, but that things will calm down after a while. As a matter of fact, there are no statistics on the number of dropouts in *Sequential FLES* and *FLEX* programs. We do know, however, that if the methods remain the same over a number of years, children get tired and bored with studying a foreign language.

IF A SCHOOL DISTRICT HAS LIMITED FUNDS AND WISHES TO IMPLEMENT A *FLEX* PROGRAM, IN WHICH GRADE SHOULD IT BEGIN?

This is a question that has to be studied at the local level. It cannot be answered in general terms because the needs of each school district differ. Perhaps one general answer is to try to work backward from the starting point in the secondary schools. For example, if the secondary school program begins in grade 7, then a grade 6 *FLEX* program might be started the first year and extended to grades 5 and 6 in the second year; grades 4, 5, and 6 in the third year; and so on.

IS GRAMMAR TAUGHT IN **FLES*** PROGRAMS? HOW CAN CHILDREN LEARN THE LANGUAGE WITHOUT LEARNING THE GRAMMAR?

Grammar, as such, is not formally taught in **FLES*** programs. Children are, however, exposed to correct forms and usage in the foreign language, and they tend to use the language functionally, as they have heard it. That is why a teacher who is highly proficient in the foreign language is essential in all types of **FLES*** programs. Although youngsters cannot quote the grammar rules, they learn how to use the language correctly in day-by-day functional situations. Furthermore, if students request specific grammar information, explanations are given in accordance with their ability to comprehend.

- There is no *one* best type of **FLES*** program.
- There are many reasons to develop **FLES*** programs.
- **FLES*** is gaining many supporters.
- More research studies support early language learning.

SELECTED **FLES*** RESEARCH REFERENCES

The following publications will be of interest to teachers, parents, school administrators, and other community members interested in learning about **FLES***. A more extensive bibliography of publications about foreign language instruction in the elementary and middle schools is presented in Appendix M. Please consult both bibliographies when seeking further information about sources cited in this book.

Alexander, L., and M. John. 1985. "Testing Oral Skills in a FLES Short Course." *FL Annals* 18 (Nov.): 235–239.

Asher, J. 1988. *Brainswitching: A Skill for the 21st Century.* Los Gatos, CA: Sky Oakes Publications.

Baranick, W., and P. Markham. 1986. "Attitudes of Elementary School Principals toward Foreign Language Instruction." *FL Annals* 19 (Dec.): 481–489.

Begley, S. 1996. "Your Child's Brain." *Newsweek* (Feb. 19): 55–61.

Bennett, W. 1988. *James Madison Elementary School. A Curriculum for American Students.* Washington, DC: U.S. Dept. of Education.

Bernhardt, E. 1992. *Life in Language Immersion Classrooms.* Great Britain: Clevedon.

Boyer, E. L. 1995. *The Basic School: A Community for Learning.* Princeton, NJ: The Carnegie Foundation for the Advancement of Teaching.

Brega, E., and J. Newell. 1967. "H.S. Performance of FLES and non-FLES Students." *Modern Language Journal* 51 (Nov.): 408–411.

Bruer, J. 1997. "The Science of Learning." *American School Board Journal* (Feb.): 24–27.

Carpenter, J., and J. Torney. 1973. "Beyond the Melting Pot." In *Children and International Education,* ed. P.N. Markun and J. L. Land, 14–24. Washington, DC: Association for Childhood Education International.

Carroll, J. 1967. "Foreign Language Proficiency Levels Attained by Language Majors Near Graduation from College." *FL Annals* (Dec.): 131–135.

Cohen, A. 1974. "The Culver City Spanish Immersion Program: The First Two Years." *Modern Language Journal* 58 (Mar.): 95–103.

Cooper, T. C. 1987. "Foreign Language Study and SAT-Verbal Scores." *Modern Language Journal* 71, IV: 381–387.

Curtain, H., and C. Pesola. 1994. *Language and Children: Making the Match.* 2nd ed. Reading, MA: Addison-Wesley.

DeLorenzo, W., and L. Gladstein. 1984. "Immersion Education à l'Américaine: A Descriptive Study of U.S. Immersion Programs." *FL Annals* 17 (Feb.): 35–40.

De Pietro, R. 1980. "Filling the Elementary School Curriculum with Languages: What Are the Effects?" *FL Annals* 13 (April): 115–123.

Donoghue, M. 1981. "Recent Research in FLES 1974–1980." *Hispania* 64 (Dec.): 602–604.

Dufort, M. 1969. "Foreign Language Attitude Scale." In *The Successful Foreign Language Teacher,* ed. R. Politzer and L. Weiss, 71–73. Philadelphia: Philadelphia Center for Curriculum Development.

Dulay, H., M. Burt, and S. Krashen. 1982. *Language Two.* New York: Oxford University Press.

Dunkel, H., and R. Pillet. 1962. *French in the Elementary School.* Chicago: University of Chicago Press.

Eddy, P. 1980. "Foreign Language in the USA: A National Survey of American Attitudes and Experience." *Modern Language Journal* 64: 58–63.

"Evaluation des Programes d'Etude de Québec." 1992. In *Evaluating **FLES*** *Programs,* ed. G. Lipton, 59–77. Champaign, IL: AATF.

Fathman, A. 1982. "The Relationship Between Age and Second Language Productive Ability." In *Child-Adult Differences in Second Language Acquisition,* ed. S. Krashen et al., 115–122. Rowley, MA: Newbury House.

Fort Lauderdale Board of Education.1990. *A Third Year Study of the Elementary Foreign Language Program.* Fort Lauderdale, FL: Fort Lauderdale Board of Education.

Foster, K., and C. Reeves. 1989. "FLES Improves Cognitive Skills." *FLESNEWS* (Spring): 4–5.

Gahala, E., and D. Lange. 1997. "Multiple Intelligences: Multiple Ways to Help Students Learn Foreign Languages." *Northeast Conference Newsletter* 41: 29–34.

Garfinkel, A. and K. Tabor. 1991. "Elementary School Foreign Languages and English Reading Achievement." *Foreign Language Annals* (Oct.): 375–382.

Genesee, F. 1987. *Learning Through Two Languages.* Rowley, MA: Newbury House.

Gifted Child Project. 1970. *French Achievement Test.* New York: Gifted Child Project, New York City Board of Education.

Ginsburg, H., and I. McCoy. 1981. "An Empirical Rationale for Foreign Languages in Elementary School." *Modern Language Journal* 65 (Spring): 36–42.

Goleman, D. 1995. *Emotional Intelligence.* New York: Bantam Books.

Hammerly, H. 1971. "Litmus Test of Second Language Acquisition Through Classroom Communication." *Modern Language Journal* 71 (Winter): 395–401.

Hammerly, H. 1989. *French Immersion: Myths and Reality.* Calgary, Alberta: Detselig Enterprises, Ltd.

Hancock, C., G. Lipton, et al. 1976. "A Study of FLES and Non-FLES Pupils' Attitudes Toward the French and Their Culture." *French Review* 49 (April): 717–722.

Johnson, C., F. P. Ellison, and J. Flores. 1963. "The Effect of Foreign Language Instruction on Basic Learning in Elementary Schools: A Second Report." *Modern Language Journal* 47, 1: 8–11.

Joint National Committee on Languages (JNCL). 1995. *The Impact of Education Reform: A Survey of State Activities.* Washington, DC: Joint National Committee on Languages.

Krashen, S. 1983. *Principles and Practice in Second Language Acquisition.* Oxford: Pergamon Press.

Krashen, S., M. Long, et al. 1982. *Child-Adult Differences in Second Language Acquisition.* Rowley, MA: Newbury House.

Lambert, W., and O. Klineberg. 1967. *Children's Views of Foreign People.* New York: Appleton-Century-Crofts.

Lambert, W., and G. Tucker. 1972. *Bilingual Education of Children: The St. Lambert Experiment.* Rowley, MA: Newbury House.

Landry. R. 1973. "The Enhancement of Figural Creativity Through Second Language Learning at the Elementary School Level." *FL Annals* 7 (Oct.): 111–115.

———. 1974. "A Comparison of Second Language Learners and Monolinguals on Divergent Thinking Tasks at the Elementary School Level." *Modern Language Journal* 58 (Jan.): 10–15.

Larsen-Freeman, D., and M. Long. 1991. *An Introduction to Second Language Research.* New York: Longman.

Lipton, G. 1969a. "The Effectiveness of Listening-Speaking-Only, as Compared with Listening-Speaking-Reading in Grade Four, the First Year of Study of French at the FLES Level, in the Acquisition of Auditory Comprehension." Doctoral dissertation, New York University, *Dissertation Abstracts International* 30/06-A, 2421.

———. 1969b. "To Read or Not to Read: An Experiment on the FLES Level." *FL Annals* 3 (Dec.): 241–246.

———. 1979. "Yes to Lex, or Elementary School FL Instruction Helps English Language Skills: Results of a Pilot Study." Unpublished paper, available from author.

———. 1996a. "**FLES*** Research Packet." Baltimore, MD: National **FLES*** Institute, University of Maryland, Baltimore County 21250.

———. 1996b. *Planning Effective **FLES*** Programs.* Baltimore, MD: National **FLES*** Institute, University of Maryland, Baltimore County 21250.

———. 1996c. *Planning Effective Spanish **FLES*** Programs.* Greeley, CO: AATSP.

———. 1996d. *Suggestions for Attracting French **FLES*** Students.* Carbondale, IL: AATF.

———. 1998. *Practical Handbook to Elementary Foreign Language Programs Including FLES, FLEX, and Immersion Programs.* 3rd ed. Lincolnwood, IL: NTC/Contemporary Publishing Company.

Lipton, G., ed. 1992. *Evaluating FLES* Programs.* Champaign, IL: Report of the FLES* Commission of AATF.

———. 1998. *A Celebration of FLES*.* Lincolnwood, IL: NTC/Contemporary Publishing Company.

Lipton, G., Morgan, R., and Reed, M. 1996. "Does FLES* Help AP French Students Perform Better?" *AATF National Bulletin* 21: 4.

Lopato, E. 1965. "FLES and Academic Achievement." *French Review* 36: 499–507.

Lundin, J., and D. Dolson, eds. 1984. *Studies on Immersion Education. A Collection for U.S. Educators.* Sacramento, CA: California State Dept. of Education.

Masciantonio, R. 1977. "Tangible Benefits of the Study of Latin: A Review of Research." *FL Annals* 10 (Sept.): 375–382.

McCaig, R. 1988. *The Effect of the Elementary Foreign Language Program on Aspects of Elementary Education: A Longitudinal Study.* Ferndale, MI: Ferndale, Michigan, Public Schools.

Nadia, S. 1993. "Kids' Brainpower." *Oregonian* (Dec. 13): 8–9.

Nash, J. 1996. "Zooming in on Dyslexia." *Time* (Jan. 29): 62–64.

National FLES* Institute. 1991. *FLES* Programs in Action* and *Study Guide.* Video. G. Lipton, project director. Baltimore, MD: National FLES* Institute, University of Maryland, Baltimore County 21250.

———. 1996. "Focus on FLES*: A Position Paper." Baltimore, MD: National FLES* Institute, University of Maryland, Baltimore County 21250.

———. 1997. "Advocacy for FLES* Packet." Baltimore, MD: National FLES* Institute, University of Maryland, Baltimore County 21250.

National Governors' Association. 1989. *America in Transition: The International Frontier.* Report of the Task Force on International Education. Washington, DC: National Governors' Association.

National Standards in Foreign Language Education Project. 1996. *Standards for Foreign Language Learning: Preparing for the 21st Century.* Yonkers, NY: National Standards in Foreign Language Education Project.

Nunan, D. 1992. *Research Methods in Langue Learning.* NY: Cambridge University Press.

Oneto, A. 1967. *FLES Evaluation: Language Skills and Pupil Attitudes in Fairfield Connecticut Public Schools.* Hartford, CT: Connecticut State Dept. of Education.

Oxford, R., and N. Rhodes, 1987. *Executive Summary: Status of U.S. Foreign Language Instruction at the Elementary and Secondary School Levels.* Washington, DC: Center for Applied Linguistics.

Ozete, O. 1980. "Milwaukee's French, German, Spanish Immersion Success." *Hispania* 63 (Dec.): 569–571.

Papalia, A. Jan. 1986. "A Synthesis on What Research Says on Early Second Language Learning." *Language Association Bulletin* 37: 11–14.

Pawley, C. 1985. "How Bilingual Are French Immersion Students?" *The Canadian Modern Language Review* 41: 865–876.

Penfield, W., and L. Roberts. 1959. *Speech and Brain Mechanisms.* New York: Atheneum Press.

Potts, M. 1967. "The Effect of Second-Language Instruction on the Reading Achievement of Primary Grade Children." *American Educational Research Journal* 4: 367–373.

Rafferty, E. 1986. *Second Language Study and Basic Skills in Louisiana.* Baton Rouge, LA: Louisiana Dept. of Education.

Rhodes, N., and A. Schriebstein. 1983. *Foreign Languages in the Elementary School: A Practical Guide.* Washington, DC: Center for Applied Linguistics.

Schinke-Llano, L. 1985. *Foreign Language in the Elementary School: State of the Art.* Washington, DC: Center for Applied Linguistics.

Singer, M. 1992. "Louisiana Evaluation Project." In *Evaluating **FLES*** Programs,* ed. G. Lipton, 10–16. Champaign, IL: AATF.

Sommerville Board of Education. 1962. *Sommerville, N.J., Public Schools Report on FLES.* Sommerville, NJ: Sommerville Board of Education.

Spilka, I. 1976. "Assessment of Second-Language Performance in Immersion Programs." *Canadian Modern Language Review* 32 (May): 543–561.

Sylwester, R.A. 1995. *A Celebration of Neurons.* Alexandria, VA: Association for Supervision and Curriculum Development.

Trites, R. 1981. *Primary French Immersion: Disabilities and Prediction of Success.* Toronto: OISE Press.

Vocolo, J. 1967. "The Effect of Foreign Language Study in Elementary School upon Achievement in the Same FL in High School." *Modern Language Journal* 51 (Dec.): 463–470.

Wisconsin Public Radio Association. 1995. "Gray Matters…The Developing Brain." Transcript of Radio Broadcast. Madison, WI: Wisconsin Public Radio Association. Available from the Radio Store, 821 University Avenue, Madison, WI 53706.

ⓥ FOR REFLECTION

We encourage administrators, classroom teachers, and parents to become active supporters of our program.

CHRISTINE BROWN (1989, 65)

Planning Effective
FLES* Programs

ORGANIZING THE PLANNING

The following *twenty-one steps* may be of help to administrators who are beginning to plan for a **FLES*** program:

1. Assess community/school interests, needs, and resources, including foreign language skills of existing school staff.
2. Organize a **FLES*** advisory or study committee.
3. Determine the resources of the school and the community with respect to finances, language preferences, secondary school programs, agencies, universities, etc.
4. Formulate realistic goals for the community. (Long-range plans have to be made concerning curriculum and articulation as well as teacher recruitment and training.)
5. Develop with the **FLES*** advisory committee a rationale for the program, a choice of one or more of the three program models, and a plan for how the school or school district will make the difficult nuts-and-bolts decisions mentioned in Chapter Four.
6. Anticipate difficulties, problems, roadblocks, and the views of people who might be opposed. Try to prepare logical responses to somewhat emotional reactions.
7. Investigate successful programs and try to discover the reasons for their success.
8. Contact knowledgeable people, particularly second-language specialists in the different types of **FLES*** programs.
9. Prepare a detailed proposal, including a plan for a pilot program, an anticipated budget (which includes start-up costs, salaries, and materials of instruction among other items), and outcomes of the program selected.
10. Arrange for coordination and supervision of the program.
11. Develop curriculum materials to fulfill realistic goals, as well as plans for articulation with upper levels. (Time for curriculum preparation should also be included in the budget proposal.)

12. Develop a plan for the recruitment and training of teachers (both preservice and in-service).

13. Promote interest by speaking to parents, teachers, principals, members of civic associations, etc.

14. Be sure to involve secondary school foreign language teachers in the study committee so that they will be supportive of the program.

15. Select and order materials of instruction for the pilot program.

16. Arrange teaching schedules.

17. Begin the pilot program and publicize it regularly.

18. Evaluate! Evaluate! Evaluate! Ask for input at all levels and at all stages of planning and implementation.

19. Be prepared for successes and failures.

20. Attempt to solve conflicts and deal with unexpected reactions.

21. After a one-year pilot program, and possibly after another year of trial and error during which necessary modifications are made, be prepared to *enjoy* the program!

These twenty-one steps may be an oversimplification of the long and arduous process (possibly nine to eighteen months) of implementing a new program. However, no matter which model is selected, **FLES*** planners need to complete all or most of these steps as they organize a **FLES*** program.

The **FLES*** advisory committee should be composed of foreign language educators representing all school levels, parents, taxpayers, administrators, business representatives, guidance counselors, specialists in elementary education, and representation from the university level. The committee could then divide the work to obtain answers to the various questions raised. They might visit other programs, gather significant information, send questionnaires, hire consultants, hold hearings, and, finally, make recommendations on the basic issues relating to such matters as the choice of the foreign language(s), the entry grade level, the involvement of all or just some of the children, and other questions, such as: Is there time in the school day for another subject? If not, what will be left out? Are there enough qualified teachers now and in the future? What is the research basis for **FLES***?

School committees are cautioned, then, to be sure that their goals are realistic and doable; to be certain that there is input from various segments of the community; to be sure that there is consensus on some of the "hot issues," such as choice of language, entry grade level, etc.; to have sufficient lead time before a program is implemented; and to be aware of the need for effective coordination and supervision of the program.

Planning for the *FLEX* Program Model

- Would it be possible to offer the foreign language to all students? Is any funding available? Is it "hidden"? (I.e., can existing funding cover some aspects?)
- What are the specific language and cultural goals? Would the limited results warrant the expenditure of time and money? How much proficiency is expected?
- Are the goals doable? Will the goals be clearly stated?
- Is it important to hire only qualified teachers?
- Should the program be devoted to only one language and culture or would it be possible to provide exposure to more than one? Which ones?
- Is it possible for elementary school teachers to teach *FLEX* using cassettes, video, and film or some form of distance learning?
- Who will be responsible for the program, districtwide and in the school(s)?
- Can the program be initiated even when there is only a little money for materials and curriculum development?
- Can the program be started with only fifteen minutes available a week? Should it be?
- How can the *FLEX* program model be evaluated? By questionnaires, examinations, interviews, etc.?
- How would this *FLEX* program compare with other *FLEX* program models in the country?
- How would the *FLEX* model contribute to the K–12 FL sequence?
- How would this model achieve the goals of the *Standards for Foreign Language Learning* (National Standards in Foreign Language Education Project 1996)?

Planning for the *Sequential FLES* Program Model

- Would it be possible to offer the foreign language to all students? The first year only? How much funding is available?
- What are the specific language and cultural goals? Are these in keeping with the needs of the community?
- Are the goals attainable? Are they appropriate? Clearly stated?
- Who is qualified to teach in this program? What are the options?
- Which language(s) will be selected? What is the rationale for the selection? Is this in keeping with the needs and wishes of the community?

- Which materials would be appropriate for this type of program (audio, video, film, television, etc.)? Are textbooks available? For one year or for more than one year? Are they culturally authentic?
- Who will be responsible for the program, districtwide and in the school(s)? Someone who knows foreign languages and **FLES***?
- Should the program be initiated without adequate materials and curriculum development?
- What is the minimum amount of time needed to achieve the established goals for this program? How will the time be found?
- How can this *FLES* program model be evaluated? By questionnaires, examinations, interviews, testing, and other ways?
- How would this *FLES* program compare with other *FLES* program models in the country?
- How would this *FLES* program compare with a *FLEX* or an *Immersion* program model in meeting the established goals?
- How would the *Sequential FLES* model contribute to the K–12 FL sequence?
- How would this model achieve the goals of the *Standards for Foreign Language Learning?*

Planning for the *Immersion* or *Partial Immersion* Program Model

- Would it be possible for all students to be in the *Immersion* model? The first year only? Is *Partial Immersion* an option? Is *Dual-Language Immersion?* For only some of the students? How much funding is there?
- What are the specific goals? Do they include language and cultural goals as well as basic subject goals? Are these in keeping with the needs of the community?
- Are the goals doable and realistic?
- Who would be qualified to teach in this program? Are there enough qualified teachers for this program model?
- Which language will be selected? What is the rationale for the selection of this language? When will English start? Does the language choice meet the needs of the community?
- How do parents feel about the *Immersion* model? Are there special concerns about progress in the curriculum and in English?
- Which materials would be appropriate for this type of model? Are there sufficient materials available not only for teaching the language itself, but also in the language for teaching math, science, and social studies? Are they all foreign materials? Would they be appropriate for the curriculum in this school district?

- Who will be responsible for the programs, districtwide and in the school(s)? What will occur in the junior high school for these *Immersion* students? Will there be an *Immersion* junior high school? An *Immersion* high school?

- Who will develop the curriculum in the several areas of *Immersion*? Will it be a translation of the English? Is this satisfactory?

- Will *Total Immersion* or *Partial Immersion* be needed to achieve the goals of the program?

- How can the *Immersion* program model be evaluated?

- How would this *Immersion* program compare with other *Immersion* program models in the country?

- How would this *Immersion* program compare with a *Sequential FLES* program or a *FLEX* program in meeting the established goals of this school community?

- How would the *Immersion* model contribute to the K–12 FL sequence?

- How would this model achieve the goals of the *Standards for Foreign Language Learning?*

Guiding Principles for Making Decisions for FLES* Programs

Decision makers should keep in mind the following guiding principles as they begin to plan appropriate programs for their school, school district, and/or school community. They are:

1. All K–8 elementary school students should have the opportunity to start the study of a foreign language before the age of ten, based on brain research studies.

2. All three program models (*Sequential FLES, FLEX-Exploratory,* and all types of *Immersion*) are valid foreign language programs, provided that they fulfill their goals.

3. There is no one best way to provide **FLES*** instruction, nor is there only one best method of **FLES*** instruction.

4. All program models contribute, in different ways, to a K–12 foreign language sequence.

Flexibility Needed

After a choice (or choices) has been made, based on the program goals and objectives, it is important to include a *flexibility* component in the model so that changes can be made when the program is not fulfilling the goals.

If flexibility is an ongoing factor, the beginning grade level can be changed (e.g., the beginning grade level can be lowered from grade 4 to grade 3), the content of the curriculum can be adjusted if it turns out to be too demanding for the time allotted to the program, and other developmental concerns can be addressed. However, if a major change seems to be indicated (such as a change from a *Sequential FLES* program model to a *FLEX* program model, or from an *Immersion* model to a *FLEX* model), it is essential that a broadly based committee be involved in studying the reasons for making such a change. I would urge that no major changes be made for at least two years before a study committee begins to look into other options. If the original study committee followed the twenty-one steps outlined earlier in this chapter, a *major* change would most likely be unnecessary.

Probably the most significant goal to be determined is the degree of proficiency to be attained. In making this determination, it is basic that any planning committee consult with **FLES*** language specialists to make certain that the committee's expectations are realistic and in keeping with what is already known about second language instruction. Variations within each major model can be arranged, such as using an itinerant specialist teacher instead of classroom teachers. Other variations include the use of television and satellite programs combined with both types of teachers. Still others involve the use of volunteers, where funding proves to be a problem. But in each case, the goals and objectives must be spelled out completely, so that no one is misled. That is central!

CAUTIONS IN PLANNING PROGRAMS

At the height of enthusiasm for a new project, policymakers and study committees may tend to overlook some of the potential problems and negative aspects. It must be stressed that before a community embarks on instituting any type of **FLES*** program, it should consider all of the implications for the next ten years. That is why both short-term and long-range goals have to be discussed, modified, changed, adapted, and developed until they represent the best thinking of the community. "What if" suppositions should be posed, "Why" questions should be pondered, and "Are we better off with the program or without it?" should be asked throughout the planning process. Careful consideration of many options will ensure an effective program.

There are a few cautions about visiting schools with **FLES*** programs. First, it is crucial to remember that ALL children speaking a foreign language are "adorable." A visiting committee must reach beyond the obvious and ask some hard-nosed questions about problems and concerns, such as: When did your program start? How has the program been evaluated? What do you like about your program? How has the program changed over the years? What would you like to change now? Is there a written curriculum? How do the students do on standardized national tests? Have you had difficulty in finding (or replacing) foreign language teachers? Are you implementing the *Standards for Foreign Language Learning*?

Suggested Guide for On-Site Visitations by FLES* Study Committees

1. Get as much information as possible ahead of time, including schedules, goals of the program, curriculum, etc.

2. Plan to observe different grades of instruction, if possible.

3. Plan to interview **FLES*** teachers, students, parents, administrators, and guidance counselors, if available.

4. Ask questions about:
   All students included in the **FLES*** program?
   Success of the program? Why?
   Expected student outcomes?
   Materials used?
   Teacher-made materials used?
   Cost of the program?
   Assessment procedures?
   Classroom space for the program?
   Place of **FLES*** in the elementary school schedule?
   Frequency and length of class sessions?
   Teacher recruitment and training?
   Written curriculum?
   Implementation of the five C's of the *Standards for Foreign Language Learning?*
   Articulation procedures?
   Modifications of the program in the past? For the future?
   Level of satisfaction for students, parents, classroom teachers, administrators, etc.?
   Problems encountered in the past and manner of solution?
   Opponents of the program?
   Other topics related to the specific school/school district?

After the goals have been set, the planners should take a very hard look at whether it is possible to accomplish those goals in the kind of program selected. **"WE MUST BE SURE TO DELIVER WHAT WE PROMISE TO DELIVER"** should be the motto of the advisory committee. Furthermore, the advisory committee must consider some of the questions posed by skeptics and those opposed to **FLES***, whatever their reasons. Such questions must be dealt with before starting a program, because they will not just disappear! (For additional cautions, see Gramer 1988.)

How to Avoid the Problems of the 1960s (Or—Follow This Blueprint of What Happened!)

It is my opinion (and that of many others) that **FLES*** programs of the 1960s and 1970s failed for many reasons:

1. **FLES*** programs grew too rapidly, without too much careful thought and planning beyond the first year.

2. **FLES*** programs made promises and set goals that were often unattainable, given the amount of *time* for instruction and the *lack of qualified teachers.*

3. **FLES*** programs failed because they did not have the support of secondary school teachers and supervisors.

4. The rationale for starting a **FLES*** program was more often based on the "bandwagon phenomenon" than on the sound and thoughtful examination of resources and goals.

5. While it is true that *funding* became a crucial factor in whether a **FLES*** program continued, taxpayers demanded to know (and rightly so) how their tax money was being spent and whether this was the most efficient way to spend it. In other words, were the results what they had been promised?

6. At that time, very little attention was given to *flexibility*, since language teaching relied heavily on pattern drills and behavioral objectives. The then-new audiolingual methodology, with its heavy reliance on pattern drills for listening and speaking activities, swept the country on all school levels. "Authorities" proclaimed that a prereading and prewriting stage should be included at all levels, and that for **FLES***, a minimum of 100 clock

hours of solely listening and speaking activities should be required. This amounted to at least one year for most **FLES*** programs. We hope that what we have learned from the failure of some programs of the 1960s will prevent us from falling into a "regimentation" trap. In the 1960s, the same methodology was used for all kinds of programs. Now we know that we *must* suit both the program type and the methodology to the goals of the program, no matter what the methodology fashion of the times may be. Now we know that we must be flexible and realistic in approach, during both planning and implementation.

7. Because opportunities for preservice and in-service training were very limited, not many **FLES*** programs had qualified teachers. Some programs relied heavily on native speakers with little training in elementary education in the United States and little exposure to second-language teaching methodology.

8. The long sequence of studying a foreign language with very little change in methodology resulted in some youngsters getting tired of and bored with studying a foreign language.

9. *Articulation* with the secondary schools was almost nonexistent, and former **FLES*** students entering secondary school programs found that they had to repeat their FL study from the beginning. This was frustrating for students and parents.

10. Since **FLES*** at that time consisted mostly of listening and speaking, with very little reading and writing, and relied mostly on songs and games, it was not taken seriously, even though most of the children learned both language and culture. Even today, in interviews with me and with other former **FLES*** teachers, some adults who are former **FLES*** students still remember their foreign language experience with great fondness.

11. At that time it was considered essential to form a "cultural island" quite apart from the rest of the elementary school curriculum. This exclusivity made such a program easier to remove than a program that was integrally related with the rest of the curriculum.

12. **FLES*** was started in the 1960s as a reaction to the surprise of Sputnik. Sputnik, readers may recall, was the first earth satellite launched by the Russians in 1957. As a result, policymakers across the nation insisted that science, mathematics, and foreign languages be expanded and supported at all levels. Federal language institutes were funded, and foreign language teachers were exposed to the new wave of audiolingual methodology, which promised more effective results in language learning on all school levels, including the **FLES*** level. It was also felt that our children needed a long time to learn difficult languages, such as Russian. By the 1970s, the pressure for early language learning

diminished and technological advancements became the object of public lobbying.

13. Failure to become an integral part of the elementary school curriculum further contributed to the erosion of **FLES***.

14. Lack of a realistic curriculum exacerbated the situation.

15. There was a lack of answers to the question, "Why **FLES***?"

16. There was a failure to say "Let's slow down," "Let's plan carefully before starting a program."

Can similar difficulties be avoided? Of course! With the involvement of a number of key people (both professional and community leaders), with a long-range public commitment, and with careful setting of realistic goals within the framework of available monies, teachers, content, time schedules, and other factors, it *is* possible to plan successful programs for the year 2000 and beyond.

- Set your goals *first.*
- Develop a program that matches your goals.
- If your program does not work, go back and adjust various aspects of it.
- Be realistic!
- Spell out long-range goals in advance.
- Set realistic, attainable goals, and make sure that they are understood and accepted by key people.
- Realize that the type of program selected must be determined by the goals.

OPTIONS IN **FLES*** DELIVERY MODELS

Fortunately, we have a number of options in delivery models to suit different types of programs and school communities. Which one is the best will have to be determined by policymakers and the **FLES*** advisory committee. The following represent the most popular delivery choices for the different types of **FLES*** programs:

OPTION 1: The use of *classroom teachers* who have a good background in a foreign language and who know the elementary school curriculum and methodology for teaching foreign languages to young children. The use of a classroom teacher who provides foreign language instruction to his or her class and possibly to one or two other classes (through a team-teaching approach) is viable in all three program models of *Sequential FLES, FLEX,* or *Immersion.* It also has the great advantage of not costing additional teaching personnel monies. Administrators should survey their school staff to discover foreign language talents.

OPTION 2: A variation of the classroom teacher option might be to combine the use of a classroom teacher with a *television* or *video* program. Prior programs indicate that the classroom teacher should have some knowledge of the foreign language because children soon tire of a single format for presentations, such as TV or video, that offers few opportunities for student-to-student communication.

OPTION 3: The use of an *itinerant foreign language teacher* who travels from class to class, and possibly from school to school. This can be effective, but usually requires additional funding for the teacher (or teachers), who often must teach twelve to fourteen classes a day—too many classes and too many children for an effective program!

OPTION 4: The *dual assignment* of foreign language teachers to both high school and **FLES*** classes, provided that such secondary school teachers get extensive training in methodology and understand younger children and how they learn. The use of high school teachers in **FLES*** classes has often been a successful solution because articulation procedures are built right into the program. The dual-assignment concept could be used to give elementary school teachers multiple responsibilities, such as bilingual and **FLES*** or ESOL and **FLES***. Other professional school personnel with a knowledge of a foreign language, such as principals, counselors, and itinerant specialists, may also be tapped to provide **FLES*** instruction.

OPTION 5: The use of *distance learning technology,* such as media programs via satellite and/or interactive cable television, is still another option. The basic technology installation is the major cost, but it may already exist in many places for other subject areas. It can be used to provide direct instruction for students as well as professional development for teachers. The advantage of interactive technology is that it offers students the opportunity for person-to-person communication and practice in the foreign language. The technology keeps getting more sophisticated, and now with computers and on-line networks, many exciting telecommunications options will be available in the not-so-distant future. (See Chapter Twelve.)

OPTION 6: The use of *volunteers* is another option. The drawback is that volunteers (whether adults or high school students) need a great deal of training. Very often, though, the most effective volunteers can be high school students, or cross-age tutors, as they are often called. These secondary school students find teaching elementary school students a rewarding experience. A student once said, "I never really understood some things about French until I taught it to kids. I love teaching, and I am going to make that my career!" The use of high school students as volunteers for **FLES*** programs is a good way to recruit future teachers.

OPTION 7: Some districts have recruited *foreign teachers* for their **FLES*** programs. Such individuals know the foreign language, but they may not necessarily know and understand the American educational philosophy, which may be quite different from what they are accustomed to in their native country. Not only will you have to provide extensive training for foreign teachers, but you will also have to deal with visas, green cards, and all kinds of international red tape. School districts in Louisiana and Kansas City, Missouri, have implemented programs with foreign teachers. (See Garcia 1990.)

OPTION 8: Another approach that is sometimes used is a *before-school* or *after-school program* using volunteers from the community. This is generally not recommended because the children view the foreign language program as an adjunct to the school day rather than a part of it, no matter who provides the instruction.

OPTION 9: Another approach, which has succeeded in Anne Arundel County, Maryland, utilizes sixth-grade elementary school teachers in a social studies/foreign language *integration* or *infusion*. Because many of these teachers have few foreign language skills, this approach requires a great deal of support and instruction in foreign language methodology. In this *FLEX* program, where the language content is very limited, the teachers use cassette recordings for self-study and in class with the children. The youngsters learn map-reading skills, practice short dialogues about travel to Canada and Latin America, and learn about customs and daily life.

OPTION 10: Magnet schools represent another delivery model. In most instances, the main objective of magnet schools is to achieve racial balance by inducing majority children to attend minority children's schools by offering special programs in math, science, or foreign language *Immersion*. They generally offer *Partial Immersion* programs. Such schools may draw students from a single school district or be a collaborative effort of several districts. Some U.S. examples of this model, which is based on the Canadian experience, may be found in Prince Georges County and Montgomery County, Maryland; Cincinnati, Ohio; Milwaukee, Wisconsin; Kansas City, Missouri; Fairfax, Virginia; and elsewhere.

This does not exhaust the list of possible options in delivery models, but it indicates that many different alternatives exist in one form or another.

CREATIVE PROCEDURES IN ESTABLISHING THE PROGRAM

In these days of budget constraints, administrators need to be creative in organizing the most cost-effective programs possible. The following suggestions may be helpful, since children should not be deprived of an early foreign language experience, if at all possible.

- Explore long-term funding from foundations, government grants, and contributions by local businesses and organizations.
- Investigate which foundations are interested in funding the teaching of less commonly selected languages.
- Adapt goals so that a less-demanding program with lower costs can be developed, provided that everyone understands the limited goals and outcomes.
- Explore long-term hiring practices that might emphasize the recruitment of effective elementary school teachers with a background in a foreign language.
- Survey the current staff to uncover hidden foreign language skills.
- Explore in-service staff development for elementary school teachers, with incentives for foreign language study and study abroad.
- Enlist the cooperation of local and/or state universities that might be able to plan for the long-term training of prospective teachers; also explore with media specialists the possibilities of satellite programs and distance learning for direct instruction of students and teacher-training programs for teachers.
- Encourage local high school and college students who excel in foreign languages to serve as volunteer peer tutors; encourage them to think about teaching at the elementary school level as a career choice.
- Explore the use of technology with elementary school classroom teachers in the form of video programs, satellite programs, university programs, etc.
- Explore the use of foreign teachers who may be residents of your school community.
- Explore with your state education department the possibility of airing **FLES*** programs on instructional television.

SCHEDULING

Once a decision has been made concerning the program model or models, and once the **FLES*** advisory committee has resolved the conflicts related to selection of students, choice of language(s), entry grade level, etc., administrators need to make decisions on scheduling. The optimum schedule for *Sequential FLES* and *FLEX* programs is a minimum of thirty minutes a day, five times a week. This schedule cannot be implemented without extensive discussions with school-based administrators and teachers. "Where will we find the time?" "What will we leave out?" The easiest solution is to work the foreign language into the social studies and/or language arts schedule to form interdisciplinary partnerships. However, effective scheduling can be organized around art, music, science, math, or the humanities. (Study the Sample Daily Elementary School Schedule on page 57.)

When the foreign language teacher is also the classroom teacher, scheduling is not a problem, because the foreign language flows naturally throughout the day, in addition to scheduled class subjects. It is important to note that the classroom **FLES*** teacher model is successful whether the program model is *Sequential FLES, FLEX, Immersion,* or *Partial Immersion.*

Unfortunately, some school districts set up schedules that are neither reasonable nor educationally sound, particularly when itinerant **FLES*** teachers teach more than fourteen classes a day. A more reasonable recommendation is to assign itinerant **FLES*** teachers to no more than seven to ten classes a day. Probably the simplest scheduling procedure is to hire competent classroom elementary school teachers, grades K–8, who are also proficient in a foreign language.

In order to implement the program(s) selected, decisions have to made about the number of sessions per week and number of minutes per session. Other questions that need answers include: Will the class have an itinerant teacher or a regular classroom teacher? How many classes will each teacher teach? Will there be joint planning time for the **FLES*** teacher and the classroom teacher(s)? One caution, however: In the 1960s, teachers who were itinerant often taught more than 150 students each day, a heavy load that interfered with their ability to get to know their students and deliver satisfactory programs. Teaching schedules must be cost-effective, but they must take into account the very real and pressing problems that an overburdened schedule might cause.

Very frequently, for *Sequential FLES* and *FLEX*, the crucial problem in scheduling is the question of which aspects of the elementary school curriculum will be left out and/or modified. There are few simple answers to this question, but often, if teachers and administrators earnestly try to find time in an extremely crowded schedule, it is possible to find thirty to sixty minutes a week. More efficiency in moving from class to class; more correlation with subjects already being taught,

A Sample Daily Elementary School Schedule

Is there room for foreign language?
(These schedules may vary from school district to school district.)

9:00	Opening Routines	Monday	Tuesday	Wednesday	Thursday	Friday
9:10–11:25	Language Arts / Reading / Spelling / Writing/Composition / Handwriting / Literature	Art 10:00–11:00		P.E. 10:30–11:00		
11:30–12:15	Mathematics		Music 11:45–12:15			
12:15–1:15	Lunch and Activities					
1:15–2:00	Social Studies					P.E. 1:15–2:45
2:05–2:50	Science				Music 2:05–2:35	
2:50–3:00	Closing Routines					

Guidelines

Math	195 minutes
Science	195 minutes
Social Studies	195 minutes

Language Arts	600 minutes
Reading	300 minutes
Writing/Comp.	120 minutes
Spelling	80 minutes
Handwriting	40 minutes
Literature	60 minutes

Art	60 minutes
Music	60 minutes
P.E.	60 minutes

such as social studies and language arts; more flexibility in scheduling; more functional use of opening and closing routines; and similar adjustments would open up the schedule a little. The difficulty is getting consensus of all parties. In this respect, **FLES*** teachers who are classroom teachers have the advantage, since the foreign language is incorporated throughout the school day, but all kinds of schedules can work.

Coordination of the **FLES*** Program

Included in any plan for developing a **FLES*** program must be a decision on who will coordinate it. Whether it is coordinated by a teacher, a supervisor, an administrator, or a chairperson, there must be someone who makes the decisions, who answers the questions and complaints (yes, once in a while there are some complaints!), who assists with hiring and firing staff, who orders materials, and who is in overall charge of the program. This person is the **FLES*** advocate. Even with the most enlightened philosophy of management, there must be one person who has the final word.

Experience reminds us that the best person for this role is a foreign language supervisor who sees the program in the entire sweep of a K–12 program. However, sometimes it is necessary for a non-foreign-language administrator to head the program. It is incumbent upon this person to become as knowledgeable as possible and to seek counsel from other foreign language people before making any major decisions.

In planning a budget, school districts should keep in mind that they must include the cost of a coordinator. The program cannot run effectively without leadership, and this position must be planned in advance or dovetailed with another, similar position. If the district elects to save money and combine **FLES*** with an already-existing position, extreme care must be taken not to overburden any one individual. Coordination of the program will take time: There must be time to arrange for teacher training and in-service; there must be time to meet with parents, administrators, and principals; there must be time to develop curriculum; there must be time to observe the program; there must be time to think of additional ways to make the program even more effective; and there must be time to make long-range plans and get consensus on them. Coordination is essential. (For additional suggestions on coordination, see Brown 1989.)

Articulation

If the goals of the program include greater foreign language proficiency as the outcome of a long sequence of study, articulation plans must be coordinated between the elementary school(s) and middle, junior, and high schools. Nothing disenchants parents and the students them-selves more when entering a new school level than to be informed that even though the students have been involved in the study of a foreign language for a number of years, they must start all over again or be placed only one level ahead of others who have never had such exten-sive foreign language experience.

The question of articulation is one of the most difficult problems when dealing with *Sequential FLES* or *Immersion*. In *FLEX* programs the situation is much simpler—most parents and students do not expect to continue the foreign language in the secondary school program. But even with *FLEX*, it is disappointing when children who have had a brief introduction to a foreign language are required to start from the very beginning. What a turn-off! Yet, from the point of view of the secondary school, when only a handful of youngsters have had exposure to a for-eign language, scheduling complexities make it impossible to keep such students in the same class to provide continuity of learning.

After three years or more of *Sequential FLES* or *Immersion*, when students with a rather strong background in a foreign language have to start all over again or decide to drop the foreign language they've stud-ied and opt for a completely new foreign language, the students' disap-pointment and that of their parents are even greater. There are few sim-ple answers to the problem. However, here are a few suggestions:

- Former *FLES* or *Immersion* students can be encouraged to work on the next stages of learning on an independent-study basis.

- Such students may be offered one class at the senior high school to continue on their proper level.

- Such students may be offered a maintenance class that will help them retain their language skills; they may then move ahead when they enter high school.

- District plans that develop an elementary school *Immersion* pro-gram should also include plans for an *Immersion* program in junior and senior high school, if at all possible.

Articulation meetings of foreign language teachers on all school lev-els can often help. Some of the topics that can be discussed at articula-tion meetings are:

Effective teaching practices	Multiple intelligences
Activities that promote proficiency	Teaching ALL students
Curriculum	Collaborative public-awareness activities
Performance assessment	
National standards	Other local, state, and regional issues
Ways to focus on the needs of students	Options for effective articulation

It is important to assess each school or school/district situation by asking some of these specific questions:

1. What are the specific language needs of the school/school community?
2. Which language(s) are favored by parents? Why?
3. Which languages are offered at the middle and senior high schools, in order to offer a long sequence, if at all possible?
4. Which language(s) can provide the greatest capability for teaching youngsters about cultural and linguistic diversity in our country?
5. Would we like to see a sole language offered in the FL sequence or more than one?

Students who have been in **FLES*** programs in grades K–8 have acquired many foreign language skills: They are able to understand the foreign language, can speak it with accurate pronunciation and intonation, can read and write it to some extent, *and* they are capable of moving ahead swiftly, based on the skills developed in their **FLES*** experience. Articulation is a *must!*

NOTE: For the **FLES*** Scale for the Evaluation of **FLES*** Programs, see Appendix A.

INVOLVING PARENTS

Parents can be helpful in supporting all types of **FLES*** programs. They can do this in the following ways:

- Help the child see foreign words in newspapers and magazines or on labels on different products.
- Purchase foreign language books and records on the child's level, although this may be primarily for enrichment.
- Encourage the child who may feel discouraged or stressed (in *Immersion* programs).
- Assist in the preparation of a class project, such as a cookbook.
- Be an advocate for the program.
- Keep in touch with the child's teacher to learn how they can help.
- Assist the teacher by going on trips related to the foreign language work.
- Assist in the preparation of assembly programs.
- Talk to the class about their experiences in the foreign culture.
- Speak to the class in the foreign language.

- Speak to the class about their work in the foreign culture and/or opportunities for careers requiring a foreign language background.
- Encourage but never force the child to speak the foreign language at home.
- Make sure that they let the child know that they are happy about the child's progress.
- Serve on an advisory board (or site-based management team) for the school.
- Speak about positive and negative aspects with parents of children who may be contemplating entrance into the foreign language program.
- Confer with the principal about various aspects of the program that may need rethinking.
- Try to give the child opportunities to participate in some aspect of the foreign culture at museums, on trips, while watching television programs, etc.
- Try to keep the entire program in perspective while resolving the day-to-day concerns.
- Get involved in other ways as the need arises.

PLANNING FOR THE CURRICULUM

The curriculum (and the scope and sequence) must suit the program and the goals selected. Consideration must be given to content, the abilities (listening, speaking, reading, writing) to be emphasized, the amount of English (if any) to be used, the instructional approaches, the link between the foreign language and other aspects of the elementary school curriculum, the development of an initial program and plans for its continuation, the thorny problem of what to do with the youngster who moves into the community without any foreign language experience, the guest speakers who could enhance the curriculum, and whether students' **FLES*** experience will be ignored or will be incorporated into the middle school and/or junior high school program.

It is difficult to make decisions about curriculum if the long-range goals are not firmly in place. If a program has been in existence in grade 7, for example, and the new elementary school program has been planned to be phased in each year, first in grade 6, next year in grade 5, and so on, it is essential to view the effect of the elementary school program on the secondary school program. If, on the other hand, a new *FLEX* program is exploratory in nature, and no one expects students to build on the early introduction, that is quite a different story. If this were the case, the limited goals and exploratory nature of the program would be understood and accepted by parents, teachers, and administrators. *Usually, when a new FLES* program is developed and implemented, plans have to be made for the revision of the secondary school program, particularly if great numbers of students are involved.*

Thus, when first planning a new program, the study committee must deal with the reality of the kind of program it will be, what the expected outcomes will be, and how this type of program fits into the short- and long-range educational sequence from a curricular point of view. If a revision of the secondary school curriculum will be required, that revision should be started long before the new **FLES*** students arrive at the secondary school. Long-range planning is a *must!*

If the study committee recommends an *Immersion* program, then long-range plans should be put in operation immediately, so that *Immersion* students can continue their program in an *Immersion* component at the middle/junior high school and even at the high school. Long-range curriculum planning must look ahead five to ten years, anticipating problems and establishing the framework for an effective articulation plan.

Spiral Curriculum

It is essential for those involved in all types of **FLES*** programs to understand the nature of language learning. Children (and adolescents and adults) rarely learn language the first time it is presented. Some of the steps in the teaching of languages are:

- Motivation for learning
- Presentation in the context of a real-life situation
- Repetition of language components
- Practice in small groups and pairs
- Personalization
- Adaptation of language to different interdisciplinary situations
- Use in all four abilities
- Practice several weeks later
- Adaptation to more sophisticated situations in a year or two

It is important that curriculum developers reenter topics, skills, vocabulary, expressions, etc., from time to time, with adaptations from year to year.

NOTE: For an overview of considerations in the development of a curriculum (K–12) in foreign languages, see Chapter Eight.

PLANNING THE BUDGET

One of the most difficult tasks for an administrator is to juggle the budget in conjunction with the goals and expected outcomes developed by the **FLES*** advisory committee. With limited funds available, the program often has to be scaled down to fit the constraints of the budget. In planning a budget, school officials might want to consider the following items:

- Instructional materials, especially for starting the program.
- Coordination and supervision of the program
- Equipment and repair costs
- Space (if special construction is needed)
- Curriculum, staff, and materials development
- Photocopying and other ways of duplicating student materials
- Teachers' salaries, if beyond the regular allotment
- Other costs related to the local situation and the program requirements

What to Do About "Budget Blues"

Over time, there are all kinds of economic swings, with resulting "budget blues" in education. How can schools/school districts maintain **FLES*** programs (or initiate new ones) under such conditions?

Each school community faces different conditions, but the following considerations may be of assistance in bolstering existing programs:

1. There is a constant need to justify and document the success of the **FLES*** program.
2. There is a constant, ongoing need to sell the program through many different public-awareness activities. (See Chapter Fourteen for information about the promotion of **FLES*** programs.)
3. There is new pressure to reevaluate the goals and delivery of **FLES*** programs in terms of reduced sources of funds for implementation, reduced funds for instructional materials, decreased supplies and equipment (and equipment repairs), scheduling problems, class-size problems, replacement of competent teachers, limited coordination and supervision of the program, and reduced funds for evaluation and assessment.

Other things to consider:

- Continue to have a "can-do," flexible approach and attitude.
- Involve the foreign language advisory council in redesigning the goals of the program while maintaining excellence. In other words, do what you are able to do and do it well!

- Examine alternative resources on the local level.
- Work with parents and other members of the school community.
- Develop alternative options.
- Examine alternative delivery systems.
- Investigate the research on technology and distance learning. (See Chapter Twelve on technology and **FLES*** programs.)
- Contact corporate and foundation sponsors.
- Network with others in the profession and on electronic bulletin boards.
- Brainstorm and be open to new ideas.

CLASSROOM SPACE AND FACILITIES FOR **FLES***

When the **FLES*** teacher is the classroom teacher, space is not a problem. When an itinerant teacher or a volunteer peer tutor is involved, some principals are forced to be very creative about finding adequate space. Realistically, placing the **FLES*** teacher in a room next to band practice is not going to foster good listening skills in the foreign language! Here, too, the school official must juggle the needs of the program with the reality of school facilities. It is the responsibility of the administrator, however, to provide the most effective learning environment possible so that teachers can teach and students can learn.

💡 FOR REFLECTION

To paraphrase a saying about winning often attributed to the football coach Vince Lombardi, *"Planning* isn't everything, it's the *only* thing."

Recruitment, Preparation, and Selection of **FLES*** Teachers

What will children remember about their **FLES*** experience? It will probably be the "process," or what happens in class. It will also be some cultural attitudes about the people(s) who speak the foreign language. If we **FLES*** teachers are "memorable" people who care passionately about children and what we teach, I think children will have very positive memories and attitudes.

Fluency or proficiency in the foreign language to be taught is the basic requirement of the would-be *FLES/FLEX/Immersion* teacher. Since young children imitate almost everything they hear, it is extremely important for teachers at this level to provide a strong model. Thus, ability in the foreign language is of great importance to the success of the program. Part of the interview for prospective teachers should be conducted in the foreign language. Furthermore, not only are oral skills needed, but written skills are important too.

INTERVIEWING PROSPECTIVE **FLES*** TEACHERS

Questions that might be discussed at an interview are the following:

1. How would you begin a **FLES*** program? What would you do the first week?
2. What are your goals for the first year? The second year? Etc.
3. How would you teach a dialogue, a narrative, drills of various kinds? How would you teach for proficiency?
4. How would you provide for individual differences and different learning styles?
5. How would you handle the disruptive pupil? The child who doesn't respond? The student who is bored?
6. How would you keep all the children interested? Motivated to learn?
7. How would you evaluate pupil achievement in the foreign language?
8. How would you evaluate your effectiveness as a teacher?
9. How and when would you introduce reading and writing skills?

10. What kinds of technology would you use?

11. How would the rest of the elementary-school program bear on what you teach in the foreign language?

12. What would be your relationship with other classroom teachers, the principal, and the parents?

13. What would you do if the children did not understand the foreign language?

14. How would you create a classroom climate for effective learning?

15. How would you help the children to be relaxed and reduce their anxiety levels?

16. How would you implement the *Standards for Foreign Language Learning* (National Standards in Foreign Language Education Project 1996)?

Although these suggested interview questions have no correct or incorrect answers, and are not meant to be exhaustive, it is possible, through questioning, to determine a candidate's philosophy of teaching, enthusiasm, understanding of youngsters in elementary and middle schools, and training in **FLES*** methodology.

Before hiring a **FLES*** teacher, more and more foreign language coordinators are interested in ascertaining whether or not the prospective teacher has the foreign language and pedagogical skills to perform successfully. They often request prospective teachers to demonstrate their teaching ability by asking them to:

1. Submit a lesson plan at the interview and discuss (reflect on) various aspects of the plan

2. Teach a **FLES*** class in the foreign language, based on a written lesson plan

3. Present a videotape of a lesson they have taught

SCREENING

Each local agency would probably wish to develop its own requirements, since few states, at the present time, have statewide requirements—although a few states are currently developing guidelines. Some states are moving toward a foreign language K–12 or K–6 and 7–12 certification. As a guide for school communities, the following criteria might be useful for initial screening of applicants:

• Proficiency in the foreign language to be taught (in all four abilities—listening, speaking, reading, and writing)

• Proficiency in another foreign language (optional)

- Knowledge of the customs and culture of the people who speak the foreign language
- Knowledge of the nature of the elementary and/or middle school youngster and the elementary school program
- Knowledge of the content of *FLES/FLEX/Immersion* programs
- Knowledge of the *Standards for Foreign Language Learning*
- Knowledge of the pedagogy for teaching foreign language to young students
- Knowledge of the methodology for teaching reading skills
- Ability to plan interesting and challenging lessons
- Knowledge of technology for **FLES***
- Ability to use a variety of materials
- Ability to relate to people of all ages
- Ability to be a cooperative player on the educational team
- Ability to enjoy working with young students
- Ability to teach, as evidenced by an approved form of student-teaching experience

It should be noted that it is easier to staff *FLES* and *FLEX* programs because there are, at present, few candidates for *Immersion* who are highly proficient in both English and the foreign language. It is generally expected that the *Immersion* teacher will be responsible for the content teaching in the foreign language and the teaching of English, although some programs have a different teacher responsible for teaching English. Based on my experience, I do not see any real need to insist on having two different teachers, since a bilingual teacher could serve as a role model for the students in the *Immersion* program. Others say that students would use more English if they knew that they could speak to their teachers in English. I do not agree. While children might, at first, test the situation, they would soon recognize that English has a definite time and place, no matter who is teaching. It is also difficult to find prospective candidates with these demanding foreign language skills who are also familiar with American elementary school procedures and practices. Just hiring a native speaker without such additional skills is not a good practice.

COMPETENCIES

Which competencies should be expected of prospective *FLES, FLEX,* and *Immersion* teachers? The following discussion might provide some insight into the range of abilities required for a successful foreign language teacher at the elementary school level.

Language Proficiency in the Foreign Language

LISTENING: Able to understand the foreign language as spoken by a native at a normal conversational tempo

SPEAKING: Able to speak the foreign language with sufficient command to communicate spontaneously on daily-life topics with a native speaker without major syntactic errors

READING: Able to read foreign language materials of a general nature with immediate comprehension (such materials as newspapers, magazines, etc.)

WRITING: Able to write foreign language material (letters, reports, summaries, etc.) with minimal errors, and has some knowledge of stylistics to express the subtleties of the language (see Appendix F)

Language Proficiency in English

The competencies in this category would be the same as those listed for the foreign language category.

Some would disagree with the notion that English proficiency is essential in the teaching of *FLES, FLEX,* and *Immersion.* Based on my experience, I find that a teacher who has personally experienced what it means to study a foreign language will be more empathetic to the students. Also, the teacher who is thoroughly familiar with both languages will be in a better position to understand and anticipate the language problems of her or his students.

Linguistics

Every **FLES*** teacher needs knowledge of the principles of phonology, morphology, and syntax, and the ability to apply those principles to strategies for second language instruction.

Methodology for *Sequential FLES* and *FLEX*

- Effective techniques for classroom management
- Unit, weekly, and daily lesson planning
- Strategies for teaching the four abilities (listening, speaking, reading, and writing) and culture
- Techniques for working with groups and in cooperative learning situations
- Error-correction techniques
- Evaluation techniques and assessment of student progress

- Procedures for teaching different types of learners
- Reinforcement and review techniques
- Procedures for group work and paired activities
- Current trends in **FLES*** second-language learning and research studies
- Effective cross-cultural strategies
- Ways to create an effective classroom climate
- Procedures for adapting texts and other materials
- Techniques for appropriate use of multimedia equipment
- Procedures for developing specific goals within the overall goals of the program
- A variety of skills, techniques, and procedures to provide a wide range of different activities in the classroom
- Use of technology
- Implementation of the *Standards for Foreign Language Learning*

Methodology for *Immersion*

- Effective techniques for classroom management
- Procedures for delivering content-based instruction in the foreign language in some or all of the subjects of the elementary school curriculum; knowledge of content and content-specific methodology
- Techniques for working with groups and in cooperative learning situations
- Evaluation techniques
- Procedures for teaching different types of learners
- Reinforcement and review techniques
- Procedures for group work and paired activities
- Current trends in *Immersion* and research studies
- Ways to create an effective classroom climate
- Procedures for adapting texts and content-specific materials
- Techniques for appropriate use of multimedia materials
- Procedures for developing specific goals within the overall goals of the *Immersion* program and the elementary school curriculum
- A variety of skills, techniques, and procedures to provide a wide range of activities in the classroom
- Use of technology
- Implementation of the *Standards for Foreign Language Learning*

American and Target Language Children's Literature

- Children's classics
- Fables and fairy tales
- Children's poetry
- Children's magazines and other contemporary materials
- Other literary materials appropriate to the goals of the program

Culture

The candidate should demonstrate a knowledge of, a sensitivity to, and an ability to contrast differences and similarities between the target culture and the American culture in

- Family life
- Social groups
- Political activities
- Kinesics
- Influence of the media
- Role of women
- Attitudes toward money, land, food, humor, and other values
- Occupations
- Leisure-time activities, such as sports
- Geography and history
- Social, educational, and governmental institutions
- Music, art, theater, and cinema
- Religion
- Cuisine
- Ceremonies, customs, and rituals
- Taboos
- Science and technology
- Other aspects as needed and/or indicated by the curriculum

Child Psychology

- Understanding of the nature of the American elementary school child
- Knowledge of how to work successfully with children, parents, and other professionals (teachers, administrators, principals, guidance counselors, psychologists, etc.)

- Knowledge of the physical, cognitive, intellectual, emotional, and social stages of the elementary school student's growth and development
- Knowledge of the different theories of learning
- Awareness of the different ways of increasing student motivation and attention span
- Awareness of the importance of the teacher's personality in creating a warm, friendly learning environment
- Ability to plan interesting and challenging lessons that will appeal to young children
- Ability to teach the foreign language to young children, as demonstrated through an approved form of student teaching
- Demonstrated success in developing rapport with young children
- Others as required by the local situation

NOTE: See Appendix F for the list of competencies recommended by the National **FLES*** Commission of AATF.

CERTIFICATION OF TEACHERS

Although most states and school districts do not, as yet, have certification of foreign language teachers at the elementary school level, teachers must be certified in some area. There are some states moving to foreign language certification in K–12, but FL certification in K–6 or 7–12 would be better. Usually, it is best to have a certified elementary school teacher with high proficiency in the foreign language. Unfortunately, there are still very few teachers with this type of background. Another alternative is to use certified foreign language teachers who are highly proficient in the foreign language and who have taken at least nine credits in elementary school methodology and curriculum, plus a **FLES*** methods course. These, too, are quite rare, but the number of qualified teachers, it is predicted, will grow, once the need is identified and publicized. *Immersion* teachers who are totally bilingual in English and the target language are also very hard to find, but here too, as more elementary foreign language programs are expanded, more teachers will seek the appropriate training to develop the required competencies. If there is a demand for training, more universities will respond with appropriate courses.

As Larew (1986) pointed out, the **FLES*** teacher is "not merely a language teacher, but is often perceived as a representative of the culture of the language she teaches, by her students." Having proficiency in the language is excellent, but many skills and competencies are required in order to perform effectively on the **FLES*** level.

TEACHER TRAINING

Preservice and In-Service Training

The FLES* Methods Course

During the preservice stage, prospective *FLES/FLEX/Immersion* teachers would benefit from an orientation to the school system and to the age level of elementary school students. The ideal situation would be a university-level *FLES/FLEX/Immersion* course, given at the university or in the district, that would give the new teacher an introduction to the field and practice in the various components of lessons. A course currently offered at the University of Maryland, Baltimore County, has the following course outline:

1. Rationale for *FLES, FLEX,* and *Immersion,* including brain research
2. Place of *FLES, FLEX,* and *Immersion* in elementary school
3. Needs of elementary school youngsters: applications to teaching foreign languages, multiple approaches, reaching all students
4. Options in **FLES***: *FLES, FLEX, Immersion*
5. Contrasting *FLEX* in elementary school and exploratory in middle school; contrasting **FLES*** and secondary school methodology
6. Techniques for the contextualized focus on **FLES***
7. Implementing the *Standards for Foreign Language Learning,* the five C's, and curriculum development
8. Techniques for teaching interdisciplinary approaches
9. Overview of materials and their use; criteria for selection and adaptation
10. Development of lesson plans: long-range, weekly, and daily; small-group activities; writing learning scenarios
11. Use of multimedia materials and technology; relationship to content and curriculum (video, computer, satellite, etc.)
12. Techniques for standards-based evaluation of student progress and grading procedures, if required; techniques for program evaluation
13. Development of activities beyond the classroom: field trips, trips abroad, community festivals, camps, etc.
14. Techniques for teaching standards-based cultural components and cultural awareness
15. Promotion of **FLES*** programs (for further information, see Moore 1996)

Other aspects of the course that should be noted are the presentation of minilessons by the participants, evaluation of materials, review of the current research from an objective point of view, mock role-playing as members of boards of education or study committees, interviews with **FLES*** and secondary school teachers, and many other activities. Guest speakers representing different points of view and different bases of experience help participants to put all ideas in perspective.

There are a number of activities that enhance learning in the **FLES*** methods course. They include the following:

1. *Micro teaching:* Teaching short parts of a lesson to members of the methods class. Sometimes individual members of the class serve as "trouble makers" whose interruptions challenge teachers.

2. *Portfolios:* Keeping a variety of materials, projects, recordings, reflections in a dialogue journal, and other items in an organized manner. Such headings as Teacher References, Student Materials, Cultural Materials, Assessment Samples, and the like can be useful at a later time (see Wolf 1996).

3. *Textbook/materials discussion and evaluation:* Using the Criteria for the Selection of **FLES*** Materials (see Chapter 15) to analyze instructional materials. **FLES*** teachers are frequently called upon to select materials (often on very short notice), and they need to develop the skills to determine which texts will be of greatest use for their students.

4. *Group problem-solving sessions:* Helping teachers to develop their skills in dealing with on-the-job challenges, such as dealing with classroom teachers, parents, supervisors, children with special needs, and others.

5. *Reflection journals:* Having teachers keep a record of their own evaluations of lessons taught, class discussions on student diversity, reactions to national standards, observation of teachers, observation of conference sessions, reactions to the language laboratory and other technology, reflections on a **FLES*** philosophy, and other important experiences.

6. *Contextualized, real-life connections in FLES*:* Keeping a list of possible age-appropriate themes, situations, and scenarios.

7. *Public relations for FLES* activities:* Developing ways to celebrate National **FLES*** Day (the first Monday of National Foreign Language Week in March); assembly programs for parents and grandparents; presentations beyond the school, such as at senior citizens' gatherings; department store language lessons; decoration of bulletin boards at libraries, etc.; as well as presentations to school board members, parents, and administrators on the value of **FLES*** (see Chapter 14).

8. *Activities with technology:* See Chapter 12.

The following represents the type of final examination that might be given at the completion of the *FLEX/FLES/Immersion* methods course; it demonstrates the skills and competencies essential for the successful **FLES*** teacher:

1. Assume that a Spanish-speaking parent comes to complain that her child is not learning anything new in Spanish *Sequential FLES*. What do you say? What do you do?

2. Invent a significant question about *FLES, FLEX*, and *Immersion* and answer it. You will be graded on the quality of the question as well as the answer.

3. Describe three cultural concepts you would teach in *FLES, FLEX*, and *Immersion*. Show how your approach would differ in each situation.

4. Write a lesson plan with explanations for each of the following (include interdisciplinary and cultural approaches):
   1 lesson plan for grades 1–2 *Immersion*
   1 lesson plan for grades 3–4 *FLEX*
   1 lesson plan for grades 5–6 *Sequential FLES*

5. Discuss the contributions of five outstanding personalities mentioned during the course. Give specific ways in which *FLES, FLEX*, or *Immersion* have been affected by these people because of what they have written, what they have proposed, etc.

6. What kinds of competencies should a teacher of *FLES, FLEX*, or *Immersion* have? How do they differ from the competencies of other teachers? What training, personality, language skills, etc., should **FLES*** teachers have? Should there be any compromises?

7. Discuss the importance of technology in *FLES, FLEX*, and *Immersion*. What is the current thought about technology? Which activities can be planned?

8. Create a learning scenario and discuss how the five C's can be included.

One example of alternative assessment for **FLES*** teacher training was developed by the 1996 participants at the National **FLES*** Institute, held at the University of Maryland, Baltimore County. Its goal was to review important concepts while demonstrating how a Jeopardy game could be an effective assessment tool in the **FLES*** classroom.

FLES* ASSESSMENT JEOPARDY GAME

HEADINGS ACROSS: The **FLES*** Institute, Guests and Participants, Facts and Statistics, Cultures and Languages, and Activities and Games

Cues related to prize amounts ranging from $100 to $500 were listed under each heading. For example:

CUE: These are the five C's.
ANSWER: What are communication, cultures, connections, comparisons, and communities?

CUE: It's what N.L.K.T. really stands for.
ANSWER: What is Native Language Kid Talk?

While methodology is extremely important, use of the foreign language is *paramount*. Therefore, even in the methods course, provision should be made for students to use the language laboratory, to join language clubs and tables designed for conversational practice, to listen to radio and television programs broadcast in the target language, and to read target language newspapers and magazines in order to keep all the skills of foreign language communication sharply honed. The most dynamic, effective teacher cannot function well in the classroom unless his or her foreign language skills are maintained and continue to grow stronger. This applies to all foreign language teachers, whether or not they are teaching *FLES, FLEX,* and *Immersion.*

Prospective teachers should be encouraged to join professional organizations so they can attend conferences; receive professional journals, listservs, and newsletters; and learn about current trends in the field.

In-Service Training: The Institute Approach

One successful way to provide in-service training for *FLES/FLEX/ Immersion* teachers is the institute approach. Institutes are held either during the summer or during the school year. A one- to three-week institute session held during the summer allows intensive practice in foreign language skills and the imparting of extensive cultural information. If the foreign language is used around the clock in real-life day-to-day situations, participants emerge from the experience with greater enthusiasm for the task and with a broad scope of additional knowledge. Hearkening to the NDEA Institutes of the past, the current breed of teacher-training foreign language institutes are sensitive to the need for immersion in the foreign languages as well as to the need for expansion of pedagogical skills.

The institute type of training is useful before service and for teachers already in service. Other types of in-service courses can be offered at the local level, devoted to the specific needs of the teachers. One such course may deal with the analysis of the current foreign culture(s); another may introduce another foreign language (Spanish for teachers of French, for example); another may present methods of teaching English and language arts for teachers of *Immersion*; another may focus on trends in developing listening and speaking abilities. These courses may be taught by knowledgeable personnel within the school district or by university faculty. The major goal is to enrich, broaden, and enhance teachers' abilities and skills.

Periodic workshops with hands-on components are extremely help-ful for teachers. Generally, it is a wise procedure to poll the teachers on their choice of workshop topics and presenters. Teachers respond more favorably to in-service programs when they have been involved in the planning. One-day workshops help to inspire teachers during the school year and usually provide them with materials and activities to try out immediately with their classes. "Make and Take" workshops are particularly popular.

Finally, a last word about teacher training. It is vital that teachers gain confidence about their own wisdom in making choices for their classes. They are the ones who are "on the firing line with students." Teachers need to learn about the theoretical bases for instruction, the pedagogical approaches and techniques, and the essentials of child psychology and growth. Teachers need to be open to new develop-ments and practices in language learning, but they also need to rely on their own experience and the experience of colleagues in the field in order to implement effective practices in their own classrooms. *Helping teachers see a wide range of options and bolstering their self-confidence in making decisions are the ultimate goals of teacher-training programs.*

Professional Growth

Teachers need opportunities for all kinds of professional growth, such as attending meetings and foreign language conferences, hearing guest speakers, observing other teachers, and, most important, meeting with peers to network and exchange ideas.

Sometimes networking among **FLES*** teachers occurs sponta-neously under informal circumstances: telephone calls, social occa-sions, encounters at foreign language conferences, etc.

Teachers also make formal plans for networking in order to share ideas and concerns, and are strengthened by the support of others involved in the same kind of endeavor. A good example of this is the FLESFEST for Wisconsin foreign language teachers. It is an informal forum for sharing activities that work, and is planned by teachers as an activity for teachers to learn from each other.

Networking with Other FLES* Teachers

Computers and electronic bulletin boards or listservs can facilitate the networking of **FLES*** teachers. They can also encourage improved artic-ulation procedures by informing FL teachers on all levels about the suc-cesses of **FLES*** teachers. One large, important listserv is FLTEACH.

Teachers may subscribe to this list (without cost) by entering this information and then following directions:

1. Send an e-mail message to
   LISTSERV@UBVM.CC.BUFFALO.EDU
2. Put nothing on the subject line
3. Message is: SUB FLTEACH (and your first name and last name)
4. Send the message (without a signature)

You will get a response in a day or two, and then you are ready to be in contact with an extensive list of foreign language teachers.

Additional Considerations for the Preparation of FLES* Teachers

1. Learning how to reach all students in **FLES*** classes, including children with learning disabilities
2. Learning about the needs of **FLES*** students
3. Knowing the components of a successful lesson: goals, motivation, presentation, practice, reinforcement, "liberated communicative practice," use of materials, assessment, etc.
4. Learning how to deal with being observed and evaluated—and how to work effectively with administrators, parents, and teachers
5. Emphasizing the use of theater and dramatic approaches in **FLES***
6. Delineating the goals and practices of elementary and secondary school foreign language programs
7. Learning how to connect with other **FLES*** professionals
8. Understanding the role of grammar and error correction
9. Teaching the culture(s) of the target language
10. Becoming aware of the *Standards for Foreign Language Learning* and understanding the process used in implementing, modifying, and evaluating programs in consonance with those standards
11. Learning how to design and implement a **FLES*** public-awareness program
12. Becoming familiar with technology
13. Learning how to understand the results of research and the criteria for evaluating research studies
14. Learning how to reflect on and evaluate oneself, and how to make reasonable assessments of one's own strengths and problems

Professional Organizations (Selected)

Contact the following organizations for assistance, conferences, workshops, newsletters, journals, and/or on-line networking with other professionals.

(AATF) American Association of Teachers of French
Mail Code 4510
Dept. of Foreign Languages
Southern Illinois University
Carbondale, IL 62901

(AATG) American Association of Teachers of German (Kinder Lernen Deutsch)
112 Haddontowne Ct., #104
Cherry Hill, NY 08034

(AATSP) American Association of Teachers of Spanish and Portuguese
University of Northern Colorado
Frasier Hall
Greeley, CO 80639

(ALL) Advocates for Learning
PO Box 4962
Culver City, CA 90231

(SLAC) Conference for Second Language Acquisition for Children
Dr. Rosemarie Benya
East Central University
Ada, OK 74820

FLTEACH, an on-line discussion group (see page 77 for procedures for subscribing)

National **FLES*** Commission of AATF
Dr. Gladys Lipton
University of Maryland, Baltimore County
Baltimore, MD 21250

National French **FLES*** Contest
Elizabeth Miller, Director
74 Tuscaloosa
Atherton, CA 94025

National **FLES*** Institute
Dr. Gladys Lipton, Director
University of Maryland, Baltimore County
Baltimore, MD 21250

National Network on Early Language Learning
Center for Applied Linguistics
Nancy Rhodes
1118 22nd St., NW
Washington, DC 20037

National Standards in Foreign Language Education Project
ACTFL
6 Executive Plaza
Yonkers, NY 10701-6801

Regional conferences:
Central States Conference
Northeast Conference
Pacific Northwest Conference
Southern Conference
Southwest Conference

A Recipe for Rave Reviews

Some time ago, I was asked, based on my experience and observations, to provide a "recipe" for **FLES*** success—something that would get **FLES*** teachers "rave reviews." The recipe follows, but as every good cook knows, a recipe can and should be adapted to individual tastes (or, in this case, to the individual **FLES*** teacher's taste and teaching style):

Blend the following ingredients:
    4 cups Planning
    5 cups Teaching Performance (exciting, effective, enthusiastic, enjoyable, and empathetic to the children)
    4 cups Pace, Tempo, Variety, Flexibility, and *Standards for Foreign Language Learning*
    5 cups Personality and Rapport with Students
    2 cups Humor
    2 cups Joie de Vivre and Charm
    Sprinkle generously with Understanding, Patience, and Knowledge

Pack all of the above ingredients (all 22 cups) into an attractive container, decorated with all the trimmings.

What will you get? You'll get "rave reviews"!!

VOLUNTEERS

When a school system determines that it is interested in a language-awareness program, or *FLEX*, but it cannot find the funds to deliver such a program, it may be feasible to use volunteers (adults or high-school and college students). In this case, as always, it is extremely important that the goals and expectations of such a program be clearly understood by everyone concerned, lest there be great disappointment at the minimal progress that students in such a program may make.

Use of Peer Tutors in a *FLEX-Exploratory* Program

Because of budgetary constraints, it is frequently possible to organize a program with cross-age tutors (students from the local high schools or colleges). Care should be taken in the selection of these peer teachers, and particular attention should be given to their training. They should agree to some kind of contract so that they will understand their responsibilities. It is recommended that the contract be signed by the volunteer, the high school foreign language teacher who is responsible for the training, and the elementary school principal. The contract should address such topics as school rules, attendance and punctuality, planning, schedules, supplies, and other pertinent procedural information. (See the sample contract, page 81.) While peer tutoring is not generally recommended unless there are limited goals and there is strong coordination for the students, it is possible to organize such a program with considerable success. The following might be used as a sample guide for high school and college volunteers.

Guide for High School and College Volunteers

It is most important that you make a good impression during your initial meeting with the elementary school principal and the classroom teacher. The following suggestions are intended to help you feel comfortable in your role as tutor:

- Be on time. Principals and teachers are busy people, and they are taking time out of their schedule to meet with you.

- Report to the main office every time you visit the school. Inform the secretary who you are and the time of your appointment.

- Dress neatly and appropriately.

- Have your materials and your letter of assignment with you.

- Take some paper and a pencil with you to take notes.

- Be sure that at the end of the first meeting you have the answers to the following questions:

  1. Where do I report when I come to the school?
  2. What time should I be at the school?
  3. Where is the room or area in which I will be teaching?
  4. Will a classroom teacher or aide be present?
  5. How will I handle problems that come up?
  6. How many students will be in the class?
  7. May I use the photocopying machine, the overhead projector, and other equipment?
  8. Are there any school rules I should be aware of?
  9. What supplies and materials are available to me? How do I get the materials I need?
  10. Will the students have paper, a notebook, or other writing materials (depending on the grade level)?

Contract for Student Volunteers in the *FLEX* Program

As a student tutor in the *FLEX* program sponsored by the foreign language department of _____ High School, I agree to abide by the following principles:

1. To become familiar enough with the school in which I am placed to observe all school rules and regulations.

2. To work closely with my cooperating teacher and to observe all classroom rules set by him or her.

3. To be responsible enough to maintain an excellent attendance and punctuality record

4. To develop a good working relationship with my cooperating teacher and with my students

5. To maintain a positive attitude toward my students, my cooperating teacher, the school principal, and other staff members at the school

6. To demonstrate my extensive knowledge of material through *careful* and *thorough* planning of activities for my students

7. To execute my plans in a well-organized and effective manner

Signatures:

_____   _____
Student Volunteer   Principal, Elementary School

_____   _____
Chair, High School   Principal, High School
Foreign Language Department

For this type of program to have some degree of success, the peer teachers need training, they need a curriculum, they need access to a picture file, they need to be able to discuss problems with their high school teacher contact, they need to learn how to plan simple lessons, they need to know how to handle general classroom routines and difficulties, and they need to get recognition for their efforts and accomplishments. A certificate of some kind is appreciated.

If the emphasis is on a districtwide effort to promote foreign languages on all levels, this type of program helps both elementary school students and high school students. However, there must be agreement, by all persons concerned, that the *FLEX* program objectives are quite simple and that in addition to the linguistic and cultural benefits, the elementary school youngsters are to be exposed to a pleasurable language-learning experience. For an overview of this type of program, see Appendix D.

Adult volunteers (parents and members of the community) may be used in this type of program, but it must be remembered that there must be training sessions for them. Knowledge of and proficiency in the foreign language is not enough. Volunteers want and need training in classroom management, sequencing and pacing of lessons, lesson planning, preparing effective and varied lessons, evaluating progress, and reviewing and reinforcing concepts, among other things.

Sample Workshop Agenda for FLES* Volunteers

1. What is **FLES***? Definitions and goals (expectations)
2. Highlights of **FLES*** methodology
3. References
4. Getting started
   a. Visit school and principal
   b. Look at classroom
   c. Ask about use of facilities
   d. Schedule of FL classes
   e. Meet teachers and other school personnel
5. Preparing an instructional program
   a. Read methods book(s)
   b. Read the National Standards for FL Learning (in summary form)
   c. Begin a picture file around thematic units and holidays
   d. Begin a transparency file around thematic units
   e. Begin making a list of TPR activities
   f. Begin making a list of learning and practice games
   g. Develop a lesson plan that includes
      • Goal(s)
      • Opening activity
      • Presentation of new materials (with visuals and actions)
      • Change of pace: TPR activity
      • Review materials
      • What did we learn today?
      • Peek at next session
      • Closing activity
   h. Plan for practice
   i. Plan for periodic review
6. Anticipating problems
   a. Behavior problems
   b. Understanding needs of children in elementary school

    c. N.L.K.T. approach
    d. Use of English
    e. Need for reentry and repetition
    f. Use of games for learning and practice
    g. Teaching four abilities and culture
    h. Writing for real-life situations
7. Follow-up

INVOLVING THE CLASSROOM TEACHER
WHO IS *NOT* A FOREIGN LANGUAGE TEACHER

When a specialized **FLES*** teacher is responsible for teaching the foreign language, it is helpful if the **FLES*** teacher enlists the aid of the classroom teacher. Sometimes this can be accomplished in a number of ways. A form of team teaching can be developed, with mutual professional respect. The foreign language specialist can provide foreign language instruction in a close working relationship with the classroom teacher, and may also assist with special foreign language events, the preparation of an assembly program, and other related activites, keeping in mind, of course, that the *classroom teacher* is responsible for the class. The classroom teacher is encouraged to provide support for the foreign language instruction in the following ways:

- Present a positive attitude toward foreign language learning.

- Prepare the youngsters for the instruction.

- Watch for topics or activities during the language lesson that can be used in follow-up activities, such as (1) playing a recording for further practice, (2) discussing an aspect of the foreign culture that may relate to a reading passage or social studies, (3) contrasting English language words and foreign language words, and (4) discussing inclusion of foreign words in the English language.

- Encourage students to explore the language and culture in greater depth.

- Plan for ways to correlate the foreign language and culture with other subjects in the elementary school curriculum; plan an interdisciplinary approach with the **FLES*** teacher.

- Encourage youngsters to bring in foreign language books from the library.

- Have students look for foreign words that have become a part of the English language (e.g., *sombrero, chapeau*) in newspapers and magazines.

- Maintain a bulletin board devoted to topics related to the foreign country or countries (current events, pictures, labels, advertisements, greeting cards).
- Develop collaborative activities, such as assembly programs and interdisciplinary activities, that reinforce some aspects of the FL curriculum; lead a school project, plant a garden (based on the foreign culture), plan a field trip, etc.
- Other activities developed jointly by the classroom teacher and the foreign language teacher.

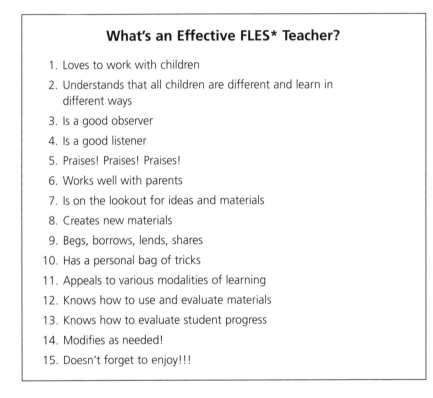

What's an Effective FLES* Teacher?

1. Loves to work with children
2. Understands that all children are different and learn in different ways
3. Is a good observer
4. Is a good listener
5. Praises! Praises! Praises!
6. Works well with parents
7. Is on the lookout for ideas and materials
8. Creates new materials
9. Begs, borrows, lends, shares
10. Has a personal bag of tricks
11. Appeals to various modalities of learning
12. Knows how to use and evaluate materials
13. Knows how to evaluate student progress
14. Modifies as needed!
15. Doesn't forget to enjoy!!!

FOR REFLECTION

It is important to reflect upon the needs that **FLES*** teachers bring to their workplace, and, therefore, the case for involving them in designing appropriate staff development activities.

PAUL GARCIA (1991, 22)

National Standards for Foreign Language Learning and **FLES*** Curriculum Development

INTRODUCTION TO THE NATIONAL STANDARDS FOR FOREIGN LANGUAGE LEARNING

After several years of study, work, and review by many members of the foreign language profession, the National Standards in Foreign Language Education Project released *Standards for Foreign Language Learning: Preparing for the 21st Century* in 1996. These national standards offer a "much broader definition of the content of the foreign language classroom. Students should be given ample opportunities to explore, develop, and use communication strategies, learning strategies, critical thinking skills, and skills in technology, as well as the appropriate elements of the language system and culture" (National Standards in Foreign Language Education Project 1996, 28).

The national standards are neither a curriculum guide nor a recommended scope and sequence, since "no single continuum of language learning exists for all students" (14). The goal of standards-oriented foreign language instruction is to prepare students who "can use the language in meaningful ways, in real-life situations" (15).

National foreign language standards are of interest to **FLES*** advocates in that they recognize the value of foreign language in elementary schools: "earlier starts with language instruction assure greater success for more students" (19). The standards also support the principle of language learning that "all children are primed to learn languages, and they will rise to meet expectations when goals are appropriately set and the conditions for learning are designed to foster achievement" (20). Furthermore, children can participate actively in language learning, since the standards indicate that "real communication is possible for young students as well as for students in high schools. The standards at all levels offer a vision of what students should know and be able to do in another language" (21).

At this writing, the language-specific foreign language associations are working on applications to their languages. These language-specific documents will reflect the necessary adaptations to the learning scenarios and progress indicators of individual languages, while keeping the consensus of the format and philosophy of the standards. Plans are also under way to work from the national FL standards to state FL frameworks, and in turn, to district and school curricula that will ultimately influence unit and lesson plans for foreign language classrooms.

TERMINOLOGY

The following terms are currently used in discussing standards-based foreign language instruction:

THE THREE MAJOR ORGANIZING PRINCIPLES: These refer to the goals, the curricular elements, and the framework of communicative modes.

THE FRAMEWORK OF COMMUNICATIVE MODES: This refers to the three modes of communication, which include the interpersonal mode, the interpretive mode, and the presentational mode (33).

THE INTERPERSONAL MODE: This represents "active negotiation of meaning among individuals" (32).

THE INTERPRETIVE MODE: This "is focused on the appropriate cultural interpretation of meanings that occur in written and spoken form where there is no recourse to the active negotiation of meaning with the writer or speaker" (32).

THE PRESENTATIONAL MODE: This is the "creation of messages in a manner that facilitates interpretation by members of the other culture where no direct opportunity for the active negotiation of meaning between members of the two cultures exists" (34).

THE PRODUCTIVE ABILITIES: These are "paths" to the communicative modes and include speaking and writing (and showing) abilities.

THE RECEPTIVE ABILITIES: These are "paths" to the communicative modes and include listening and speaking (and viewing) abilities.

CULTURAL KNOWLEDGE: This includes knowledge about culture from the interpersonal, interpretive, and presentational points of view (33).

KNOWLEDGE OF THE LINGUISTIC SYSTEM: This includes "the use of grammatical, lexical, phonological, semantic, pragmatic, and discourse features necessary for participation in the Communicative Modes" (33).

THE WEAVE OF CURRICULAR ELEMENTS: This demonstrates the graphic form of the broader focus on foreign language content, the language system, the five C's, and other aspects of language learning, strategies, and knowledge (29).

LEARNING SCENARIOS: These represent a variety of unit topics that help teachers make the transition to standards-oriented instruction (24). (A sample learning scenario is included in this chapter.)

SAMPLE PROGRESS INDICATORS: These are suggested criteria for grades 4, 8, and 12 "that define student progress in meeting the standards, but are not themselves standards" (23). (See Chapter Thirteen.)

THE FIVE C's: These refer to the five goal areas of foreign language education—communication, cultures, connections, comparisons, and communities—which the national standards describe as follows.

THE FIVE C'S OF FOREIGN LANGUAGE EDUCATION[1]

The purposes and uses of foreign languages are as diverse as the students who study them. Some students study another language in hopes of finding a rewarding career in the international marketplace or government service. Others are interested in the intellectual challenge and cognitive benefits that accrue to those who master multiple languages. Still others seek greater understanding of other people and other cultures. Many approach foreign language study, as they do other courses, simply to fulfill a graduation requirement. Regardless of the reason for study, foreign languages have something to offer everyone. It is with this philosophy in mind that the standards task force identified five goal areas that encompass all of these reasons: *Communication, Cultures, Connections, Comparisons,* and *Communities*—the five C's of foreign language education.

Communication

Communication is at the heart of second language study, whether the communication takes place face-to-face, in writing, or across centuries through the reading of literature.

Cultures

Through the study of other languages, students gain a knowledge and understanding of the *cultures* that use the language and, in fact, cannot

---

[1] Reprinted with permission. National Standards in Foreign Language Education Project. 1996. Executive Summary of *Standards for Foreign Language Learning: Preparing for the 21st Century.* Yonkers, NY: National Standards in Foreign Language Education Project.

truly master the language until they have also mastered the cultural contexts in which the language occurs.

Connections

Learning languages provides *connections* to additional bodies of knowledge that may be unavailable to the monolingual English speaker.

Comparisons

Through *comparisons* and contrasts with the language being studied, students develop insight into the nature of language and the concept of culture and realize that there are multiple ways of viewing the world.

Communities

Together, these elements enable the student of languages to participate in multilingual *communities* at home and around the world in a variety of contexts and in culturally appropriate ways.

"Knowing how, when, and why to say what to whom"

All the linguistic and social knowledge required for effective human-to-human interaction is encompassed in those ten words. Formerly, most teaching in foreign language classrooms concentrated on *how* (grammar) to say *what* (vocabulary). While these components of language are indeed crucial, the current organizing principle for foreign language study is *communication*, which also highlights the *why*, the *whom*, and the *when*. So, while grammar and vocabulary are essential tools for communication, it is the acquisition of the ability to communicate in meaningful and appropriate ways with users of other languages that is the ultimate goal of today's foreign language classroom.

Learning Scenarios

Standards for Foreign Language Learning provides a great many learning scenarios to help teachers get involved in standards-based instruction. In a learning scenario, several elements must be in place:

- A real-life situation serves as the basis of the scenario.
- The scenario presents a problem, challenge, information gap, etc.

Learning Scenarios Outline: FLES* K–8

TITLE:

TARGETED STANDARDS:

DESCRIPTION OF THE SCENARIO (AN INTEGRATED CURRICULUM):

- Students' motivation (information or service gap, etc.)
- **FLES*** teacher's role
- Collaboration with teachers in other areas
- Communicative components
- Cultural components
- Interdisciplinary components—connections
- Comparisons
- Community activities
- Group and paired activities
- Culminating activity and/or product
- Class, group, and individual assessment and evaluation

REFLECTION:

1. Reflection by students on both the process and the product of the scenario (selected examples):
   - Students reflect on the learning process and their own acquisition of information and understanding
   - Students engage in conversations about the theme(s)
   - Students reflect on their abilities to use the FL in connection with the scenario
   - Students reflect on difficulties they have encountered and how they (and peers and resources) have helped in overcoming them
   - Students express their impressions of new information and comparisons
   - Students tell about what they have learned
   - Students further their knowledge, as appropriate
   - Students read and discuss different aspects of the scenario
   - Students use the FL within the school and/or in the community
   - Students create a product of their learning (e.g., a poem, a skit, a diorama, a poster, a brochure, a cartoon, a map, a bookmark, a bumper sticker, an activity to benefit the community, an e-mail message, a menu, etc.)
2. Overview statement of reflection about the scenario by the teacher (selected examples):
   - Goals of the scenario
   - Procedures used

continued on page 90

- Success in working with targeted standards
- Assessment of student progress in language and accuracy
- Collaboration and cooperation of students
- Collaboration of teachers in different subject areas
- Success in interdisciplinary aspects of the scenario
- Success in promoting higher levels of thinking skills
- Creativity promoted in the culminating activities and the products

- Students are actively involved in all the steps of the learning scenario: planning, assignment of tasks, research, and specific activities regarding the culminating activity or product, using the foreign language.

- Students learn aspects of the foreign language that relate to the theme of the scenario (and also review others that are related to or provide scaffolding for the new materials).

- Students work individually, in pairs, and in small groups on different components of the learning scenario.

- Some interdisciplinary and cultural activities are included as part of the learning scenario.

- Assessment is built into the scenario both as an ongoing procedure and as part of the culminating activity or product.

- Reflection on the part of students and teacher plays a major role in the process of the learning scenario.

The planning for the learning scenario can take the form of a paragraph describing the challenge, the procedures involved, and the culminating activity or product. It may also take the form of a planning web. Let us assume that the theme of the learning scenario is a class party to celebrate Monet's birthday.

Sample Learning Scenario[2]

The local museum is featuring paintings by Monet. The class is planning a trip to the museum and a class party to celebrate Monet's birthday. The class is divided into groups to gather information about Monet, his paintings, his home in France, etc., and to create a short skit to illustrate his life. Once the information has been shared with the entire class, groups are again formed to plan the class party, using the FL for communication and presentation.

---

[2] Inspired by Harriet Saxon, of Rutherford, NJ, who has her students plant a "Monet garden."

Reflection:

1. Students visit the museum to see Monet's work and draw pictures demonstrating Monet's style for a class exhibit.

2. Students research aspects of Monet's life and create a short skit, in the FL, for presentation at the class party. Students compare Monet's style of painting with those of U.S. artists.

3. This scenario includes the five goals of communication, cultures, connections, comparisons, and community (the visit to the museum).

NOTE: Chapter Nine includes a description of planning for a class party.

In anticipation of a trip to a local museum featuring paintings by Monet, this scenario addresses the following goals from the national standards: communication (about Monet's life and the class party), cultures (content of Monet's paintings), connections (research about Monet's life and the context of his paintings), comparisons (comparing his style of painting with those of painters in the United States), and community (visiting a local museum).

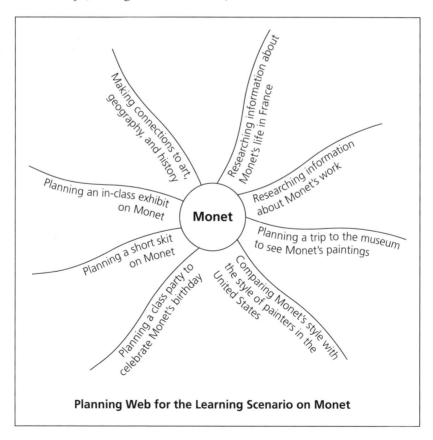

Planning Web for the Learning Scenario on Monet

Implications of National FL Standards for **FLES*** Programs (*Sequential FLES, FLEX,* and *Immersion*)

This is a selected list; other implications may emerge as more teachers use the standards in their local areas.

- There will be recognition of the importance of the early start provided by teaching foreign language in elementary school.
- There will be recognition of the broader contexts of foreign language education.
- There will be confirmation that all **FLES*** students can learn a foreign language.
- Implementation will depend upon state and local FL frameworks.
- Implementation will also depend upon budget allocations for teachers, curriculum development, and teacher training.
- The various **FLES*** program models (*Sequential FLES, FLEX,* and *Immersion*) have the potential of fulfilling the standards and progress indicators for grades 4 and 8, and helping to fulfill those for grade 12. Of course, there will be variations in the degree of achievement, based on number of contact hours and frequency of FL instruction, as well as on the preparation of teachers.
- While the standards are the result of professional consensus, many research projects are needed to document the results of standards-based foreign language programs.
- Real communication in real-life situations will be provided.
- Culture and language learning are interdependent.
- Language abilities (listening, reading, speaking, and writing) are linked to the three modes of communication.
- The weave of curricular elements indicates the interrelationships of the various components of foreign language learning and the five C's.
- The learning scenarios present a focus on the purpose for the various language-learning components, including culminating activities and/or products.
- Interdisciplinary content and the development of critical thinking skills help to integrate the elementary school learning experience for children.
- **FLES*** curriculum development must include important aspects of the national FL standards, including real-life scenarios and assessment procedures that are geared to the progress indicators for grades 4 and 8.

Following are the national K–12 standards that continue through page 107. It is important for **FLES*** practitioners to see the scope of foreign language learning from kindergarten through grade 12.

STANDARDS FOR FOREIGN LANGUAGE LEARNING[3]

Communication

STANDARD 1.1 Students engage in conversations, provide and obtain information, express feelings and emotions, and exchange opinions.

This standard focuses on interpersonal communication. In most modern languages, students can quite quickly learn a number of phrases that permit them to interact with each other. In the course of their study, they grow in their ability to converse in a culturally appropriate manner. Students who come with a home background in the language may have already acquired such abilities. Students of non-European languages may face greater challenges in this area than students of languages more closely related to English.

Sample Progress Indicators, Grade 4

- Students give and follow simple instructions in order to participate in age-appropriate classroom and/or cultural activities.

- Students ask and answer questions about topics such as family, school events, and celebrations in person or via letters, e-mail, audio, or video tapes.

- Students share likes and dislikes with each other and the class.

- Students exchange descriptions of people and tangible products of the culture, such as toys, dress, types of dwellings, and foods, with each other and members of the class.

- Students exchange essential information such as greetings, leave-takings, and common classroom interactions using culturally appropriate gestures and oral expressions.

Sample Progress Indicators, Grade 8

- Students follow and give directions for participating in age-appropriate cultural activities and investigating the function of products of the foreign culture. They ask and respond to questions for clarification.

---

[3] Reprinted with permission. National Standards in Foreign Language Education Project. 1996. *Standards for Foreign Language Learning: Preparing for the 21st Century.* Yonkers, NY: National Standards in Foreign Language Education Project.

- Students exchange information about personal events, memorable experiences, and other school subjects with peers and/or members of the target cultures.

- Students compare, contrast, and express opinions and preferences about the information gathered regarding events, experiences, and other school subjects.

- Students acquire goods, services, or information orally and/or in writing.

- Students develop and propose solutions to issues and problems related to the school or community through group work.

Sample Progress Indicators, Grade 12

- Students discuss, orally or in writing, current or past events that are of significance in the target culture or that are being studied in another subject.

- Students develop and propose solutions to issues and problems that are of concern to members of their own and the target cultures through group work.

- Students share their analyses and personal reactions to expository and literary texts with peers and/or speakers of the target language.

- Students exchange, support, and discuss their opinions and individual perspectives with peers and/or speakers of the target language on a variety of topics dealing with contemporary and historical issues.

STANDARD 1.2 Students understand and interpret written and spoken language on a variety of topics.

This standard focuses on the understanding and interpretation of written and spoken language. Standard 1.2, unlike Standard 1.1, involves one-way listening and reading in which the learner works with a variety of print and non-print materials. For students who come to language learning with no previous background in the language, the context in which the language is experienced and the ability to control what they hear and read may impact the development of comprehension. As a result, for some learners, the ability to read may develop before the ability to comprehend rapid spoken language. In addition, content knowledge will often affect successful comprehension, for students understand more easily materials that reflect their interests or for which they have some background. In contrast, students with exposure to the language through home life may be quite advanced in their understanding of the spoken language and less advanced in terms of their ability to read. The reading aspects of this standard make it particularly relevant to the classical languages. Reading may also develop less rapidly for languages with non-Roman writing systems.

Sample Progress Indicators, Grade 4

- Students comprehend main ideas in developmentally appropriate oral narratives such as personal anecdotes, familiar fairy tales, and other narratives based on familiar themes.

- Students identify people and objects in their environment or from other school subjects, based on oral and written description.

- Students comprehend brief, written messages and short personal notes on familiar topics such as family, school events, and celebrations.

- Students comprehend the main themes and ideas and identify the principal characters of stories or children's literature.

- Students comprehend the principal message contained in various media such as illustrated texts, posters, or advertisements.

- Students interpret gestures, intonation, and other visual or auditory cues.

Sample Progress Indicators, Grade 8

- Students comprehend information and messages related to other school subjects.

- Students understand announcements and messages connected to daily activities in the target culture.

- Students understand the main themes and significant details on topics from other subjects and products of the cultures as presented on TV, radio, video, or live presentations.

- Students understand the main themes and significant details on topics from other subjects and products of the cultures as found in newspapers, magazines, e-mail, or other printed sources used by speakers of the target language.

- Students identify the principal characters and comprehend the main ideas and themes in selected literary texts.

- Students use knowledge acquired in other settings and from other subject areas to comprehend spoken and written messages in the target language.

Sample Progress Indicators, Grade 12

- Students demonstrate an understanding of the main ideas and significant details of live and recorded discussions, lectures, and presentations on current or past events from the target culture or that are being studied in another class.

- Students demonstrate an understanding of the principal elements of non-fiction articles in newspapers, magazines, and e-mail on topics of current and historical importance to members of the culture.

- Students analyze the main plot, subplot, characters, their descriptions, roles, and significance in authentic literary texts.

- Students demonstrate an increasing understanding of the cultural nuances of meaning in written and spoken language as expressed by speakers of the target language in formal and informal settings.

- Students demonstrate an increasing understanding of the cultural nuances of meaning in expressive products of the culture, including selections from various literary genres and the visual arts.

STANDARD 1.3 Students present information, concepts, and ideas to an audience of listeners or readers on a variety of topics.

This standard focuses on the presentation of information, concepts, and ideas in spoken and written modes. This standard, in most cases, is concerned with one-way speaking and writing. Students with little or no previous experience in the language are likely to produce written and spoken language that contains a variety of learned patterns or that looks like English with words in the other language. This is a natural process. Over time, students then begin to acquire authentic patterns and to use appropriate styles. By contrast, home-background students write in ways that closely resemble the spoken language. Moreover, they control informal oral styles well. Over time, these learners develop the ability to write and speak using a variety of more formal styles.

Sample Progress Indicators, Grade 4

- Students prepare illustrated stories about activities or events in their environment and share these stories and events with an audience such as the class.

- Students dramatize songs, short anecdotes, or poetry commonly known by peers in the target culture for members of another elementary class.

- Students give short oral notes and messages, or write reports, about people and things in their school environment and exchange the information with another language class either locally or via e-mail.

- Students tell or retell stories orally or in writing.

- Students write or tell about products and/or practices of their own culture to peers in the target culture.

Sample Progress Indicators, Grade 8

- Students present short plays and skits, recite selected poems and anecdotes, and perform songs in the language for a school-related event such as a board meeting or PTA meeting.

- Students prepare tape or video recorded messages to share locally or with school peers and/or members of the target cultures on topics of personal interest.

- Students prepare stories or brief written reports about personal experiences, brief personal events, or other school subjects to share with classmates and/or members of the target cultures.

- Students prepare an oral or written summary of the plot and characters in selected pieces of age-appropriate literature.

Sample Progress Indicators, Grade 12

- Students perform scenes and/or recite poems or excerpts from short stories connected to a topic from other disciplines such as world history, geography, the arts, or mathematics.

- Students perform scenes from plays and/or recite poems or excerpts from short stories commonly read by speakers of the target language.

- Students create stories and poems, short plays, or skits based on personal experiences and exposure to themes, ideas, and perspectives from the target culture.

- Students select and analyze expressive products of the culture, from literary genres or the fine arts.

- Students summarize the content of an article or documentary intended for native speakers in order to discuss the topics via e-mail with other users or speakers of the language.

- Students write a letter or an article describing and analyzing an issue for a student publication.

- Students prepare a research-based analysis of a current event from the perspective of both the U.S. and target cultures.

Cultures

STANDARD 2.1 Students demonstrate an understanding of the relationship between the practices and perspectives of the cultures studied.

This standard focuses on the practices that are derived from the traditional ideas, attitudes, and values *(perspectives)* of a culture. Cultural practices refer to patterns of behavior accepted by a society and deal with aspects of culture such as rites of passage, the use of forms of discourse, the social "pecking order," and the use of space. In short, they represent the knowledge of "what to do when and where." It is important to understand the relationship between these practices and the underlying perspectives that represent the culture's view of the world.

For example, in some Asian cultures members are positioned (a *perspective*) on a hierarchical scale based on age, social status, education, or similar variables. In those cultures, the exchange of business cards (a *product*) that provides key information is a helpful *practice*. Because these cards facilitate social interaction and are treated with respect in those cultures, one should not scribble another name or telephone number on the business card (taboo *practice*). The information on the card also directly affects the nonverbal behavior *(practice)* of those involved in the communicative interaction, as well as the choice of linguistic forms *(products)* that indicate status.

The following progress indicators relate to learning activities based on the culture studied:

Sample Progress Indicators, Grade 4

- Students observe, identify, and/or discuss simple patterns of behavior or interaction in various settings such as school, family, and the community.
- Students use appropriate gestures and oral expressions for greetings, leave-takings, and common classroom interactions.
- Students participate in age-appropriate cultural activities such as games, songs, birthday celebrations, story telling and dramatizations.

Sample Progress Indicators, Grade 8

- Students observe, analyze, and discuss patterns of behavior typical of their peer groups.
- Students use appropriate verbal and nonverbal behavior for daily activities among peers and adults.
- Students learn about and participate in age-appropriate cultural practices such as games (role of leader, taking turns, etc.), sports, and entertainment (e.g., music, dance, drama).

Sample Progress Indicators, Grade 12

- Students interact in a variety of cultural contexts that reflect both peer-group and adult activities within the culture studied, using the appropriate verbal and nonverbal cues.
- Students learn about and participate in age-appropriate cultural practices, such as games, sports, and entertainment.
- Students identify, analyze, and discuss various patterns of behavior or interaction typical of the culture studied.
- Students identify, examine, and discuss connections between cultural perspectives and socially approved behavioral patterns.

STANDARD 2.2 Students demonstrate an understanding of the relationship between the products and perspectives of the cultures studied.

This standard focuses on the *products* of the culture studied and on how they reflect the *perspectives* of that culture. *Products* may be tangible (e.g., a painting, a cathedral, a piece of literature, a pair of chopsticks) or intangible (e.g., an oral tale, a dance, a sacred ritual, a system of education). Whatever the form of the product, its presence within the culture is required or justified by the underlying beliefs and values *(perspectives)* of that culture, and the cultural *practices* involve the use of that *product*.

For example, in the United States, youth has traditionally been valued more than old age (a *perspective*). As a result, *products* that purport to prolong youth and vitality (e.g., face creams, high fiber breakfast cereals, and "exercycles") have become an integral part of our culture. At the same time, *practices* that are perceived as prolonging youth and health are encouraged: school children exercise to meet the goals of the President's Physical Fitness Award; teenagers go on crash diets; whole segments of the population invest in running shoes and jogging togs *(products)*.

Sample Progress Indicators, Grade 4

- Students identify and observe tangible products of the culture such as toys, dress, types of dwellings, and food.

- Students identify, experience, or read about expressive products of the culture such as children's songs, selections from children's literature, and types of artwork enjoyed or made by their peer group in the cultures studied.

- Students identify, discuss, and produce types of artwork, crafts, or graphic representations enjoyed or made by their peer group within the cultures studied.

- Students recognize themes, ideas, or perspectives of the culture.

Sample Progress Indicators, Grade 8

- Students experience (read, listen to, observe, perform) expressive products of the culture (e.g., stories, poetry, music, paintings, dance, and drama) and then explore the effects of these products on the larger communities.

- Students search for, identify, and investigate the function of utilitarian products (e.g., sports equipment, household items, tools, foods, and clothing) of the culture studied as found within their homes and communities.

- Students identify, discuss, and analyze themes, ideas, and perspectives related to the products being studied.

Sample Progress Indicators, Grade 12

- Students identify, discuss, and analyze such intangible products of the target culture as social, economic, and political institutions, and explore relationships among these institutions and the perspective of the culture.

- Students experience, discuss, and analyze expressive products of the culture, including selections from various literary genres and the fine arts.
- Students identify, analyze, and evaluate themes, ideas, and perspectives related to the products being studied.
- Students explore the relationships among the products, practices, and perspective of the culture.

Connections

STANDARD 3.1 Students reinforce and further their knowledge of other disciplines through the foreign language.

Learning today is no longer restricted to a specific discipline; it has become interdisciplinary. Just as reading cannot be limited to a particular segment of the school day but is central to all aspects of the school curriculum, so, too, can foreign language build upon the knowledge that students acquire in other subject areas. In addition, students can relate the information studied in other subjects to their learning of the foreign language and culture. Students expand and deepen their understanding of and exposure to other areas of knowledge, even as they refine their communicative abilities and broaden their cultural understanding. The new information and concepts presented in one class become the basis of continued learning in the foreign language classroom. In the lower grades, for example, students in a science class are introduced to the range of vocabulary related to weather, seasons, and temperatures. At the same time, the foreign language class continues this presentation with the months of the year, seasons, and weather vocabulary in the foreign language. By comparing the weather conditions in the foreign country with those at home, students have acquired new knowledge at the same time that they have deepened their understanding of previous information.

Interdisciplinary reinforcement can occur at all levels of the school curriculum. At various stages, the foreign language teacher could teach more than the names and events presented in the history class and geographical place names by introducing students to journalistic accounts of historical events or literary depictions of individuals living at that time. Furthermore, in addition to the concepts and processes introduced in science and the achievements of artists and musicians studied in art, students could read documentation in various reference materials, the descriptions of success and failure in biographical sketches of various individuals, as well as the autobiographical accounts documented in personal letters and diaries of those historical figures. Prior discussion of works of literature in the English class enables students to have a better understanding of various genres—from the detective story to the sonnet—and literary conventions when they encounter similar texts in the language classroom. Even the manipulations and story problems taught in math provide content and a basis for discussion and exploration in the foreign language classroom. Students who are grappling with a science problem are aided in their attempts to understand it by relating it to their peers in the language classroom. When integrated into the broader curriculum, foreign language learning contributes to the entire educational experience of students.

Sample Progress Indicators, Grade 4

• Students demonstrate an understanding about concepts learned in other subject areas in the target language, including weather, math facts, measurements, animals, insects, or geographical concepts.

Sample Progress Indicators, Grade 8

• Students discuss topics from other school subjects in the target language, including geographical terms and concepts, historical facts and concepts, mathematical terms and problems, and scientific information.

• Students comprehend articles or short videos in the target language on topics being studied in other classes.

• Students present reports in the target language, orally and/or in writing, on topics being studied in other classes.

Sample Progress Indicators, Grade 12

• Students discuss topics from other school subjects in the target language, including political and historical concepts, worldwide health issues, and environmental concerns.

• Students acquire information from a variety of sources written in the target language about a topic being studied in other school subjects.

• Students combine information from other school subjects with information available in the foreign language in order to complete activities in the foreign language classroom.

STANDARD 3.2 Students acquire information and recognize the distinctive viewpoints that are only available through the foreign language and its cultures.

As a consequence of learning another language and gaining access to its unique means of communication and ways of thinking, students acquire new information and perspectives. As learners of a foreign language, they broaden the sources of information available to them. The have a "new window on the world." In the earlier stages of language learning, they begin to examine a variety of sources intended for native speakers, and extract specific information. As they become more proficient users of the foreign language, they seek out materials of interest to them, analyze the content, compare it to information available in their own language, and assess the linguistic and cultural differences.

Sample Progress Indicators, Grade 4

- Students read, listen to, and talk about age-appropriate school content, folktales, short stories, poems, and songs written for native speakers of the target language.

Sample Progress Indicators, Grade 8

- Students use sources intended for same-age speakers of the target language to prepare reports on topics of personal interest, or those with which they have limited previous experience.

Sample Progress Indicators, Grade 12

- Students use a variety of sources intended for same-age speakers of the target language to prepare reports on topics of personal interest, or those with which they have limited previous experience, and compare these to information obtained on the same topics written in English.

Comparisons

STANDARD 4.1 Students demonstrate understanding of the nature of language through comparisons of the language studied and their own.

This standard focuses on the impact that learning the linguistic elements in the new language has on students' ability to examine their own language, and to develop hypotheses about the structure and use of languages. From the earliest language learning experiences, students can compare and contrast the two languages as different elements are presented. Activities can be systematically integrated into instruction that will assist students in understanding how languages work.

Sample Progress Indicators, Grade 4

- Students cite and use examples of words that are borrowed in the language they are learning and their own, and they pose guesses about why languages in general might need to borrow words.

- Students realize that cognates enhance comprehension of spoken and written language and demonstrate that awareness by identifying commonly occurring cognates in the language they are learning.

- Students are aware of the existence of idiomatic expressions in both their native language and the language being learned and talk about how idiomatic expressions work in general.

- Students demonstrate an awareness of formal and informal forms of language in greetings and leave-takings and try out expressions of politeness in other languages and their own.

- Students report differences and similarities between the sound and writing systems of their own language and the language being learned.

- Students demonstrate an awareness of the various ways of expressing ideas both in their own language and the language being learned.

Sample Progress Indicators, Grade 8

- Students recognize the category of grammatical gender in languages, and their spoken and written language reflects that awareness.

- Students hypothesize about the relationship among languages based on their awareness of cognates and similarity of idioms.

- Students demonstrate an awareness of ways of expressing respect and communicating status differences in their own language and the language they are learning.

- Students demonstrate awareness that languages have critical sound distinctions that must be mastered in order to communicate meaning.

Sample Progress Indicators, Grade 12

- Students recognize that cognates have the same as well as different meanings among languages and speculate about the evolution of language.

- Students demonstrate an awareness that there are phrases and idioms that do not translate directly from one language to another.

- Students analyze elements of the target language, such as time and tense, and comparable linguistic elements in English, and conjecture about how languages use forms to express time and tense relationships.

- Students report on the relationship between word order and meaning and hypothesize on how this may or may not reflect the ways in which cultures organize information and view the world.

- Students compare the writing system of the target language and their own. They also examine other writing systems and report about the nature of those writing systems (e.g., logographic, syllabic, alphabetic).

STANDARD 4.2 Students demonstrate understanding of the concept of culture through comparisons of the cultures studied and their own.

As students expand their knowledge of cultures through language learning, they continually discover perspectives, practices, and products that are similar to and different from those in their own culture. They develop the ability to hypothesize about cultural systems in general. Some students may make these comparisons naturally, others learn to do so. This standard helps focus this reflective process for all students by encouraging integration of this process into instruction from the earliest levels of learning.

Sample Progress Indicators, Grade 4

- Students compare simple patterns of behavior or interaction in various cultural settings.

- Students demonstrate an awareness that gestures are an important part of communication and that gestures may differ among languages.

- Students compare and contrast tangible products (e.g., toys, sports equipment, food) of the target cultures and their own.

- Students compare and contrast intangible products (e.g., rhymes, songs, folktales) of the target cultures and their own.

Sample Progress Indicators, Grade 8

- Students contrast verbal and nonverbal behavior within particular activities in the target cultures and their own.

- Students demonstrate an awareness that they, too, have a culture, based on comparisons of sample daily activities in the target cultures and their own.

- Students speculate on why certain products originate in and/or are important to particular cultures by analyzing selected products from the target cultures and their own.

- Students hypothesize about the relationship between cultural perspectives and practices (e.g., holidays, celebrations, work habits, play) by analyzing selected practices from the target cultures and their own.

- Students hypothesize about the relationship between cultural perspectives and expressive products (e.g., music, visual arts, appropriate forms of literature) by analyzing selected products from the target cultures and their own.

Sample Progress Indicators, Grade 12

- Students hypothesize about the origins of idioms as reflections of culture, citing examples from the language and cultures being studied and their own.

- Students compare nuances of meanings of words, idioms, and vocal inflections in the target language and their own.
- Students analyze the relationship of perspectives and practices in the target cultures and compare and contrast these with their own.
- Students analyze the relationship between the products and perspectives in the cultures studied and compare and contrast these with their own.
- Students identify and analyze cultural perspectives as reflected in a variety of literary genres.

Communities

STANDARD 5.1 Students use the language both within and beyond the school setting.

This standard focuses on language as a tool for communication with speakers of the language throughout one's life: in schools, in the community, and abroad. In schools, students share their knowledge of language and culture with classmates and with younger students who may be learning the language. Applying what has been learned in the language program as defined by the other standards, students come to realize the advantages inherent in being able to communicate in more than one language and develop an understanding of the power of language. Well-developed language applications increase not only the marketability of the employee, but also the ability of the employer to meet the expectations of the customer. Many of the Progress Indicators for Standard 5.1 are repeated at Grades 4, 8, and 12 not only to emphasize that the activity may be similar, but also to indicate that spiraling of tasks and competencies advances with age. As students have opportunities to use language in response to real-world needs, they seek out situations to apply their competencies beyond the school setting.

Sample Progress Indicators, Grade 4

- Students communicate on a personal level with speakers of the language via letters, e-mail, audio, and video tapes.
- Students identify professions which require proficiency in another language.
- Students use the language to create imaginary situations.
- Students present information about the language and culture to others.
- Students write and illustrate stories to present to others.
- Students perform for a school or community celebration.

Sample Progress Indicators, Grade 8

- Students discuss their preferences concerning leisure activities and current events, in written form or orally, with peers who speak the language.
- Students interact with members of the local community to hear how they use the language in their various fields of work.
- Students present information about the language and culture to others.
- Students participate in club activities which benefit the school or community.
- Students write and illustrate stories to present to others.
- Students perform for a school or community celebration.

Sample Progress Indicators, Grade 12

- Students communicate orally or in writing with members of the other culture regarding topics of personal interest, community, or world concern.
- Students participate in a career exploration or school-to-work project which requires proficiency in the language and culture.
- Students use community resources to research a topic related to culture and/or language study.
- Students present information about the language and culture to others.
- Students participate in club activities which benefit the school or community.
- Students write and illustrate stories to present to others.
- Students perform for a school or community celebration.

STANDARD 5.2 Students show evidence of becoming life-long learners by using the language for personal enjoyment and enrichment.

Language is an avenue to information and interpersonal relations. Each day millions of Americans spend leisure time reading, listening to music, viewing films and television programs, and interacting with each other. By developing a certain level of comfort with the new language, students can use these skills to access information as they continue to learn throughout their lives. Students who study a language can use their skills to further enrich their personal lives by accessing various entertainment and information sources available to speakers of the other language. Some students may have the opportunity to travel to communities and countries where the language is used extensively and, through this experience, further develop their language skills and understanding of the culture. Many of the Progress Indicators for Standard 5.2 are repeated at Grades 4, 8, and 12 to emphasize that the activities may be similar. However, the sophistication and ease with which the activities are performed depend greatly on the student's age and abilities.

Sample Progress Indicators, Grade 4

- Students read materials and/or use media from the language and culture for enjoyment.
- Students play sports or games from the culture.
- Students exchange information about topics of personal interest.
- Students plan real or imaginary travel.
- Students attend or view via media cultural events and social activities.
- Students listen to music, sing songs, or play musical instruments from the target culture.

Sample Progress Indicators, Grade 8

- Students consult various sources in the language to obtain information on topics of personal interest.
- Students play sports or games from the culture.
- Students exchange information around topics of personal interest.
- Students use various media from the language and culture for entertainment.
- Students attend or view via media cultural events and social activities.
- Students listen to music, sing songs, or play musical instruments from the target culture.

Sample Progress Indicators, Grade 12

- Students consult various sources in the language to obtain information on topics of personal interest.
- Students play sports or games from the culture.
- Students read and/or use various media from the language and culture for entertainment or personal growth.
- Students establish and/or maintain interpersonal relations with speakers of the language.
- Students attend, or view via media, cultural events and social activities.
- Students listen to music, sing songs, or play musical instruments from the target culture.

FLES* CURRICULUM DEVELOPMENT

Overview of Considerations in the Development of a FLES* Curriculum

1. New national trends, including national FL standards, in the teaching of foreign languages (K–12)

2. Current status in the school and school district

   Languages, grade levels, selection of students, articulation; state and local frameworks

3. Directions and special needs for the future at the local level

4. Philosophy statement

5. Goals and student outcomes (assessment of student achievement)

6. Curriculum constraints in the school district
   Curriculum tied to one text?
   Fully articulated program?
   Testing? (At school level? Districtwide?)
   Required grammar?
   Multimedia support available?
   Philosophy to include the four abilities and culture?
   Integration with other subjects of the curriculum?
   Local celebrations, holidays, events?
   Other?

7. Components of a NEW curriculum
   Focus on language functions and practical applications to real-life situations (basic communication abilities)
   Role of grammar at all levels
   Productive/receptive content
   Minimum requirements; challenges for gifted language students
   Culture
   Goals: increasing enrollments, improving achievement, and maintaining students at upper levels
   Use of the textbook and...is there time for functional real-life language activities in the FL classroom?
   What are the teacher behaviors? The student behaviors?
   What kind of progress is expected from level to level? How will it be demonstrated?
   What is a spiral curriculum? Is it appropriate?
   What is a comprehensive curriculum plan?
   At all levels, consider:
   Students
   Teachers
   Content
   Materials and equipment

Time schedule
Testing
Articulation
Four abilities
Culture
Technology
Results of research
Assessment (progress indicators)
The five C's of the *Standards for Foreign Language Learning*
The three communicative modalities
A variety of approaches
Other?

Planning Curriculum for a FL Continuum

All Kinds of	Lead to	Higher Proficiency
FLES* Programs		Levels

1. Students show a lack of fear in using the FL.
2. Students have interest in continuing their study of the FL.
3. Students develop good FL study skills.
4. Students gain from the integration of learning through an interdisciplinary approach.
5. Students acquire cultural knowledge and appreciation.
6. Students use accurate patterns in real situations.
7. Students demonstrate enjoyment and a sense of progress.
8. Students understand the value of FL study.
9. All **FLES*** programs contribute (in different ways) to the continuum of FL instruction.
10. All **FLES*** programs need a conceptualized focus on **FLES***.
11. All **FLES*** programs build productive and receptive abilities in varying degrees, depending upon the amount and frequency of instructional contact time and the goals of the program.

Decisions About the Format of the Curriculum

In discussing the emergence of the national FL standards, Jackson (1996, 120) points out that "the standards are broad, far-reaching, and exciting. They represent a concerted effort on the part of the profession to speak in a unified voice and create a clear blueprint for the future. They lay the groundwork and provide the underpinnings for developing state frameworks, local curricula, and classroom practice."

There are many different types of formats for a **FLES*** curriculum. It is important to utilize the goals of the program in deciding which elements should be included. The following categories often appear in **FLES*** curriculum documents:

Unit title

Student outcomes

Materials and text references

Content

Language functions, such as agreeing, apologizing, asking for information, giving excuses, complaining, asking for help, etc.

Productive abilities

Receptive abilities

Communicative activities

Cultural components

Interdisciplinary components

Comparison components

Communities components

Assessment

Other categories, as needed

Guiding Questions for the Categories That Often Appear in FLES* Curriculum Documents in the Preparation of an Instructional Unit

STUDENT OUTCOMES FOR THE UNIT

What are the goals of the overall program? Which communicative abilities are included (e.g., comprehension, speaking, reading, writing)? What are the expected outcomes for each year of instruction? How are these outcomes related to the state and local curriculum frameworks? How are the objectives of the program related to the national FL standards? How is students' progress assessed? How is this related to the progress indicators described in the national FL standards?

MATERIALS AND TEXT REFERENCES FOR THE UNIT

Which materials are appropriate for the various units? Is a wide variety of materials used (text, reading materials, cassettes for listening, pictures, real objects, realia, videos, computer programs, etc.)? Are the materials helpful in furthering the objectives of the unit? Are the materials useful in implementing the five C's of the national FL standards? Do the materials reflect real-life situations? Are the materials effective in implementing the learning scenario of the unit? Do the materials reflect accurate, authentic cultural information?

CONTENT OF THE UNIT

What kinds of content are stated in the learning scenario? What other kinds of content are implicit (but not stated) in the learning scenario? How is the content for this unit related to the student outcomes? How is the content for this unit related to the preceding and following units? Which content, knowledge, and abilities are required before proceeding with new material? Which topics need to be reviewed before initiating the new content?

LANGUAGE FUNCTIONS OF THE UNIT

Which language functions will be included in the unit? How are these related to previous and future language functions? How are the language functions related to real-life situations? Which structural items are to be taught with respect to the language functions? How are these language functions related to the five C's of the national FL standards?

PRODUCTIVE ABILITIES AND RECEPTIVE ABILITIES

Which aspects of speaking and writing are to be included in this unit? Which aspects of listening and reading? How are they related to the learning scenario for the unit? How are they related to the language functions of the unit? How are they related to the content of the unit? How are they related to the various materials used? What are the various formats that will be used in conjunction with speaking and writing? With listening and reading? Will students be given opportunities for individual and/or group creative expression?

COMMUNICATIVE ACTIVITIES

Which specific activities related to the learning scenario for the unit will help develop communicative abilities? Will individual, paired, and group activities be included? Which aspects of technology will be used? Are these communicative activities related to real-life situations? Are some learning games included? Are these communicative activities related to the five C's of the national FL standards?

CULTURAL COMPONENTS

Which aspects of the target culture(s) will be included in this unit? Are the various components of culture included (day-to-day customs, comparisons, new developments, etc.)? Are the cultural components part of the communicative activities and the content of the unit? Are cultural activities planned (role-plays, storytelling, etc.)? Are research activities needed to acquire additional cultural understanding?

INTERDISCIPLINARY COMPONENTS

Which specific interdisciplinary components are inherent in this unit? Which are implied? How will interdisciplinary components be included? Direct teaching? Individual, paired, and group research activities?

Reflection activities? How are the interdisciplinary components related to the language functions? The productive activities? The receptive abilities? How are they related to the cultural components?

COMPARISON COMPONENTS

Does this unit lend itself to various comparison options? Comparison of cultural components? Comparison of activities? Comparison of linguistic elements? Others? How will comparison components be included? Direct teaching? Individual, paired, and group research activities? Reflection activities? How will students demonstrate comparisons to others? Which interdisciplinary descriptors will be used (pie charts, bar graphs, etc.)?

ASSESSMENT

How will assessment procedures be related to students' outcomes? To the content of the unit? To the language functions? To the productive and receptive abilities? To the other categories in the unit? Will students be tested in the same manner in which they were taught? Will alternative assessment tools be developed and used? Upon completion of the unit, will it be clear to the teacher and the students (and to the parents and administrators) whether or not the students have learned the various components of the learning scenario?

The format of the curriculum for an *Immersion* program will follow the school/school district curriculum for the specific curriculum area, such as mathematics, science, social studies, health, etc. Following the lead of Quebec and Canadian curriculum formats, many U.S. *Immersion* programs contain sequential language development (in the foreign language and in English) to ensure accuracy and functional language performance. Omaggio (1993, 154–155) reports that "spoken and written French of both early- and late-*Immersion* students have fallen short of native-like proficiency, even after 5,000 or more hours of instruction." Experts recommend that language development be integrated with content instruction. Following are two sample formats of curriculum.

FLEX Japanese Unit

Geography
Map of Japan
"Fuji Find" Word Search
"My Day" Video Review Sheet
U.S.A./Japan Comparison Diagram: Graphic Organizer

Greetings
Greetings from Japan
"Mum's the Word" Word Find
"What Can I Say?" Activity
Take-Home Page

Numbers
"Kanji Counting" Activity
"Air Mail" Activity
"Celebrate" Activity

Origami
"Origami" Reading
"Fold and Find" Activity
"Samurai Helmet" Directions

Cognates
Japanese Connections
"Mixed Messages" Activity
Japanese Writing Systems
"Write in Japanese" Video Review Sheet

Hiragana Chart

Katakana Chart
"Fun With Japanese Writing" Activity Suggestions

Song Lyrics
"Big Bird in Japan" Video Review Sheet
"Tokyo Sunday" Video Review Sheet
"Pagoda Passage" Game Board and Instructions
"Letter to Japan" Writing Prompt

Holiday Images

Reprinted with permission. Prince Georges County, MD, Public Schools, Foreign Language Office.

Elementary School Russian Curriculum Unit VI: Shopping in Moscow

Outcomes	Prerequisite knowledge	Materials	Content	Skills	Activities	Interdisciplinary connections	Assessment
Students will: 1. expand their vocabulary to include words associated with shopping for food, clothing, and other souvenirs. 2. express their preferences for goods to be purchased in a variety of shopping situations. 3. read to obtain information about goods and services. 4. write to inform about goods and services.	• Basic food and drinks • Clothing • Numerals • Souvenirs • City locations • Means of transportation	• Toy money (rubles) • Plastic food and drinks • Russian souvenirs • City maps • Clothing • Videos • Scale	1. Food and drinks 2. Souvenirs 3. Clothing 4. Verbs related to shopping 5. Money 6. Kilograms and grams	1. Decision making 2. Cooperate with others during role-playing 3. Classifying 4. Planning 5. Being aware of necessary resources	*Students will:* 1. role-play vendors and customers, dialoguing about selling and purchasing different goods. 2. In their journals, create a shopping guide providing: a. names of different shopping places; b. locations of these places; c. available transportation; and, d. lists of goods and services. 3. after reading shopping guides created by their peers, dialogue about their shopping plans for the day. 4. participate in various games using vocabulary associated with shopping. 5. view and discuss a cartoon about shopping.	*Social Studies* • Skills/processes—interpret maps. • Participate in cooperative learning activities. • Content-related text—discuss to gain and verify information about a topic. • Expository text—clarify information and concept (interpretive stance). • Functional text—respond to functional print in the environment. • Write to inform—advertisement, lists. • Conscious language choices—nouns, verbs. *Mathematics* • Money—count combinations of bills and coins up to $100 and apply to real-life situations.	*Students will:* 1. work in pairs to prepare for a shopping trip in Moscow by discussing choices of: a. shopping locations; b. determining the means of transportation to the selected shopping locations; and, c. writing a list of goods to be purchased. (Outcomes 1 and 3 and 4). 2. role-play different shopping situations between customers, vendors and/or assistants by: a. selecting the goods to be purchased; b. determining the cost of the goods; and, c. purchasing the goods with rubles (Outcomes 1 and 2).

Reprinted with permission. Harford County Public Schools, Foreign Language Office, Bel Air, MD 21014.

What Is the Content of FLES*?

The content selected for foreign language in the elementary school depends on the goals of the program. But it also depends on the abilities of the youngsters, the resources and materials, the teachers, the schedule, and what is a realistic expectation leading to some degree of proficiency.

The content of *Sequential FLES* or *FLEX* is by no means limited to those forms of organization of content described above. Some others come to mind:

- Learning scenarios
- Holidays in the foreign culture
- Video, film, and computer programs
- A mini-trip to the foreign culture
- An interdisciplinary unit, such as a joint foreign language-social studies unit (e.g., a unit in French paired with a unit on Canada or a unit in Spanish paired with a unit on Latin America)
- Total physical response
- Letters and tapes sent to and received from pen pals in the foreign culture
- Foods in different cultures
- Songs in the foreign culture
- The five C's of the *Standards for Foreign Language Learning*
- A combination of all those already mentioned

The curriculum is the organization of the content. It must be vitalized by an enthusiastic teacher using a broad range of teaching techniques appropriate to the age and abilities of the youngsters in his or her class. Essentially, however, if a *Sequential FLES* or *FLEX* program is to be successful, there must be a long-range curriculum in which the specific content is spelled out in detail.

Content at Kindergarten to Grade 4

Content at this early level moves slowly, devotes shorter periods of time to the foreign language in *Sequential FLES* and *FLEX*, and has very short lesson segments. Since children's attention span is brief at this level, teachers find that they must change activities every three to four minutes in a twenty-minute lesson. Activities alternate from listening and being seated to moving around or singing and dancing or role-playing. The content revolves around the children's daily activities at school and at home, including pets and animals in the zoo. This age group likes number and counting games and reading-readiness activities. By grade 3, they can apply some of the word-attack skills they have learned in English to reading in the foreign language, but they need special instructions when it comes to sound-letter correspondences. The content of a lesson in grade 1 would reflect some of the content in the elementary school curriculum and might include:

- Numbers 1–11; counting with a ball
- Telling time
- Using a toy clock to tell time
- TPR: movement to illustrate the arms of the clock at various times of the day
- Listening to a story
- Playing "live" tic-tac-toe (children standing on X and O places in the classroom)

The content would also reflect the *Standards for Foreign Language Learning*.

Content at Grades 4 to 8

The content at grades 4 to 8, depending on when the foreign language was started, would be on a more sophisticated level and would follow the topics listed earlier. There would be reading and writing activities, and some TPR activities would be successful at this level, too, such as "live" tic-tac-toe. The content of a lesson in grade 5, for example, in a class that had started in grade 4, might include:

- Reviewing numbers 1–31
- Learning to tell time
- Playing Buzz
- Completing a worksheet on time, writing in the time as pictured
- Listening to a story
- Dramatizing the story
- Reading parts of the story
- Writing answers to questions about the story
- Discussing time for meals in the United States and in the foreign culture

As in all grades, the content would reflect both the content of the elementary school curriculum and the *Standards for Foreign Language Learning*.

Content in Immersion *Programs*

The foreign language content in *Immersion* programs revolves around the daily use of the foreign language for the purpose of communication and instruction. Even in early grades, teachers focus on the sound system, on phonics, and on reading readiness activities. In grades 2 and 3, word-attack skills in the foreign language are developed and practiced, as well as reading and writing activities appropriate for the regular elementary school curriculum. Specific terms and vocabulary in the foreign language are presented to facilitate instruction in the content areas of social studies, science, math, and other areas. Because science and math are manipulative, the children get more time for these subjects in grades 1, 2, and 3. Basically, the content in *Immersion* programs is controlled by the district elementary school curriculum, so much of this content is supposed to mirror what other children in the same grade level are studying in English, except that *Immersion* students are expected also to be functionally fluent in the foreign language when they complete grade 6.

Immersion programs also focus on English language skills, depending on when they are introduced. Many of the programs introduce English in grade 3, while the content of the elementary school program is continued through the medium of the foreign language. When *Immersion* programs delay the introduction of English language arts until grade 4 or even grade 5, parents worry about students' progress in reading and spelling. Research studies indicate that some students experience some lag in English language skills—language arts and reading (Dulay, Burt, and Krashen, 1982)—but that most of them will make up such deficiencies by the end of the elementary school grades. Concerning differences in achievement in second language reading, Genesee (1987) indicated that such differences may be due to "grade level, student ability, socioeconomic status and other factors." Studies are under way at this time in Canadian *Immersion* programs concerning the best time to introduce English language skills. In view of my own experience with bilingual and *Immersion* programs, I recommend that English skills be started *no later than* grade 3 in *Immersion* programs.

The Thematic FLES* Curriculum

Depending on the initial grade of instruction, in a thematic approach the teacher may move through three or more years of sequential, spiral learning, with each year reviewing and expanding previous work as well as introducing additional themes. For example, a three-year spiral curriculum might include some of the following topics:

Year One: Themes, Language Functions, and the Five C's

SCHOOL: Greetings, days of the week, equivalent names in the foreign language, classroom objects, colors, numbers, weather, time

FAMILY: Members, age, pets, names, relationship

OCCUPATIONS: Names, places of business

HOUSE: Different types of homes, rooms, furniture, television

Year Two: Themes, Language Functions, and the Five C's

Review and expand themes in year 1.

CLOTHING: Articles of clothing, colors, plurals

TOYS: Different types of toys, colors, activities, games

HOME: Expansion of rooms, furniture, activities in the home, pets, and other animals, computers (games, World Wide Web, etc.)

FOOD: Different types of food, meals, plurals, likes and dislikes, telling time, numbers

NEIGHBORHOOD: Buildings, different places, directions

Year Three: Themes, Language Functions, and the Five C's

Review and expand themes in years 1 and 2.

GOING TO A RESTAURANT: Expansion of food, ordering meals, amenities in a restaurant

GOING SHOPPING: Shopping for food, shopping for clothing, shopping for toys

TRAVEL: Visiting relatives, taking a longer trip; expansion of occupations connected with travel

ENTERTAINMENT AND RECREATION: Movies, sports, seasonal activities; comparing sports in the target cultures with those in the United States; computers (key pals, World Wide Web, etc.)

In planning curriculum, there exists a strong relationship involving thematic topics, language functions, learning scenarios, and the five C's of the *Standards for Foreign Language Learning.* All of these are involved in creating real-life scenarios.

Included in a thematic curriculum must be the necessary vocabulary, idiomatic expressions, verbs, adjectives, adverbs, and exclamations with which to build dialogues, stories, questions and answers, personalized items suggested by the children, and other local interests and activities. If the community boasts a football team, then many of the language activities will focus on the team and its comings and goings. If the community sponsors an exchange program, then there will be many opportunities for developing cross-cultural contrasts, particularly with day-to-day activities.

However, no matter which themes are included in the curriculum, the most important goal is to give children the opportunity to use what they have learned—first in familiar situations, but then in unfamiliar situations. For example, after a unit on going shopping has been completed, students might be given the following situation, or a form of learning scenario:

> SETTING: You are shopping for food for dinner with your friend. You have the equivalent of $8.00. The total for what you want to buy is the equivalent of $10.50.
>
> TASK: What would you say to your friend? What would you say to the vendor? What would you do? What would your key pal in Marseilles do in a comparable situation?

In order to deal effectively with the problem, students need to be able to use numbers, names of food items, courtesy expressions, etc., in a real-life situation. Many other situations could be developed by the teacher and the students, too, which could be placed in a Situation Box (see Chapter Eleven). Periodically, youngsters can select one of the situations for performance. At first, the children might rehearse the situation; later on, groups of children might be able to perform the situation spontaneously.

Situations usually involve some of the following communication functions (there are many more):

Complaining about...

Disagreeing...

Getting angry about...

Feeling happy about...

Apologizing about...

Refusing...

Accepting...

Praising...

Getting (and giving) information for an "information gap"...

Persuading...

Expressing feeling in situations...

Getting sleepy when...

Misplacing your lunch...

Losing your homework...

Getting a present...

NOTE: For many sample learning scenarios, see *Standards for Foreign Language Learning: Preparing for the 21st Century* (National Standards in Foreign Language Education Project 1996, 67–94).

The Interrelationship Between FLES* Curriculum, National Foreign Language Standards, and Assessment

It is important to remember that there is a very strong bond between **FLES*** curriculum, the national standards described in *Standards for Foreign Language Learning*, and assessment. Each does not exist in a vacuum. Each helps students to make progress in their acquisition of the foreign language and culture.

Throughout this chapter, this interrelationship has been stressed. Whether we are discussing the goals of the program, the content of the curriculum (as stated in the learning scenario for each unit), the classroom activities that reflect the five C's of the *Standards for Foreign Language Learning*, the communicative and receptive abilities, the ongoing assessment of student progress, or the many different activities

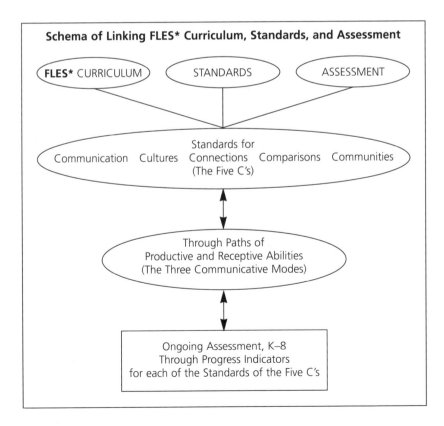

Schema of Linking FLES* Curriculum, Standards, and Assessment

FLES* CURRICULUM   STANDARDS   ASSESSMENT

Standards for
Communication Cultures Connections Comparisons Communities
(The Five C's)

Through Paths of
Productive and Receptive Abilities
(The Three Communicative Modes)

Ongoing Assessment, K–8
Through Progress Indicators
for each of the Standards of the Five C's

that take place in different **FLES*** classrooms, there is a continued interweaving and linking of these three elements.

Obviously, careful planning must precede classroom instruction to ensure that students acquire a cohesive **FLES*** language-learning experience in any of the program models and at any and every level of **FLES*** instruction.

For selected sources of **FLES*** curriculum, see Appendix L.

⚲ FOR REFLECTION

Standards are intended to serve as a gauge for excellence as states and local districts carry out their responsibilities for curriculum in the schools.

National Standards in Foreign Language
Education Project (1996, 95)

What Approaches Are Used in All Types of **FLES*** Programs?

Focus on Children

In discussing the various approaches to the teaching of **FLES*,** the overarching principle is the focus on the needs and interests of children. It is also important for teachers to recognize the various strengths and challenges of children (and multiple intelligences) as they engage in language-learning activities (see Chapter Two).

FLES* students vary in their skills, needs, and abilities. Within the same class, **FLES*** teachers have students with differing multiple abilities and intelligences. Gardner (1993) has identified seven intelligences: musical, bodily kinesthetic, logical-mathematical, linguistic, spatial, interpersonal, and intrapersonal. Gardner "makes the case for the plurality of intellect...individuals may differ in the particular intelligence profiles with which they are born and...they differ in the profiles they end up with. I think of the intelligences as raw, biological potentials." Thus, the study of a foreign language is not a solely cognitive experience!

FLES* teachers generally teach ALL students, including students with dyslexia, attention deficit disorders, hearing, speech, and visual challenges, and many other individual differences. How then do **FLES*** teachers help ALL students to be successful foreign language learners? The following **FLES*** practitioners' reports of successful, innovative solutions to this challenge are representative of the work of many, many **FLES*** teachers who have made a foreign language accessible to all students:

- Miller (1995) states that teachers can organize success for students through a multisensory approach—something that **FLES*** teachers have been practicing and perfecting over the years.

- Hurst (1996) indicates that it is incumbent upon **FLES*** teachers to provide structured practice activities involving consonant and vowel sounds in Spanish, through the use of phoneme cards. This, according to Hurst, provides a successful experience for students, so that they can go on to different kinds of communicative activities. This approach is particularly helpful to students who have auditory and visual difficulties.

- Kennedy and DeLorenzo (1985) believe that "a *FLEX-Exploratory* language class can play a crucial role in making children aware of the world beyond their own neighborhoods." This appeals to many children who, in the past, were denied access to foreign language programs.

- The most fundamental principles of teaching ALL students success-fully are based on children's experiences, both in and out of school. Lucietto (1994) offers concrete suggestions for helping **FLES*** students understand their "uniqueness as individuals" through a number of personalized activities.

- Gramer (1993) offers a number of concrete, practical suggestions for reaching all students in the **FLES*** class: "a) create mnemonic devices; b) add visualization to abstractions; c) create as many forms of sensory input as possible; d) build in a lot of repetition; e) alter the method of presentation; f) provide immediate reinforcement; g) alternate expectations by accepting student limitations and provide success for everyone at some level."

- As mentioned earlier, Gardner (1993) indicates that there are seven different kinds of intelligences. All seven play important roles in the classroom, and all teachers need to be aware of them as they try to make plans to accommodate individual children's differences.

Gardner's Multiple Intelligences

1. *Linguistic:* spoken or written word activities
2. *Logical-math:* numbers, calculations, logic, classifications, critical thinking
3. *Spatial:* visual aids, colors, visual organizers, mind maps
4. *Musical:* music, environmental sounds, rhythms
5. *Bodily kinesthetic:* whole body, TPR activities
6. *Interpersonal:* peer or cross-age friendships, sharing, group situations, cooperative activities
7. *Intrapersonal:* reactions, feelings, memories, student choices

How Do Your Students Learn?

What are your students' learning strengths?

- Visual learners?
- Auditory learners?
- Motor learners?

- Kinesthetic learners?
- Tactile learners?
- Analytic learners?
- Global learners?
- Left-brain learners?
- Right-brain learners?

Many other factors:

- Chemistry of the class
- Native Language Kid Talk (N.L.K.T.)
- Temperature of the classroom
- Season of the year
- Pre- or post-holiday
- Pre- or post-school event
- Early in the day
- Last period of the day
- Too much listening required
- Too much sitting required
- Too few interactions
- Good or poor memory skills
- Learning styles in a culture
- Male or female achievement attitudes
- Personal problems—lack of sleep, state of health, food, drugs, learning disabilities, etc.

All Children Can Learn!

1. Explore different ways to reach ALL students.
2. Honestly believe that ALL children can learn—some in different ways.
3. Find ways to appeal to all the senses, if possible.
4. Discover ways to appeal to the different intelligences of children.
5. Use topics of interest to children—things children talk about at home, at recess, on the playground—the N.L.K.T. approach.
6. Use real-life situations and scenarios for teaching and for assessment of student progress.
7. Provide more to do for gifted students (challenging projects, appeals to higher-order thinking skills, service projects for other classmates and children in other classes and grades).

8. Explore alternative ways to review, reteach, and practice (e.g., different visuals, different classroom organization, using partners and small groups).

9. Sneak in all kinds of review by recombining themes (e.g., weather and clothing, clothing and colors, interdisciplinary science activities and mathematics and sports).

10. Use TPR and rhythm activities in different ways, because children learn through their muscles!

11. Create a "joy in learning" classroom that is both nonthreatening and challenging.

12. Listen carefully to children's comments—there's a lot of wisdom in those young minds!

13. Focus on reaching ALL children!

Specific Approaches in the FLES* Classroom

There is no one *best* way to teach **FLES***. Happily, there is a wide choice of different approaches that help to vitalize the classroom. Teachers (and students) find that following only one approach or one method soon leads to boredom on the part of the children (and probably the teacher, too!). The following selected approaches help the teacher to be more creative and can be adapted to individual teacher and class needs and styles. All kinds of materials and technology can be used with these approaches. More details on how to use these approaches may be found in Chapters Ten and Eleven.

The Standards-Oriented Approach

This approach involves the five C's of foreign language study: communication, cultures, connections, comparisons, and communities. "The standards for foreign language learning require a much broader definition of the content of the foreign language classroom. Students should be given ample opportunities to explore, develop, and use communication strategies, learning strategies, critical thinking skills, and skills in technology, as well as the appropriate elements of the language system and culture. The exact form and content of each of these elements is not prescribed in the present document. Instead, the standards provide a background, a framework for the reflective teacher to use in weaving these rich curricular experiences into the fabric of language learning" (National Standards in Foreign Language Education Project 1996, 28). For additional information about the standards defined by the National Standards in Foreign Language Education Project, see Chapter Eight.

The Communication Approach

With the advent of the proficiency movement in the teaching of foreign languages on all school levels, the emphasis on communication is widely accepted as an important goal of all kinds of **FLES*** programs. No longer do we have mindless repetition of drills as in the past (although some drills still have a role). The goal of giving students many opportunities for understanding and speaking the foreign language in different real-life situations is well accepted in all types of **FLES*** programs, for *communication and culture are the central goals at this level.* While it is important to use a variety of approaches, a variety of strategies, and all kinds of instructional materials and multimedia equipment, we must never forget that interpersonal communication and intercultural understanding are the building blocks of all types of **FLES*** programs.

The Cultural Approach

The culture (or cultures) of the target language adds a broader perspective to language learning. Learning about the day-to-day activities of youngsters in the target culture makes the foreign language more meaningful to young students. Besides, cultural components can be incorporated into the linguistic aspects by including such elements as greetings, famous personalities of the target culture(s), and celebration of holidays and historical events. Other cross-cultural topics might include food, times for meals, dress, homes, toys, family life, customs, rituals, heroes and heroines, folk stories, sports, leisure-time activities, and nonverbal communication. The differences as well as the similarities between the two cultures are of great interest to children.

The people-to-people aspects of teaching culture are vital to the success of the program. That is why language and culture in **FLES*** are extremely important and should give youngsters the tools for communicating with people from other cultures. Some of the commonly accepted procedures include pen pals through the mail, key pals through computers (e.g., *le Minitel*), audiocassette and video exchanges, and satellite simultaneous exchanges. The latest technology is truly bringing the world closer to our children! (See Chapter Twelve.)

The Conversation/Dialogue Approach

All types of **FLES*** programs utilize dialogues and/or dramatic situations at some time or other, although there is less emphasis on memorization of dialogues now than in the past. In the dialogue approach, children communicate in different situations and learn how to adapt dialogues to suit other situations. In the conversation/dialogue approach, role-playing is *key*, and children learn the language, culture, and sometimes the elementary school content through the reenactment of, for example, historical events.

With a dialogue approach, basic structures, vocabulary, and idiomatic expressions can be used and practiced in the context of a specific topic or conversation. The context can be a conversation between two or more people in a natural setting that reflects the interests of the students. The most productive conversations also contain some significant cultural aspects or implications, including gestures and customs. An effective dialogue is one that can be adapted to *new* and *different* settings while retaining the basic structures.

The steps in the dialogue approach are clarification of the setting or situation, presentation, presentation of new words/expressions, repetition, and applications. Other suggestions may be found in Chapter Eleven and Appendix C.

The Story, or Narrative, Approach

The advantage of using a story approach is that it enables the teacher to use or adapt authentic folktales that reflect the foreign culture. The steps for presenting a story are similar to those for presenting a dialogue. An additional step is conversion of the story to a dialogue.

In the narrative approach, some of the topics that have to be touched on are:

- The story line
- The characters
- The action
- The scenes
- The crisis
- The solution(s)
- The endings(s)

Storytelling by Children

Storytelling can be done as a class project, with groups of children working on different sections of the story.

Children love to recount what happened to them...what they saw on television...what they ate...what they bought...where they went... These stories can be spontaneous and simple.

Problem: Many teachers do not want to use this approach because of the past tense. A simple way to get around the past tense is to start a narrative by saying: "Today is Tuesday." Then the story can be told in the present tense without the past-tense complications. Gradually, as the children gain more experience with the language, they can learn the first- and third-person forms of the past tense.

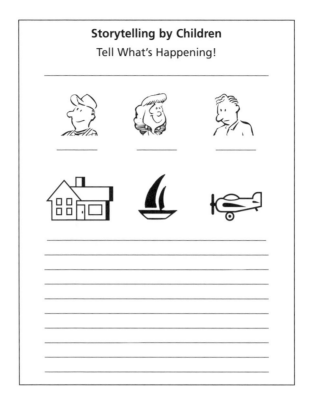

Storytelling by the Teacher

The teacher can use a story technique from time to time to bring new excitement to the learning process. The teacher tells a story (usually a folktale that is rich in the foreign culture) and dramatically teaches vocabulary through actions, gestures, and props. SPECIAL NOTE: There should be a short refrain that is repeated periodically throughout the story, so that after a while the children naturally chime in and repeat the refrain without being asked. Such a refrain in Cinderella, for example, might be "She is so sad; she can't go to the ball!"

After the story, the teacher checks comprehension by asking questions. Then the teacher might divide the story into four or five different sections, assign each section to a different group, and have each group dramatize their part of the story. Vocabulary and key phrases are taught to the class prior to this assignment. Then the assignments might be rotated to different groups, so that *each* group has an opportunity to work on all the segments of the story. Sometimes (but not always) there is a performance of the story for others to enjoy, too.

The teacher could ask more gifted language students to change the ending of the story, or to change the roles of the characters, or to see how the story would work in 1999 or in 1604 or in 2500.

Additional steps with the story approach might be the development of the cultural content through additional pictures; map and globe studies to identify the locale; discussion of the effects of geography and weather on the life of the people in the story; cross-cultural contrasting of family life in the foreign culture in the story with that in the United States; role-playing not only parts of the story but also life in the foreign culture as depicted or as inferred by the children; checking on false assumptions by questions and research or defending assumptions based upon some parts of the story, etc. Naturally, the more sophisticated activities will be limited to upper-level **FLES*** students.

Using Authentic Children's Literature for Storytelling by Teachers

Types of Authentic Literature

- Stories, proverbs, songs, poems, plays, historical events, current events, jokes, letters, articles, videos, riddles, raps, advertisements, etc.

Benefits for Children

- Authentic sounds and rhythm of language
- Increased vocabulary
- Use of language in meaningful situations
- Culture linked to language
- Learning how to get the gist and make inferences
- Introduction to short conversations
- Review of material already learned
- Creative thinking about changing the ending of the story
- Remembering the sequence of the story
- Variety of follow-up activities in pairs and small groups
- Potential lead-in to additional expansion of language and additional units

---

The Learner-Centered Approach

Much of the time at the **FLES*** level, teachers teach the *whole* class, and this can be very effective. However, in light of current thinking about how young children learn and how they need many different opportunities to use the foreign language in real-life situations, teachers are encouraged to try different approaches in classroom arrangement and in learner-centered instruction, such as:

- Small-group interactions
- Cooperative learning in small groups
- Partner practice or paired activities
- Presentations by students
- Activities during which a student is in charge, such as a warm-up
- Activities in which students make visuals for practice sessions
- Activities in which students plan and direct games
- Activities in which the classroom becomes a marketplace or a department store
- Activities that help students make decisions
- Activities that promote communication
- Opportunities for students to ask questions and state personal preferences and options

The Individualized/Personalized Focus

It is difficult to teach **FLES*** without an individualized and personalized approach. The children, no matter on which grade level, want to relate everything to their own frame of reference. Therefore, successful **FLES*** teachers use the children's birthdays, preferences in food and clothing, and favorite movie and video stars to practice the language and the content of the curriculum. This approach keeps the youngsters on their toes and keeps them interested!

Guidelines for Student-Led Activities

- Small groups of varying levels of ability
- Roles of students: leader, recorder, observer, member of the group
- Task/problem to be worked on in the foreign language
- Leader keeps the communication and ideas going
- Recorder reports to the whole group and keeps a record
- Group grade

Steps in the Learner-Centered Approach

- Know your students.
- Have a specific purpose.
- Prepare students, space, materials, and equipment.
- Arrange the room effectively.
- Train assistants (students, student teachers, aids, etc.).

- Define routines.
- Prepare charts (To Do, More to Do...).
- Select student leaders and train them. Make sure they know their responsibilities and what they are to do when there is a problem. Make sure that each student gets a chance to be a group leader.
- Discuss small-group and partner practice with the class—rationale, responsibilities of each member of the group, outcomes, etc. Discuss standards for attention to task.
- Begin with short sessions (four to five minutes).
- Follow with class discussion about problems.
- Discuss teacher responsibilities.
- Discuss evaluation of students' work (group and individual).
- Discuss use of materials.
- Discuss use of technology.
- Discuss situations in which help is needed and/or required.
- Have students discuss their reactions. Ask them what they learned.
- Think about your reactions as a teacher:

    Is it difficult to give up center stage?

    Do you see real learning taking place?

    Do you think more learning would occur if *you* did the teaching?

    Does all of this go against your personality?

    What do students really learn?

    What are the problems? Can they be solved?

Activities in Pairs and/or Small Groups

1. Learning dialogues
2. Adapting dialogues
3. Working on a project
4. Giving a dictation or spot dictation
5. Asking/answering in a specific situation
6. Creating skits, riddles, jokes, etc., for oral presentation and/or for a class newspaper (also cheers, jazz chants)
7. Listening (lab or mini-lab situation, using records, magnetic card reader, TV, etc.)
8. Playing FL games
9. Creating FL games (to drill, to stimulate student talk, etc.)
10. Working on reports (e.g., current happenings)

11. Preparing materials (e.g., for bulletin board, for reviewing vocabulary)
12. Interviewing native speakers
13. Preparing a group presentation (e.g., cooking flan)
14. Planning a class field trip (e.g., to a museum)
15. Reporting on a movie or video to the class
16. Planning a party to celebrate a cultural event
17. Making costumes for a skit
18. Working with the Situation Box (e.g., pull out situations at random and role-play)
19. Planning a mini science experiment for the class
20. Preparing test items for a quiz
21. Preparing a conversation for videotaping
22. Planning a debate about a hot issue
23. Creating a group jazz chant (or rap) in the foreign language, then teaching it to the rest of the class. Add a little TPR as the whole class performs the jazz chant or rap and marches around the room, clapping hands.

Other suggestions for using the learner-centered approach may be found in Chapter Ten.

The Cooperative Learning Approach

Cooperative learning is a trend that encompasses all areas of the curriculum. Stated very simply, it encourages students to help one another in the learning process and reduces a great deal of the competition that can sometimes hinder the learning process.

Applied to all types of **FLES*** programs, cooperative learning is an excellent approach, since communication and interaction among students is a highlight of this technique. Four or five students, grouped according to their needs, attempt to solve a problem, practice a situation, brainstorm ideas for a class assembly program or presentation, or interact in any other real-life situation. This provides the motivation for students to participate wholeheartedly in the group activity. The most effective topics involve a puzzle or problem or an information gap.

A *leader* is selected, a *recorder* writes down the important ideas, and other members of the group participate actively, using the foreign language. When students have only a limited base in the foreign language (i.e., limited skills in reading and writing, limited vocabulary and expressions), the teacher first teaches some of the essential components that will be used in the activity so that the students can function for a short period of time on their own. What is really helpful in this activity is that the esprit de corps becomes operational—that is, the individual students in the group help one another to further the functioning of the entire group. They express ideas, agree, disagree, correct each other, and generally try to produce an outstanding *group effort*. Some teachers grade students on the group's product, rather than on individual participation. This practice, too, helps students to work together and communicate with one another.

Some of the major concepts in cooperative learning are:

1. All students function in a leadership role from time to time.
2. Students are capable of resolving their own problems through group decision making.
3. Students learn how to work together and collaborate on a specific group task.
4. Because this is a group assignment, students learn how to contribute to a group product.
5. Groups are most effective when they represent heterogeneous groups of students—different backgrounds, different abilities, different capabilities, different genders, etc.
6. Students help one another within the constraints of the communication skills they have acquired.
7. There is a wide range of ways to implement cooperative learning in **FLES*** classes, depending on the needs of the students and the skills of the teacher in organizing group activities.
8. The teacher needs to plan several practice sessions with groups so that they understand that they need to be on task and that they need to work together politely, with a minimum of discord or distraction.
9. An essential component of cooperative learning is for students to evaluate how the group is functioning and how effective their individual role is in the group's activities and progress.
10. The teacher's role during the group sessions is primarily to motivate the activity, to be of assistance, to observe the functioning of each group, to encourage participation, to note major errors in the foreign language for future whole-class instruction, to suggest sources of information, and to plan future whole-class instruction as well as small-group and paired activities.

A treasure hunt is an excellent way to encourage groups of children to work together on a common problem with a common goal. First, the teacher has to prepare the classroom with hidden objects. Second, he or she has to be sure that the students recognize the names of the objects they will be looking for. Third, the children have to be instructed that when they find the hidden object, they must be very quiet so that they do not give away the information to the other groups.

After all the groups have found the objects, the teacher calls on the first group that finished the hunt to announce where the objects are located. Of course, the first group gets a prize!

After a while, more able students can work together as a group to prepare the classroom for the treasure hunt.

Sample Class Treasure Hunt

Cosas para encontrar en la sala de clase:

algo azul	algo verde
algo suave	algo que vive en el agua
etc.	

The Higher-Order Thinking Skills Approach (H.O.T.S.)

Across the curriculum, educators insist upon giving *all* students opportunities for reaching, intellectually speaking. Teachers are encouraged to be on the lookout for opportunities that will help develop higher cognitive skills while still reviewing vocabulary and expressions. Asking children to comment on the differences and similarities between a horse and a dog, for example, does not only reinforce vocabulary, but can also stimulate higher levels of thinking skills. Showing pictures of different animals can further reinforce vocabulary. However, going a step further and asking children to categorize the various animals (those with four feet, those with two feet, etc.) will add a more sophisticated dimension to the language lesson and will integrate it with the skills-development program of the entire elementary school curriculum.

Other opportunities are afforded by the kinds of questions teachers ask their students. The hierarchy of questioning and other strategies for including H.O.T.S. in the classroom is (from low to high):

- Identifying vocabulary and expressions
- Retelling and organizing ideas
- Applying rules and central ideas
- Analyzing, including classifying, comparing, contrasting, and drawing conclusions
- Synthesizing, including predicting, solving, and creating new ideas
- Evaluating, including giving opinions, setting priorities, and making decisions

In order for students to develop a reservoir of different approaches to different situations, they need a classroom environment of inquiry and group processing of ideas. Student-centered activities are helpful in carrying out these goals.

Additional H.O.T.S. activities may be found in Chapter Ten.

The Total Physical Response Approach (TPR)

Experience and research support the thesis that children learn through physical motions. Seefeldt and Barbour (1994) state that "children learn through their senses including their muscles." Children like to learn with all kinds of motion, with moving around, with pantomime as well as words. They cannot sit quietly for long periods of time and need frequent changes of activities. Obviously, the attention span will be longer as children get older and mature, but even sixth graders are not able to sustain attention to language learning for more than ten minutes at a time for a particular segment of a lesson. That is why the recommended lesson plan contains many short segments. (See Chapter Ten.)

The following is an example of a TPR activity suitable for a **FLES*** class, much like a Gouin series, which was in use in the seventeenth century:

Levez-vous.	Je me lève.
Allez à la porte.	Je vais à la porte.
Frappez à la porte.	Je frappe à la porte.
Ouvrez la porte.	J'ouvre la porte.
Fermez la porte.	Je ferme la porte.

After listening to the commands and performing the actions, the children repeat both the commands and the responses, using appropriate actions with their fingers and hands. Then several children say the words and perform the actions. Using the "comprehensible input" approach, the commands, the responses, and the actions will be modeled by the teacher and the motions modeled by the children, without production or speaking. If the time for listening and understanding is sufficient, many of the children will have learned both the commands and the responses (including the motions) with ease. The teacher must be alert for those with special needs and special learning styles who will need additional assistance, perhaps in the form of drills and group work.

A TPR File

Teachers should begin to collect all kinds of TPR activities that are related to different aspects of the elementary school curriculum. For example, when working on locations in social studies, students may pick a card from a file (or listen to a cassette) that says:

Je vais à Rouen pour acheter une bicyclette.

The student goes to the map of France and points to the city of Rouen, then draws a picture on the board or pantomimes a bicycle.

Additional TPR activities may be found in Chapters Ten and Fifteen.

The Drama Approach: Dramatizing and Role-Playing

Children of all ages enjoy role-playing and dramatizing activities. They enjoy dramatizing folktales, and they get pleasure from activities that put them into the shoes of children in foreign cultures. All kinds of communicative activities, dialogues, stories, anecdotes, commercials, events of daily family-life, and the like can be converted into some kind of dramatic form. The rehearsals are wonderful ways to have numerous repetitions and drills! Through play, repetition, and practice, youngsters can absorb tremendous quantities of communicative expressions in the foreign language.

Even some of the nuances of language can be emphasized through drama techniques. Changing intonation patterns of the same sentence can help youngsters understand different patterns of meaning. Learning how to change one's voice so that it sounds like a five-year-old and later like a ninety-year-old can also convey much meaning, without, of course, including stereotypical behaviors. Some simple role-playing strategies can be:

• Asking permission to do something at home, then at school

• Creating a scene with a complete conversation

• Creating a scene with just a few words of conversation

• Creating a scene that expresses different emotions, such as happiness, sadness, boredom, anger, etc.

• Playing charades in the foreign language, with a narrator

In preparing a charade, each group of students needs to discuss and plan how they will present their charade to the rest of the class and how the narrator will describe their actions.

Dramatizing the simple, familiar tale of Cinderella or some of the fables of La Fontaine can be an exciting experience in the classroom and can also serve as a presentation at a community fair or in the auditorium. When dramatizing something for the public, it is wise to use a story that is familiar. Although putting on a "production" requires a great deal of preparation on the part of the teacher (mostly by simplifying the language), it has tremendous appeal for the children and for the parents, grandparents, administrators, school board members, and others in the audience. Good public relations and good presentation of students' foreign language skills!

The Humor Approach

Children in the elementary and middle schools enjoy humor—and learn quite readily through this approach. Although this approach does not necessarily use jokes throughout the program, it does capitalize on humor that deals with plays on words, double meanings, intonation, spelling, and situational guessing of meaning. After several years of study, children can then tell amusing anecdotes and events within the limits of their vocabulary and language proficiency. Many teachers use this approach to help students clarify meaning and heighten understanding. Amusing visuals also help students remember vocabulary and expressions.

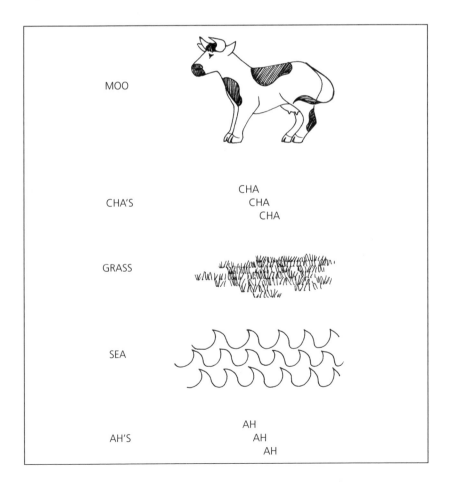

Unfortunately, this approach is rarely used...but children seem to be naturally jovial and enjoy all kinds of humor. Obviously, the teacher has to set the ground rules before undertaking a lesson involving the humor approach, as children may mistakenly take the humor to be a sign of liberation from acceptable classroom behavior!

Sometimes it involves a dialogue that can be converted to a humorous setting; sometimes it involves a funny situation linked to the situation approach. Sometimes it involves a serious discussion and demonstration of advertisements that are funny in our culture and that may or may not be funny in the target culture. (Often, what is funny in the target culture may not be funny in our culture, and vice versa.)

Cartoons are a good way to use humor. Children can insert comments in the balloons of a comic strip that have been whited out by the teacher. Often, children's humor is not particularly funny to adults, so the teacher has to be a good sport, provided the humor is in acceptable taste. The traditional elephant jokes or any of the current comic strips are fun to have children work with.

Obviously, the humor approach can often be combined with another approach, thus enhancing the growth of language and culture in a pleasurable fashion. As with humor on any level, it should be used sparingly, and is particularly well received when it is least expected! Try it! It might be fun for the children and the teacher!

Q: Why is the Statue of Liberty's hand eleven inches long?

A: If it were one inch longer, it would be a foot.

Empowering FLES* Students Through an Interdisciplinary Approach

The interdisciplinary approach is of great value to students in that it helps to integrate all school learning. Furthermore, it represents one of the goal areas recommended by the *Standards for Foreign Language Learning*—connections. This approach necessitates team planning so that the **FLES*** teacher will be aware of what the students are studying in math, science, social studies, and the other subjects of the curriculum.

Most administrators encourage an interdisciplinary approach because it helps students to identify relationships, to understand all kinds of events during a single time period, and to grasp concepts as they relate to other concepts in other disciplines.

FLES* educators have long recognized the importance of relating foreign languages to the other areas of the curriculum. The interdisciplinary approach gives students a more integrated view of their own learning by enabling them to see the interconnections between the various subjects they study. For example, when they study weather and temperature in science and use weather expressions in the foreign language classroom, there is reinforcement of learning and a strong sense of related learning.

There are a number of excellent descriptions of the **FLES*** interdisciplinary approach. Saxon (1992) writes about an effective interdisciplinary activity that includes planting a "Monet garden" by the French classes. This then becomes an integrated activity with French, science, and art. It also involves the collaboration of other teacher specialists, such as the art and the science teachers, who present background information about Monet's life and work and discuss some of the scientific principles of growing plants.

Another highly successful interdisciplinary unit is one written by DeBuhr (1993). Because there is an important schoolwide unit about animals, the Jungle Unit, it becomes a unit of study for French classes.

On the first day of the Jungle Unit, the children are greeted "with a room lavishly decorated with all manner of 'jungle' animal pictures as well as Rousseau paintings." The chairs are arranged to simulate a safari bus. "Through a commentary in French on the animals they will encounter on their trip, my students receive a continual supply of 'comprehensible input' in the target language," writes DeBuhr. Beyond identification of the animals, the students review numbers, colors, adjectives of size, and animal body parts, and they research the eating habits of the animals. Of course, the unit includes a visit to the zoo, with a commentary in French, as well as a discussion of naturalists who would like to see animals in the wild rather than in zoos.

Interdisciplinary units can be implemented by teachers in all three program models: *Sequential FLES, FLEX-Exploratory,* and *Immersion.* Each program model, however, has different goals and expectations for a specific interdisciplinary unit. The following interdisciplinary planning unit (web) has the potential to be useful to all three program models, and might involve six to eight lessons:

THEME: Caterpillars and Butterflies

LANGUAGE: Spanish

GRADES: 1–3

Language Arts

- Basic vocabulary: *la oruga, días de la semana, tener hambre, comer, un capullo, convertir, una mariposa; pequeño, grande, gordo, bello, feo,* etc.
- *La Oruga Muy Hambrienta* by Eric Carle; teacher reads the book aloud, students role-play the story and create skits

- Teacher and class create a jazz chant about caterpillars and butterflies
- Students write poems, in Spanish, about caterpillars and butterflies.

Art

- Weaving or string art
- Class mural of stages from caterpillar to butterfly
- Students create landscape pictures with caterpillars and butterflies.

Science

- Discuss size, shape, habitat, stages of growth, food, etc., of different types of caterpillars and butterflies.
- Butterfly farms (in Costa Rica, for example)
- Relationship of caterpillars and butterflies to plants
- Cautions about removing caterpillars and butterflies from natural environments

Social Studies

- Using maps, locate the natural habitats of different types of caterpillars and butterflies.
- Students do research on the contributions of caterpillars and butterflies.

Mathematics

- Counting by sixes; compare butterflies with spiders; counting by eights
- Play Buzz using sixes.
- Students create mathematical problems using caterpillars and butterflies.
- Classification of different types of caterpillars and butterflies

Physical Education

- Students simulate the stages of growth from caterpillar to butterfly.
- Teacher and class create a "Caterpillar to Butterfly Dance."

Music

- Teacher and class create a "Caterpillar to Butterfly Song" in the FL.

Another example of an interdisciplinary planning unit (web), about hats, involves foreign language, social studies, science, physical education, mathematics, language arts, art, and music:

Theme: Hats

Science
- What are hats used for?
- Temperature
- Weather
- Different fabrics (natural and invented)

Social Studies
- Hats around the world
- Ceremonial hats
- Customs (tipping one's hat…)
- Courtesy about hats

Language Arts
- Expressions (throwing one's hat in, hats off…)
- Fairy tales in which one of the characters wears a distinctive hat ("Robin Hood," "Little Red Riding Hood," etc.)
- Creative poetry and composition about hats
- Reading stories in which hats are involved

Music
- "My Hat Has Three Corners"
- "Sur le pont d'Avignon"
- Other songs

Art
- Making a class collage of different hats

Physical Education
- Mexican hat dance
- Other dances in which hats are involved

Mathematics
- Counting hats by twos, by the dozen, etc.
- Hat sizes in United States and in the foreign country
- Cost of hats

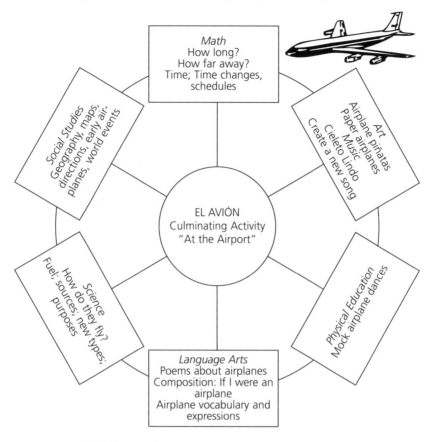

Interdisciplinary Planning Web or Unit around the Airplane and Transportation (approximately 4 weeks)

Specifics of the Interdisciplinary Approach

THE CONTENT-ENRICHED APPROACH

The goals for the development of skills and abilities in the elementary school curriculum can be achieved through the other subjects studied and **FLES***. Such skills and abilities as oral and written communication and self-expression, the learning of language concepts, reading and writing skills, and understanding the meaning of symbols and abstract ideas (to name a few) can all be integrated to some degree with the study of the basic vocabulary and expressions of the target language in a content-enriched approach.

In the area of *language arts,* children in **FLES*** can be encouraged to

• Read books about the foreign culture in English and in the target language

- See the influence of the foreign language on English in such words as *chauffeur, fiesta,* and *kindergarten*
- Write and prepare assembly programs on themes about the target culture(s)
- Read about the lives of famous people from the target culture(s)
- Write letters to pen pals in the foreign culture(s)
- Dramatize international events and folktales
- Research various aspects of the foreign culture by reading, interviewing, writing for information, etc.
- Set up displays about the foreign culture(s)
- Go on field trips (to museums, restaurants, etc.)
- Discuss current events in the foreign culture(s)
- Listen to and speak with guest speakers from the foreign culture(s)
- Write letters of appreciation to guest speakers

  In the area of *social studies*, children in **FLES*** can be encouraged to

- Enhance their map skills by locating areas where the foreign language is spoken
- Discover place names in the United States that have foreign origins, such as Montpelier and Laredo
- Study a unit on early explorers from the foreign culture(s)
- Research the contributions of people in the foreign cultures to the American Revolution, the United Nations, etc.
- Explore the foreign culture for similarities to and differences from our own with respect to:

  Family life

  Politics

  Kinesics

  Media

  Roles of men and women

  Attitudes toward money, land, humor, food, etc.

  Careers and occupations

  Leisure activities, such as sports and TV

  Geography and history

  Institutions

  Architecture

  Religion

  Food, nutrition, and cuisine

  Ceremonies, customs, and rituals

Taboos and superstitions

Science, mathematics, and technology

Other topics

- Learn similarities and differences in concepts and vocabulary. For example, the word *bread* may have different conceptual bases from *le pain* in French, *el pan* in Spanish, etc.

- Identify the contributions of the foreign cultures to English through borrowed words and expressions

- Compare holiday celebrations in the United States and in the foreign culture(s)

- Discuss current political events in the foreign culture(s)

- Identify gestures and meanings in the United States and the foreign culture(s)

- Discuss person-to-person relationships in the family and outside the family (including the use of the familiar forms in the foreign language) and "personal distance" for comfortable conversations in different cultures, etc.

- Explore the origin of customs and ceremonies in the target culture(s) and the significance of the symbols and colors on the flags of different countries.

Similarly, other subjects in the elementary school curriculum can be enriched:
- Art projects similar to projects in the foreign culture can be worked on, such as weaving, etc.

- Music offers all kinds of folk songs, popular music, etc.

- Physical education offers games, sports, folk dances, etc.

- Mathematics and science include the study and origin of the metric system, the rate of exchange of foreign currency, famous mathematicians and scientists, etc.

For example, if a fourth-grade class is studying about a cold area (like Alaska) in social studies, all other aspects might come into play in the foreign language:

SOCIAL STUDIES: Location of land and sea areas; foreign-language-speaking people; history, famous people.

MATH: Temperature readings (Fahrenheit and centigrade); differences in temperature between Alaska and the local school area

SCIENCE: Clothing for cold temperatures; new materials that are lightweight and that keep people warm; housing; coping with the cold (animals and humans); protection of the environment

PHYSICAL EDUCATION: Dances to keep warm

LANGUAGE ARTS: Poetry and prose about living in the cold; jazz chants and songs about the cold

ART: Pictorial living (banners, artwork, mobiles, posters, collages); art of Alaska

THE CONTENT-RELATED APPROACH

In the content-related approach, the content of a subject or subjects is taught in the foreign language, somewhat as it is in *Partial Immersion*. For example, the entire content in science could be taught in the foreign language, since there are many experiments and hands-on activities. A more modest way to introduce the content-related approach would be to teach minilessons in science or mathematics or social studies as part of the foreign language lessons. Holiday celebrations, historical events in the target culture, and current news events lend themselves to the implementation of the content-related approach from time to time.

The content-related approach can be used in connection with many of the cultural aspects of the target culture(s) dealing with

- Holidays
- A pretend minitrip to the country
- Discussion and tasting of food in different cultures
- Songs in different cultures
- Map and globe study
- Graphing and charting
- Categorizing, classifying, and other H.O.T.S. (higher-order thinking skills)
- Other aspects of the elementary school curriculum

Used by teachers with a solid background in the foreign language *and* the content area, the content-related approach can, from time to time, add variety and heighten student interest in the **FLES*** program.

Sample Content-Related Unit, Grade 4
(approximately 3 weeks)

CONTENT

1. Directions: north, south, east, west; crossing rivers, oceans, lakes, mountains, plains
2. Travel by train, car, bus, plane, bicycle, and on foot

ACTIVITIES

Looking at a map of the United States, Canada, and Mexico, students and teacher make various statements about directions (all in the foreign language):

- Here is the United States on the map.
- Here is Canada, to the north of the United States.
- Here is Mexico, to the south of the United States.
- Washington, DC, is the capital of the United States.
- Mexico City is the capital of Mexico.
- The president of the United States is _____.
- The president of Mexico is _____.

Students could dictate in Spanish a story about children traveling from San Francisco to Mexico City, crossing rivers, lakes, mountains, and plains.

Students, in groups, could then describe the trip, using different types of transportation: train, car, bus, plane, bicycle, and on foot. They could make scrapbooks for the group, showing maps, places visited en route, road signs they would pass, etc., depending on the information they found while doing research.

As a culmination, each group could dramatize one aspect of the trip (amusing or historical in nature, or demonstrating some of the difficulties encountered, etc.). This would help reinforce the social studies concepts as well as the functional use of Spanish.

For sample content-related lesson plans, see Appendix E.

It is important to note the difference between an interdisciplinary approach, which is taught from time to time, and a content-based approach, which attempts to cover one or more curriculum areas of the elementary school curriculum in a kind of *Partial Immersion FLES**. Both attempt to reach out to other areas of the curriculum; however, with the interdisciplinary approach, the goal is an integrated, holistic curriculum that is delivered to children by reaching into many subject areas and through many modalities of learning. The goal, too, is not to cover but to reinforce the content of the other disciplines, and to weave it together so that children come to understand meaningful relationships, past and present. The foreign language teacher can touch on any aspects that correlate well.

We need research on how much content is really understood, grasped, and internalized by the children, if taught in the foreign language:

- What are the results of content-based or (*Partial Immersion FLES*) instruction on the development of students' foreign language skills?

- What are the results of content-based (or *Partial Immersion FLES*) instruction on students' achievement in the content area(s), compared with the achievement of students who have studied the content area(s) in English?

The greatest drawback to the content-based (or *Partial Immersion FLES*) approach is that many **FLES*** teachers do not have the knowledge of the content and do not know the approved methods of teaching some of the subject disciplines. Often, curriculum specialists of other areas fear that foreign language teachers with little background in science and mathematics, for example, will "interfere" with the regular science and mathematics curriculum, concepts, and methodology.

The Global Awareness Approach

In these days, when events that take place all over the world enter our living room rapidly via television or some other form of telecommunications, it is interesting for the children to try to answer some of their questions about different places and different issues. Some of these questions can be researched by groups of children; some of the issues can be discussed; but the most important attitude to encourage is that there may not be a right or a wrong answer—*let's find out!* Naturally, some of the vocabulary has to be taught before students can tackle this kind of discussion, even on a very simple level.

Some sample issues follow:

- World energy issues.
- People who speak English with a foreign accent are _____.
- To get from New York City to Paris, you can ride your bicycle.
- There are no foreign words in the English language.
- Children in the United States and children in Germany celebrate the same holidays.
- In Italy, the dogs respond to Italian.
- Studying a foreign language is necessary if you want to be a doctor.
- A child who speaks Russian couldn't be my friend.
- Everything we need is right here in the United States.
- World environment issues.
- All people in the world are _____.
- World hunger problems.
- It would be fun to stay with a Japanese family in Japan.
- It would be hard to learn how to say *hello* in Chinese.
- You can swim to Argentina from Boston.

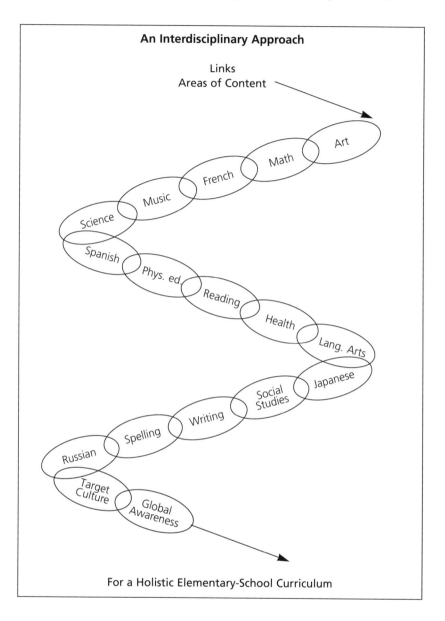

An Interdisciplinary Approach

Links
Areas of Content

Art
Math
French
Music
Science
Spanish
Phys. ed.
Reading
Health
Lang. Arts
Japanese
Social Studies
Writing
Spelling
Russian
Target Culture
Global Awareness

For a Holistic Elementary-School Curriculum

The Native Language Kid Talk Approach (N.L.K.T.)

What Do Kids Like to Talk About?		
Self	Sports	Funny things that happened
Family	Heroes, heroines	
Friends	Music	School, classes
Feelings	Fashions	Technology
TV, movies	Shopping	Space
Computer games	Pets	?

The N.L.K.T. approach stresses the value, according to Lipton (1994c), of including in the **FLES*** curriculum the kinds of things students talk about in their native language, such as sports, music, school events, teachers, school life, homework, parents, siblings, family life, friends, computer games, TV, videos, movies, shopping, fashions, pets, feelings, and many other topics.

Some teachers find that personalized questions help to gain student interest in the foreign language, such as: "Who is your favorite actor/actress?" or "What do you think will happen next to Bart Simpson's family on TV?" or "What do you do when you're happy? When you're sad?" Other teachers use famous names to illustrate familiar topics, such as the names of the members of the Spanish royal family. Activities using this approach include having the students role-play the family life of a famous family (with specific attention to cultural aspects that are the same as and different from family life in the United States); asking students to gather information by doing research in books and on the Internet and then having them correspond with key pals in the foreign culture to validate the information; as well as many other communicative activities.

All three program models (*Sequential FLES, FLEX-Exploratory,* and *Immersion*) may deal with the topic of family life in similar, yet different ways. For example, in French, in the *FLEX-Exploratory* program model, students learn how to identify the members of the family, including the extended family. They construct family trees and work with the teacher in developing a class skit about family life. They will, perhaps, focus on famous families in francophone countries, as well as on their own families. In the *Sequential FLES* program model, students may have the time to work in cooperative learning groups for the purpose of creating their own skits about family life, and possibly make comparisons between family life in the United States and in several francophone countries. They will be able to focus on the importance of family life in several different cultures—for example, in France, in Canada, in Senegal, and in Martinique. In the *Immersion* program model, family life would undoubtedly be part of a social studies unit on Canada, for example, with an emphasis on furthering the concepts required by the elementary school social studies curriculum.

While the theme of family life may be handled quite differently in each of the three program models, a number of *basic* learnings may also emerge in all three models:

- Identification of family members
- Understanding of relationships within the family
- Learning about the roles of family members
- Learning French names
- Learning about the use of *tu* and *vous*
- Learning the names of famous families in francophone countries
- Applying geography and map skills to study francophone countries
- Learning about famous families from the past in francophone countries
- Dramatizing skits about family life in francophone countries
- Role-playing events in historical families, such as, for example, in Marie Antoinette's family
- Writing to pen pals to confirm concepts of family life
- Writing/communicating with key pals

This brief analysis illustrates the ways in which one topic may be handled in the three program models. Of course, individual teachers may develop their own procedures. Thus, activities, techniques, and strategies will vary from class to class and from teacher to teacher. But in all three program models, students will acquire linguistic knowledge, as well as gain valuable insights into cross-cultural phenomena.

With sufficient preparation of basic N.L.K.T. vocabulary and expressions for the students, **FLES*** teachers in all three program models may organize small groups to work on a *real, functional experience,* such as a class party or celebration. It may be a party to celebrate the completion of a thematic unit, a local sports event, a historical event, or the birthday of a famous person in the target culture. What a sense of empowerment the students will have when they have successfully implemented their plans! Small groups of children could be asked to consider the following aspects of planning the class party:

1. Program
2. Decorations and arrangement of the room
3. Refreshments and clean-up

4. Entertainment and costumes

5. Guests and invitations

6. Research on the theme (for grades 4–6)

7. Others, as needed

Some of the planning in the foreign language (after the teacher has presented appropriate vocabulary, expressions, and questions, and students have had opportunities to practice them) might include discussion of the following:

- What do we need?
- How much does it cost?
- Who is going to take care of…?
- What are we going to say?
- What is in our skit?
- Are we going to sing?
- Do we need help?
- Other important questions

Invitations might look like this:

L'Invitation

Quand? _____

Où? _____

À quelle heure? _____

Pourquoi? _____

_____

R.S.V.P. _____

FLES* teachers may adapt these suggestions to other types of class activities. For example, some **FLES*** teachers and their classes provide outreach activities by preparing programs at senior citizens' homes, public libraries, local hotels, and other places in the community. The type of planning described above can be used to create different real-life opportunities for the children.

¡Vamos a cantar!

The Music/Song Approach

Children enjoy listening to and participating in music and songs, and the songs are particularly useful when they are representative of the culture(s) of the target language. Music generally appeals to youngsters and often helps reinforce pronunciation and intonation of the foreign language as well as vocabulary and expressions. The music/song approach can often be used as the new presentation of the day, as a change of pace, and as a review. Long after the vocabulary and structures have been forgotten, students may very well remember the words and melody of a song, particularly if hand and body motions are included in the learning process.

For those teachers who say that they cannot sing, there are many other ways to introduce the music approach: using recordings, playing the guitar, etc. The advantage of using the music approach from time to time is that it helps the class come alive, particularly through clapping hands, tapping feet, and other movement activities, and it still contributes to and reinforces the development of foreign language skills.

The Praise Approach

How Many Ways Can You Praise Students in the Foreign Language?

Do you always say the same things when students perform well in the foreign language? Why not use praise as a means of getting more language across to the students? You know how easily they pick up everything you say—why not vary your praise language according to the response and/or the performance?

Say these in the foreign language you teach! Others, too!

Super!	You're trying very hard!	Congratulations!
That's right!		Good job!
That's great!	That's better!	That's it!
Exactly!	I knew you could do it!	Good!

Good work!	Wow!	Superb!
Not bad!	Sensational!	Right on!
I think you've got it!	Excellent!	Keep it up!
That's coming along!	Wonderful!	Marvelous!
Great!	Perfect!	Well done!
Nice going!	Terrific!	Etc., etc., etc.

Why don't you draw up a list of praise expressions in your foreign language and use them!

Magnifique!	Wunderbar!	¡Magnífico!
_____	_____	_____
_____	_____	_____
_____	_____	_____
_____	_____	_____

CHALLENGING ALL STUDENTS BY USING A VARIETY OF APPROACHES

Although there are many approaches to use in the teaching of foreign languages at the **FLES*** level, some teachers fall into a routine and provide little variety in their lessons. It is highly recommended that teachers use a variety of approaches to keep students motivated and interested.

Often, it is possible to use several approaches in combination. For example, in the following survey technique, these approaches are interfaced:

- The communication approach
- The higher-order thinking skills approach
- The interdisciplinary approach and the content-based approach
- The TPR approach (if students move into groups according to the survey)
- The cultural approach (if a survey is conducted in the target culture)

Other approaches can be included according to the class situation.

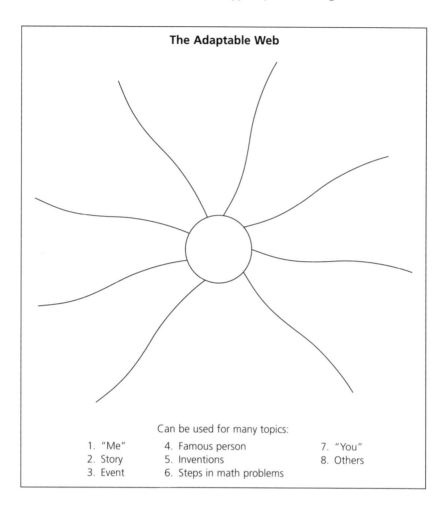

The Adaptable Web

Can be used for many topics:

1. "Me"	4. Famous person	7. "You"
2. Story	5. Inventions	8. Others
3. Event	6. Steps in math problems	

Conducting a Class Survey

- Number of children wearing purple?
- Number of children who like spinach?
- Number of children whose name begins with *M*?
- Number of children who have a birthday in August?
- Number of children who have been to Germany?

Record the results in a chart, thus developing categorizing skills.

Have the children dictate the results as an experience story; then continue with questions and answers about the information. This survey technique can be repeated from time to time, using different questions and different topics.

- There is no *one* way to teach **FLES***.
- Methodology is determined by the goals, the participants, and the teacher.
- The primary abilities are listening, speaking, reading, and writing, plus culture, for the purpose of communication.
- A variety of different approaches to teach the four abilities and culture are used with great success in **FLES*** classes.

♀ FOR REFLECTION

Elementary school foreign language teaching features the use of a wide variety of techniques designed to actively involve students in language use.

JUDITH SHRUM AND EILEEN GLISAN (1994)

FLES* Methodology: Inside the FLES* Classroom

How Do Children Learn Foreign Languages?

Children learn foreign languages differently from adolescents and adults. They rarely attempt to analyze the foreign language. They learn through real objects, in context with a thought or a situation. Children like doing things while they are learning, such as showing something, bringing something, following directions, etc.

Children's attention span is relatively short. That is why in **FLES*** programs, activities should change every four to five minutes; with younger children, it should be even more frequent.

Children really like a meaningful situation that includes some of their interests. When Batman was in vogue, it was fun to include this character in conversations, drills, and other types of activities. When Bart Simpson was the children's favorite bad boy on the block, they loved including him in their **FLES*** activities. Children, however, are very fickle. What is "in" one month will be "out" the next. It is incumbent upon the teacher to keep up with the children's parade of personalities since what they talk about with one another outside of the **FLES*** class will be of interest to them during the foreign language sessions.

Teachers must remember that listening to a great deal of comprehensible input is necessary before students can produce even small amounts of the foreign language.

Comprehensible Input

FL Production

Helping Children Learn

Children learn through their

☑ minds	☑ abilities	☑ muscles
☑ senses	☑ experiences	☑ feelings

Children learn in different ways. Teachers too seldom know how children learn and often lack the time to offer instruction in different modalities. Certainly, using the Total Physical Response approach helps reinforce learning, and teachers would be wise to use this approach often, when the content and the situation call for this helpful and enjoyable form of learning.

Other strategies are helpful, too. Many teachers find that in presenting new work of any kind (language, science, mathematics, etc.) it is helpful, if memory is involved, to point out or to elicit from the children ways in which they can remember. Mnemonics have proved to be helpful. Most Spanish language teachers remember the "shoe verbs" that highlight the stem changes. Teachers have encouraged children to use the traditional shoe to remember the stem-changing verb forms, but have also encouraged the children's creativity by having them design different types of shoes: ballet slippers, hockey skates, etc.

Sample Shoe Verb
(for stem-changing verbs in Spanish)

In teaching K–8 students, it is important to keep in mind the following factors:

1. Age and maturity levels of the students
2. Attention span
3. Memory span
4. Immaturity in making generalizations
5. Immaturity in understanding cross-cultural and community issues
6. Immaturity in making connections and comparisons
7. Learning styles and multiple intelligences

Obviously, these factors vary in individual students, based on the students' previous experience with the foreign language and culture. Every effort should be made to reach all children by using **FLES*** methodology, which includes age-appropriate approaches and activities, and the goals of the *Standards for Foreign Language Learning* (National Standards in Foreign Language Education Project 1996). We have to examine different methodologies, and extract those elements that work with our specific students. We have to accept the fact that one specific method will not always work with all students, all classes, all levels, all...anything!

OVERVIEW OF THE **FLES*** CLASSROOM

In the 1960s, there was a lockstep in **FLES*** methodology, namely: listening and speaking only for 100 clock hours of instruction, no matter which language, no matter which grade level, no matter which materials were being used. Fortunately, today there is greater openness to all aspects of **FLES*** methodology, with the purposeful matching of approaches and methodology to goals, outcomes, and needs of learners.

Some of the general characteristics of an effective class session in a foreign language are similar to those in any other subject area, such as members of the class engaged and interested in the lesson, and members of the class actively participating in the lesson by raising their hands and answering questions, performing actions in response to TPR commands, role-playing, listening with understanding, working in pairs, speaking, reading, and writing, to name just a few of the ongoing activities.

The classroom environment is conducive to learning activities, and there are effective classroom management routines in evidence. The seating arrangement varies according to the activity: sometimes whole-class instruction, sometimes small groups, sometimes paired activities, sometimes some of the children working with a computer or audiovisual equipment. The most important aspect of the classroom environment has to do with teachers helping children to feel at ease—comfortable yet challenged—encouraging, praising, helping them learn.

ASPECTS OF **FLES*** METHODOLOGY

An Overview of What Happens in the FLES* Classroom

1. Words and expressions are taught in context, not in isolation.
2. There is an emphasis on the integration of productive and receptive abilities and culture.
3. Associations are made between the foreign language and the object, action, or concept, rather than the English equivalent.

4. A wide range of materials of instruction are used during the class session, including audio, visual, manipulative, etc.

5. The emphasis is on functional communication activities in real-life situations, based on the national FL standards.

6. Grammatical structures are learned by imitation and repetition; there is evidence of error correction.

7. Each lesson includes a great deal of systematic review, reentry, and reinforcement of previously introduced material.

8. The pace of the lesson is lively and is maintained by well-timed changes and transitions from one activity to the next.

9. The cultural component is interwoven with the linguistic activities.

10. The children are encouraged to speak to one another in the foreign language, within the constraints of vocabulary and structure.

11. Although both the children and the teacher recognize that they are engaged in the development of foreign language skills and understandings, the teacher appeals to the children's interests and humor to motivate the youngsters and enhance the learning activities.

12. Evaluation is an ongoing and integral part of the teaching and learning process.

13. There are choral, group, and individual repetitions of the foreign language.

14. The children role-play conversations, songs, poems, stories, and historical and current events.

15. The children learn how holidays are celebrated in the different cultures.

16. There is an interdisciplinary approach, with integration of the foreign language with the subjects of the elementary school curriculum, such as music, art, science, physical education, mathematics, and social studies.

17. There is some content-based instruction to reinforce the concepts of other subjects in the curriculum.

In *Immersion* Programs

1. Many of the procedures and activities mentioned above are useful in *Immersion* and *Partial Immersion* classes.

2. The foreign language is used throughout the day in full *Immersion* classes or for half the day in *Partial Immersion* classes.

3. All instructions are given in the foreign language and the children are expected to respond in the foreign language, although some children use English for a short time.

4. By the end of the first year, children usually understand almost everything, except for presentations of new work and vocabulary.

5. Preparation for teaching any new topic, no matter what the subject area, involves teaching children the vocabulary they will need for understanding the new topic. The use of concrete objects and gestures helps to convey meaning.

6. The teaching of reading in the foreign language parallels the methods used in the teaching of reading in English. For some languages, such as French, extra attention must be paid to sound-letter correspondence. For example, in the word *beaucoup, eau* is pronounced like *o, ou* is pronounced like *oo,* and the *p* is silent.

7. There are many manipulative activities for reinforcing the new vocabulary in the teaching of math and science.

8. The foreign language is not taught, per se; it is the medium of instruction. Children learn to understand, speak, read, and write the foreign language as they study some or all aspects of the elementary school curriculum.

9. There is evidence of error correction of the foreign language in the classroom.

10. There is evidence of the teaching of cross-cultural understanding.

RECENT TRENDS IN **FLES*** INSTRUCTION

Some of the recent trends in **FLES*** instruction are:

- The *Standards for Foreign Language Learning* stress real-life communication, cultures, connections, comparisons, and communities.
- There is no one *best* way to teach foreign language.
- There is more "student talk" than "teacher talk."
- No English (or very little) is used by the teacher; no English is used by the students.
- The teacher uses a wide variety of methods in presentations, in practice, in repetitions, in review, in testing, in homework, etc.
- There is abundant use of TPR in all aspects of learning and at all levels.
- A variety of instructional materials is used: audio, print, and multimedia.
- Authentic cultural materials are used whenever possible.

- The teacher uses procedures for encouraging students and for alleviating student anxiety.
- There are special procedures for challenging gifted students.
- There are interdisciplinary and/or content-based approaches.
- Implementation of the goal of person-to-person communication can be observed in the lesson.
- The teacher uses small-group, paired, and individualized instruction and cooperative learning for practice in the foreign language.
- There is an infusion of global-awareness concepts.
- Activities to stimulate higher-order thinking skills (H.O.T.S.) are used in the classroom.
- There is wide use of all kinds of technology.
- There is evidence of the adaptation of instructional materials to meet the needs of the students.
- Real, concrete objects help children understand the foreign language.
- There is emphasis on activities for the real world of children.
- There is recognition of the impact of technology on FL learning.
- There are short segments because children's attention span is short.
- Children learn in a meaningful context.
- An informal approach is used, with an emphasis on comprehension and speaking the language.
- Listening activities (listening to the teacher, to recorded voices, to dialogues, poems, stories, questions) provide comprehensible input.

Other integrated activities include:

- Singing songs
- Reading labels around the room
- Reading simple sentences
- Writing simple sentences and labels
- Writing letters and invitations
- Reciting conversations and poems
- Preparing skits and dramatizations
- Learning about different ways of living
- Learning about holidays in different cultures
- Learning about folktales in different cultures
- Integrating language with different subjects in the curriculum, such as music, art, science, etc., through interdisciplinary activities
- Enriching and expanding knowledge about famous people as they relate to the language being studied

- Incorporating many of the approaches discussed in Chapters Nine and Eleven

THE CLASSROOM ENVIRONMENT

The ambience of the classroom is conducive to effective teaching and learning. If the decorations are interesting and attractive and are used as aids to the teaching/learning process, learning is enhanced. Posters, pictures, dolls, collages, streamers, charts, maps, costumes, menus, flash cards, etc., help to make an appealing environment of the place(s) where the foreign language is spoken. Sometimes, in the elementary school classroom, it can be little more than a corner with a bulletin board. Sometimes it can be a foreign language area, shared by different grades. In all cases, however, it should be changed frequently, and items on display can be used in developing stories, dialogues, and real-life situations. Samples of children's work are particularly effective for encouraging students and for sharing their accomplishments with other students, parents, administrators, etc.

Another aspect of the classroom environment is the seating arrangement of the students. For some lessons, the teacher will want to have a full-class environment. On other occasions, when the teacher wishes to have partner practice, the youngsters can be seated by twos. Other times, there will be small groups of four or five, for the specific purpose of rehearsing a dialogue, doing research together, planning scenery for a dramatization, etc. If the school has equipped the foreign language area with a listening corner, a group of three or four students may listen to a cassette tape or language master cards with headsets. Others may work on a computer.

Other basic components of the foreign language classroom may include:

- All kinds of student work on display
- A picture file of the important thematic topics (food, clothing, etc.)
- A box containing different articles of clothing
- Records, cassettes, CDs
- Tapes (video and audio)
- Books and magazines (appropriate for this level)
- Foreign language newspapers
- Flags
- A transparency file based on thematic topics (food, clothing, etc.)
- A "professions box" with hats and clothes for all types of professions
- Other props for situational and communicative activities

Reducing Student Anxiety

The most important aspect of the classroom environment has to do with helping students feel at ease, comfortable yet challenged by interesting activities. The teacher's manner should be friendly, encouraging, and helpful, so as to minimize any anxiety on the part of the children. Some teachers start the lesson with music (culturally authentic, of course!). Other teachers have a special hat (sombrero?) or special puppet who speaks only the foreign language. If the children are entering the classroom from another room, the teacher is there to greet them and comment in a friendly fashion about their individual interests. During the lesson, a change-of-pace activity is a must (usually one involving movement). This usually consists of some physical activity or repetition of familiar material. Such an activity tends to reduce the anxiety level, and the children are then ready to engage in other activities related to the lesson. Humor is also an important aspect of the classroom environment, although it should never be at the expense of any of the students. Finally, an element of surprise in a lesson (a funny TPR, such as "Put the pencil on your friend's head," or a new puppet or a cartoon about snow in June) can capture the children's interest. When children learn to expect that there will be such surprises, when they understand that laughter can be incorporated into the class work, they will enjoy the process of language learning as well as the results. They also enjoy making suggestions for different aspects of the class activities.

Another way to encourage students is to praise their efforts. *Très bien, excelente,* and *wunderbar* are helpful, except when teachers fall into a pattern of praising every response with the same brush (or same expressions). Students quickly learn that there will be no differentiation between praise for an ordinary response to a review warm-up question and praise for a response using a new concept. Then, too, the student who volunteers a question or response (never having done so before) merits unusual praise. I recently came across a list of eighty-eight different ways to give praise in English! Surely *FLES/FLEX/Immersion* teachers can develop ten or twelve or more expressions that can be interspersed judiciously so that they convey real appreciation and encouragement. (See the Praise Approach in Chapter Nine.)

Don't hesitate to tell children when they are wonderful, fantastic, extraordinary, unbelievably good, going in the right direction, great, really getting it, trying very hard, stupendous, marvelous, spectacular, tremendous, terrific, beyond your wildest dreams! However, match your praise to the different kinds of success that children achieve.

Motivating Students to Learn

For every activity in school or in life, there must be motivation. Even at the *Sequential FLES/FLEX/Immersion* level, the teacher should be cognizant of the need to find different ways to interest the children in the concepts being addressed. There is a phenomenon identified as the "four-minute barrier"—a short time during which contacts are established, affirmed, or rejected.

If we think of this barrier in terms of the daily lesson, we should examine what teachers do during the first four minutes of class. Does the teacher, for example, check attendance or homework, or distribute papers or books? Is there something repetitive or predictable about the way the teacher begins each lesson? True, sometimes it is comforting to students to know what to expect. On the other hand, does the teacher plan something different for those first four minutes, something to establish a motivation for learning? Why not rouse curiosity, why not set the stage for learning, why not excite the thirst for knowledge, why not rivet students' attention upon what is to follow? How to do this? Consider some of the following:

- Discuss a real-life problem that is age-appropriate.
- Show a short film (3 to 5 minutes).
- Sing a song, substituting new words.
- Have the teacher or a student dress as a famous historical figure from the target culture(s).
- Have the students guess what is in a gift-wrapped box.
- Write a secret message on the board in the foreign language.
- Pantomime a message.
- Each day for two weeks repeat a future date that relates to an undisclosed event.
- Unroll a new poster.
- Bring in a new puppet.
- Post a new banner.
- Read a short paragraph in the foreign language and stop at a crucial point.
- Other procedures that inventive teachers can create!

These strategies and many, many others can help motivate students for learning and make the "four-minute barrier" an important segment of an effective lesson.

Is it possible to identify the various components of successful classroom motivation? Here are a few guiding questions:

- Is the teacher's personality encouraging?
- Does the teacher have a sense of humor?
- Is there a brisk pace and a variety of activities?
- Is the content sufficiently challenging and interesting to the students? (Are there ways to make it interesting?)

- Is there enrichment for some students and attention to the needs of others?
- And finally...Did the children learn something today, and do they *want* to come back for more?

Classroom Management

Before the Lesson

1. Plan carefully.
2. Have all your materials ready.
3. Check all the equipment, if possible.
4. Say to yourself: "This is going to be an exciting lesson for the children, and they are going to learn a lot!"

During the Lesson

1. Begin immediately—those first four minutes are crucial to the success of the lesson.
2. Begin with something that will capture the children's attention.
3. Involve the children as much as possible by personalizing, by using TPR, by using hand motions that you have taught them to respond to, and by making sure that you have taught routines for distributing paper and books, lining up, sitting down, putting things away in the desk, etc.
4. If the routines have not been firmly established, take the time to work with the children on one component, then go on with the lesson. Working on the routine may mean having the children respond several times to make sure that they understand.
5. If there is a disruptive student, try to figure out why that student is disruptive. If he or she wants attention, find ways to give him or her attention (and praise) in some part of the lesson. If the student cannot understand, and there may be others in this category, make sure that you are using a sufficient number of visuals, gestures, real objects, etc., to convey meaning.
6. Make sure that you include examples that use the children's names and the names of some of the TV personalities whom the children admire.
7. Make sure that you have planned short segments (3 to 5 minutes). If you find that attention is waning, *change* the activity. It is usually wise to go from a quiet activity to a more active one; from an oral activity to a reading or writing one; from a TPR activity to a quiet one, etc.

8. Check to see that you provide variety, interest, change of pace, and a great deal of *encouragement* and *praise* during your lessons.

9. Near the end of the lesson, give a brief summary of the new work and praise the children for the progress they have made.

10. Have all kinds of repetition: whole class, by rows, half the class, boys, girls, children wearing red, children whose birthday is in March, etc.

11. Praise—praise—praise those students who are doing well, responding well, following TPR commands, etc. Once in a while, a surprise form of praise (a pencil, a sticker, etc.) can be given.

After the Lesson

1. Be a reflective teacher. Evaluate for yourself whether the routines are working well, whether you started the lesson promptly, whether you had a great deal of variety in the lesson, whether you were able to reach some of the less-motivated students, whether all or most of the children learned something, etc.

2. Do not get discouraged! If a lesson doesn't work out well, there could be many reasons for the problem. Did the students just come from physical education activities? Is this the last half hour of the day? Is this just before or after lunch or recess? Is the chemistry of the class such that it is difficult to change the learning patterns right away? Have the children been together in the same class for many years? Are *you* tired? Do *you* have other problems on your mind?

3. Try to talk to other teachers and other school personnel about specific problems. This can give you new insights about the class, the students, and the school.

4. Don't become discouraged if the children do not learn the first time something is taught! Repetition and more repetition in different ways can help from time to time.

5. Plan to try a different kind of lesson with different approaches next time! *It will get better!*

TPR Techniques and Strategies

How to start:

Hand motions in response to a story

Simon Says

Catch the ball or beanbag, etc.

Tug-of-war across a pretend river

Use simple commands and vocabulary; use recombinations of commands and vocabulary; use funny commands.

Creating a TPR Activity

TITLE:

PURPOSE:

ACTIVITY: Teacher does...; Students do...

TIME:

MATERIALS:

VARIATIONS:

A TPR file could include some of the following activities:

TPR DRAMATICS

- List two things (superstitions, mechanical devices that annoy you, childhood memories, tics or habits that irritate you); find someone who has similar things on his or her list
- Freeze of group tableau: role-play different events (historical or current)
- Fragmented telephone conversations (e.g., "No, no trouble at all.")
- Interviews with famous people
- A plane trip

TPR CREATIVE ACTIVITIES

- Brainstorming new practical uses for things (a sock, a paper clip, a bandage, etc.)
- Live tic-tac-toe, Twister
- Obstacle course
- Cheers for the team
- Jazz chants or raps
- Situations (e.g., a picnic)
- Amnesia (pin name on back)
- Drills with props
- Relay races
- Treasure hunt
- Cocktail party (Each student receives a slip of paper containing a biographical sketch, such as: You are 32 years old. Your name is

_____. You are married and have one child. The goal is to find out how people at the party are connected. [Another student might have a slip of paper identifying him or her as the spouse of the first player.]) A variation of this might be matching famous people with their work, e.g., Bizet with *Carmen*.

- Unusual conversations, e.g., between two dogs, two pencils, two shoes of a pair, etc.
- Fairy godmother who grants three wishes
- Which animal would you like to be?
- Demonstrate "feelings" individually or as a group
- Assign ordinal numbers or names of fruits; everyone changes places on command

STORY ACTION

Distribute cards with the names of the different characters in the story. When you read the story, the child with the name on his or her card stands up and twirls around each time his or her name is mentioned. A variation could be that the child jumps twice in place. Another variation could be to assign one character to four or five children in order to get more student participation. For example, you read the story of The Three Bears. The characters are Mama Bear, Papa Bear, Baby Bear, and Goldilocks. One or more students would stand up and twirl around each time the name of one of the characters is mentioned. More-advanced students could tell the story, thus conducting the activity.

A TPR SERIES

Going to the movies—commands:

1. Call up your friend.
2. Say you'll meet her at three o'clock.
3. Meet at the movies.
4. Buy the tickets.
5. Show your ticket to enter.
6. Buy soda and popcorn.
7. Go into the theater—it's dark—stumble.
8. Find a good seat.
9. Sit down.
10. Watch the previews and yawn.
11. Eat the popcorn.
12. Drink the soda.
13. Watch the film.
14. This part is funny...laugh.

15. This part is sad...cry.
16. Wipe your tears.
17. The film is over. Get up.
18. Stretch.
19. Say good-bye to your friend.
20. When you get home, call another friend.
21. Tell him or her about the movie.

UNEXPECTED TPR COMMANDS
1. Put your right hand on your left ear and jump three times.
2. Take your notebook and throw it in the wastebasket.
3. Point to a plate of food you dislike and make a face.

ADDITIONAL IDEAS FOR TPR

- Play all kinds of games to provide opportunities for movement.
- Incorporate visual aids into TPR activities. Ask students to place the visual aids in various parts of the room, on top of desks, etc.
- Balls, balloons, flash cards, and toys can all be props in moving-around-the-room activities in response to commands. These would also include counting and clapping activities.
- Dramatize familiar stories (fairy tales or TV programs). For example, in French, Guignol puppets offer very strong TPR possibilities, with their characteristic punching and hitting activities. Some adaptations may have to be made for the classroom, however.
- Role-play familiar daily activities containing many motions, such as stretching upon awakening, brushing teeth and hair, getting dressed, eating breakfast, etc. Other activities could include going to the doctor, going to the supermarket, going to the restaurant, etc.
- Use props of all kinds, such as clothing, table settings, hats, puppets, tools to denote different occupations, etc.
- Use Jazzercise and other physical exercises to establish the rhythms of the language.
- Play games, such as relay races, to focus on the vocabulary and comprehension activities being studied.
- Conduct simulated tours around the classroom, the school, and the school community, using the content being studied.
- Present fashion shows, festivals, and pageants as culminations of units on clothing, food, holiday celebrations, etc.
- Create a marketplace in the classroom, with different types of stores and services. Students move around, purchasing things with fake

money, bargaining in some cases, and learning about the differences between shopping at home and abroad.

- Create motions by eliciting ideas from the children as they learn a new dialogue, poem, song, etc.
- Simulate travel in space, with conversations to and from ground control.
- Develop "motion mnemonics," using a recorded rhythm instrument, for learning vocabulary.
- Create a "home" in the classroom in order to role-play family life in the foreign country and in the United States.
- Plan a program for presentation to the rest of the school on such themes as:
  1. Songs and dances of the foreign culture
  2. Dramatization of folktales from the foreign culture
  3. Dramatization of travel in the foreign culture
  4. Dramatization of a scene at the United Nations
  5. Programs for special holidays
  6. Dramatizations of the lives of famous people from the foreign culture
  7. Quiz program about people and places in the foreign culture
  8. Dramatization of well-known current events as seen by people in the foreign culture
  9. "Who Am I?" programs—interviews with people from the foreign culture

TRY THESE MOTIVATIONAL STRATEGIES!

Try to use these ideas from time to time:

1. Amusing poems or songs
2. Riddles
3. Jokes
4. Outlandish adjectives, for humor
5. Relay games
6. Praise of all kinds
7. Puppets
8. "Teacher has a sore throat" technique, whether or not you do. It does wonders for developing student-led activities!
9. Repetition (different ways each time)

10. Movement—movement—movement (use TPR)

11. Real names of students in dialogues and situations

12. Surprises...DO THE UNEXPECTED!

13. Personalized activities based on individual preferences

14. Prizes (only once in a while)

15. Unusual props

16. The technique of "let them talk" (in the foreign language, of course) about topics of interest to children (Native Language Kid Talk)

17. The technique of dressing up as a well-known person

18. Ordinary props used in unusual ways

19. Strategies that help students learn

20. The technique of changing students' seats; changing the format of the class (pairs, groups, etc.)

21. Other strategies that capitalize on local events of interest to children

REPETITION AND THE NEED TO STIMULATE CREATIVE LANGUAGE IN REAL-LIFE SITUATIONS

Whether repetition is used for developing comprehension or as a model for students to imitate, it is an extremely important component of teaching foreign languages to young children. In *Sequential FLES* and *FLEX*, it is crucial. In *Immersion* programs, since language is the means of communication and instruction, the sheer volume of time devoted to language provides a broad base for learning both the language and the content areas. Still, repetition plays a role in *Immersion* programs, since not all students in *Immersion* programs have the same ability for learning.

In *Sequential FLES* and *FLEX*, care must be taken to vary the types of repetition, even of the same content. This can be accomplished by changing some elements in the materials, by changing some visuals (posters changed to transparencies, for example), by changing the manner in which something is repeated (softly, loudly, boys only, girls only, etc.), by changing hand signals, by having students record the content, and many other ways. The key word is *variety*.

Someone once commented that the way to teach foreign language to children was the "What's the color of George Washington's gray horse?" approach. This implies that students need to *hear* and comprehend the language before they are able to produce it. They cannot make it up out of thin air! Thus, if a teacher held up a picture of a gray horse, she or he would first have to teach the word for *horse*, then the color *gray*, then possession, and establish that this was George Washington's gray horse before asking the question, "What's the color of George Washington's horse?" This process of teaching the new vocabulary and structures would take a number of repetitions on the part of the teacher and the students.

If teachers continue to repeat the same thing over and over again, however, boredom becomes an unwelcome visitor to the classroom. Every language teacher wrestles with this problem, and here are a few suggestions for stimulating language activities:

Use a variety of materials, such as pictures, signs, key words, sequence materials (arranging pictures and/or words of a story in sequence), TV schedules, advertisements, stuffed animals, labels on food and other items, photographs, sounds, videos, transparencies, etc.

Personalize the language concepts in order to give students many different opportunities to express their ideas, thoughts, and feelings, such as:

I am happiest when _____.

I would like to be _____.

My friends can be sure that I will _____.

If I had a million dollars, I would _____.

Right now I am thinking _____.

I hate _____.

I get angry when _____.

Change the activity when the children get restless (probably after ten minutes at the most!). Using a TPR activity tends to ease the tension.

Include change-of-pace activities, which need not depart drastically from the goals of the lesson. For example, numbers could be practiced by counting backwards, counting by twos, using arithmetical operations, bouncing a ball, throwing a beanbag, giving dates of birth for members of the class and famous people, etc.

Include songs, which, in addition to providing a pleasurable change of pace, help to reinforce pronunciation, structures, and vocabulary.

Plan games that help to teach, review, and reinforce language skills and provide a change of pace during the lesson. Some simple games that require little preparation include numbers to be guessed, Simon Says, Reverse Simon Says, Guess Whose Voice It is, Guess Who Has the Picture of the Dog, and others.

Have students role-play, from time to time, the part of the teacher for a short segment of the lesson. The things you will observe about yourself! Your voice, your gestures…

Use partner practice to reinforce learning.

Use cooperative learning to get students involved in learning through group motivation and group enthusiasm.

Create and use jazz chants (raps). This can be amusing and rhythmic as the children clap their hands or snap their fingers and repeat a chant they have created on a topic of interest to them. This is a good way for them to express personal feelings. For example:

La escuela, la escuela,
No me gusta, no me gusta;
Prefiero la playa
Me gusta la playa
No me gusta la escuela…

Or:

It's hot…it's hot
The temperature is high
I'd rather be at the beach
To cool it…
To cool it…

Use sounds. Another way to encourage children's creative ideas is to have them listen to a tape with different sounds on it (some familiar, some unfamiliar). Then encourage them to describe what they think they are hearing or to invent an event, a dialogue, a narrative, etc., about the sounds.

TIPS FOR THE NEW **FLES*** TEACHER (OR HOW TO GET SOME CLASSROOM "MAGIC")

1. Look forward to teaching the language and have the children look forward to learning it.
2. Introduce yourself in the foreign language. Use a special hat; show on a map where people speak the language.
3. Bring a puppet (a sock puppet will do) and introduce it in the foreign language.

4. Bring a calendar with the month in the foreign language.

5. Have students keep a foreign language notebook to store pictures, calendars, illustrated activities, weather charts, etc.

6. Think of a number of things to do in any one lesson, however short. Read to the children. Have students repeat words and use motions, listen, dramatize, role-play, sing, dance, illustrate, copy a short sentence, make greeting cards, etc.

7. Do not become discouraged if the children do not remember too well from lesson to lesson. It takes a lot of practice, a lot of review, and a lot of *patience* on your part.

8. Always try to have a surprise for the children, such as something in a box for a guessing game. This is a good review of vocabulary previously taught.

9. Make sure that the children learn something new in every lesson, as well as review other items that were presented previously.

10. Develop a set of hand motions to signal the children

    • When to listen

    • When to repeat

    • When to answer as a whole class, as a row, or as a group

    • When to imitate certain motions

    • Other responses as needed

11. End the lesson with hint of what will be happening in the next lesson.

12. Use a variety of materials: pictures, charts, real objects, toys, hats, puppets, and all kinds of recordings, tapes, videos, etc.

13. Use "something old and something new" as a guide in planning.

14. Try to have children listen to a variety of voices: male, female, young, old.

15. Use as many different reading materials as possible: magazines, readers, newspapers, poems, comic books, cartoons, brochures.

16. Give students opportunities to express themselves while learning, such as starting a statement and having students complete it in different ways. For example, "Summer makes me feel _____."

17. Have students move around in response to the foreign language.

18. Try to build an integrated lesson around the productive and receptive abilities and culture.

19. Give individual children an opportunity to conduct a game.

20. Remember—**FLES*** represents the *beginning* stages of FL learning—encourage continuing study of the FL.

Planning Lessons

What are some of the essential components of a **FLES*** lesson?

- Warm-up, using familiar material
- Periodic review and reteaching
- Part of learning scenario and/or unit
- New work or new presentation based on a functional situation
- Related to the five C's of the national FL standards
- Songs, games, changes of pace
- Pupil-to-pupil conversations and partner practice
- Variety of materials
- Informal, nonthreatening environment
- TPR or motion activities
- Variety of lesson formats
- Some form of summary of the new work
- Evaluation (not necessarily testing) of what was actually learned
- Plans for next lesson
- Follow-up activities
- Inclusion of some form of cultural component
- Inclusion of the four abilities (listening, speaking, reading, writing), if appropriate to the class and the goals of the program
- Evidence that the lesson is pleasurable for teacher and students

A Typical Lesson Plan Format (Basic)

Lesson	Time
(Goal or goals of the lessons, based on unit plans or learning scenarios and related to the five C's of the national FL standards)	
Warm-up of familiar material (greetings, health, weather, numbers, etc.)	3 minutes
New material, including culture	7 minutes
Change of pace (song, TPR, etc.)	2-3 minutes
Applications, including cultures, connections, comparisons, communities	8–10 minutes
Review of previous material	5 minutes
Productive and receptive abilities	5–7 minutes
Summary and plans for follow-up	2 minutes
Peek at the next lesson	2 minutes

Comments About the Lesson Plan Format

1. This type of lesson plan could be adapted for use in a fifteen- to forty-five-minute lesson.
2. Each segment could be changed to fit the special needs of the class.
3. Attractive audio and visual materials enhance each of the segments.
4. Movement activities (TPR) are a *must*.
5. This plan could be used in a *Sequential FLES* program as well as in a *FLEX* program.
6. *Immersion* and *Partial Immersion* classes follow a lesson plan appropriate for teaching the subject area, such as mathematics, science, etc.
7. Be sure to give students a peek at the content and activities in the next lesson!

For sample lesson plans, see Appendix E.

Tips on Teaching in *Immersion* Programs

Plan, Plan, Plan

- Set goals for both content and language.
- Look at both English and FL materials.
- Create new materials appropriate to your class.
- Plan to motivate the children to learn.

Teach, Reteach, Revise, Reteach

- Use concrete materials to convey meaning.
- Use appropriate praise.
- Try different approaches and strategies.
- Vary activities (sitting, listening, speaking, role-playing, TPR, partner practice, etc.).
- Check for comprehension (through questions, responses, nonverbal actions, etc.).
- Appeal to multiple senses of learners (and multiple intelligences).
- Cover the *major* aspects of the curriculum for the grade.
- Assess progress frequently.
- Keep a portfolio for each student to document progress.

- Exchange ideas with colleagues.
- Be creative—collect pictures, activities, and strategies.

Steps in Teaching in *Immersion* or *Two-Way Immersion* Classes or Using the Content-Based Approach

1. Know the content and the materials that will be used.
2. Know *how* to teach the content (standard approved practices in teaching mathematics, science, etc.).
3. Know your group of children.
4. Plan the lesson carefully; plan the sequence of the lesson and the approximate time for each segment.
5. Prepare the children for learning:
   - Teach the vocabulary and expressions; use concrete objects.
   - Review the concepts they already know that relate to the topic.
   - Use demonstrations with real and easily recognized objects.
   - Use manipulatives wherever possible.
   - Use oral before written.
6. Clarify meaning as the lesson proceeds; make sure that students understand by providing opportunities for responses of all kinds.
7. Involve the children as much as possible; encourage them to ask questions as well as answer them.
8. Use all kinds of hands-on activities.
9. Provide "memory jogs" (this looks like…; we'll remember this because…).
10. Test informally, for diagnostic purposes.
11. Reteach if necessary.
12. Review periodically and tie in concepts with future lessons.
13. Look for ways to tie the learning to the target culture(s) by comparing and/or contrasting.
14. Make sure the children practice in small groups and/or pairs.
15. Use all kinds of appeals to higher-order thinking skills.

Reflecting About Lesson Planning and Teaching

Planning the Lesson

- Think about the next lesson and its place in the learning sequence (previous lesson, following lesson).

- Think about the place of this lesson in the learning scenario or unit plan. Which of the five C's does it address? Which national FL standards?
- Think about scaffolding activities that can help prepare for the new learning.
- Think about the time needed for each segment of the lesson.
- Always think of motivating activities.
- Reflect on specific questions, commands, and activities.
- Think of the lesson's teacher goals and student goals.
- Which materials will be used?
- Will there be any problems?
- Can you plan anything that will help?

Teaching the Lesson

Be aware of:

- The pace of the lesson
- Student interest and participation
- Handling the unexpected
- Accomplishing the goals
- What and how much the students have learned
- The students' sense of accomplishment
- The teacher's sense of accomplishment

Reflecting About the Lesson

- In general, how do YOU feel about the lesson?
- Check back on your planning activities and your awareness of what was happening while you were teaching the lesson.
- How well did the lesson work? Were the goals accomplished? How well?
- Did anything unexpected occur? How did you handle it?
- Did you complete everything you planned?
- Did you check to see how well the students learned?
- Do you need to reteach, review, or give students more practice time?
- Do you need to modify the next lesson?
- Use the following checklist to help you evaluate the lesson.

DO YOU KNOW A GOOD **FLES*** LESSON
WHEN YOU TEACH ONE?

- Are students actively participating in the foreign language, individually, in paired groups, in small groups, and in whole-class activities?
- Is this lesson related to the five C goal areas of the national FL standards?
- Are the youngsters given the opportunity to use the foreign language with one another in functional situations during the lesson?
- Are the students encouraged to use the foreign language (depending on the goals of the program and the grade level of the students) in all the productive and receptive abilities?
- Are the students challenged with activities for promoting higher-order thinking skills?
- Are many of the new trends and techniques for **FLES*** in evidence in the classroom?
- Is there a variety of activities in short segments, using a rapid pace?
- Are there review and reinforcement activities as well as presentation of new material in each lesson? Is there evidence of effective planning?
- Do you emphasize *communication* and *cultural* activities?
- Are topics integrated with other subjects in the curriculum?
- Is a variety of instructional and multimedia materials used by both you and the students? Are the materials appropriate, attractive, and appealing to children?
- Do you motivate students throughout each lesson and each segment of the lesson? Are you energetic, enthusiastic, and dynamic?
- Do you use authentic language and cultural components?
- Is ongoing evaluation in evidence? Do you correct major individual errors in an encouraging manner? Is accuracy encouraged? Is evaluation performance-based rather than grammar-based?
- Are cultural topics woven into each lesson?
- Is the textbook adapted and modified to suit the curriculum and the ability of the students? Is a variety of materials used?
- Do you have effective classroom routines so that everyone is on task during the entire lesson? Is every minute used?
- Is the homework explained clearly? Is the homework checked and explained during the class lesson?
- Do you use the FL at all times? Do the students?
- Do the students appear to look forward to the next foreign language class?
- Do you assist individual students, both for remediation and for enrichment? Are gifted students given challenging assignments?

- Have the students learned something new?
- Do you look forward to the next foreign language class?
- If you had an administrator/supervisor in class, would she or he have learned some expressions in the foreign language this lesson, particularly if she or he did not know the foreign language? Would she or he have enjoyed the foreign-language-learning experience?

FOLLOW-UP AND REINFORCEMENT OF LEARNING

Teachers find that much better results are obtained when there is some provision for follow-up and reinforcement of learning. Whether it is called homework or extra-credit work or out-of-school games or assignments, it is still helpful for children to have many opportunities to practice the language in situations that are meaningful for them.

Consider these ways to reinforce learning:

1. Encourage children to find pictures to illustrate what they have learned and to keep picture dictionaries.
2. Have children make a calendar for a month (or longer) to illustrate some of their activities at home and at school.
3. Assign children to find "foreign" words in newspaper articles, magazines, advertisements, etc.
4. Have children make a family tree, labeling each person in the foreign language. They might use actual photographs of family members. They could make a booklet entitled "Me."
5. Ask the children to practice a dialogue with a relative or friend.
6. Have the children teach vocabulary or a conversation to someone else.
7. Encourage children to bring in favorite toys that can be used in adapting a situation.
8. Have children bring in materials (objects or artwork or written projects) for a bulletin-board display. A child-made map or diorama is useful, too.
9. Ask the children to bring in materials made in a foreign country for a cultural display.
10. Assign children to write letters to their pen pals and to bring in materials to be sent to a class pen pal in a foreign country.
11. Develop a class foreign language newspaper with student contributions of articles, cartoons, drawings, etc.
12. Have children make greeting cards for their friends and families.

13. Ask the children to keep a weather record in the foreign language, thus practicing dates, months of the year, days of the week, and weather expressions.

14. Have children listen to recordings in the foreign language (perhaps a fairy tale recorded by the teacher or a native speaker).

15. Encourage the children to create their own "restaurant" with special menus for different days of the week.

16. Have children create a game based on a class lesson to practice colors, numbers, etc. They could also create follow-the-dots puzzles to practice numbers and the names of objects.

17. Have the children make up riddles in the foreign language to try to stump their classmates.

18. Ask the children to think up different types of TPR activities, especially humorous or surprising ones.

19. Have the children think of different ways to end a familiar story.

20. Ask the children to think about "What if?" situations, such as: "What if the Eiffel Tower were in Chicago?"

21. Relate the learning to current television favorites or situations.

22. Have students step into the target culture for a few minutes each lesson by singing, dancing, looking at video or slides, etc.

23. Have youngsters guess what is in the Mystery Box each week.

24. Focus on current happenings in the target culture.

25. Create novel ways to foster student-to-student communication in the FL.

26. Graphic pictures of vocabulary words are fun and also reinforce the memory process. Words in Spanish, such as

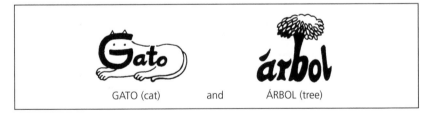

GATO (cat)   and   ÁRBOL (tree)

can be pictorialized to enhance learning. Very often, using an acronym (the first letters of a series of words combined to form new words) is a good example of something that helps students learn. Even if the new word is invented, it can be helpful, such as BRAVA for some of the major colors in Spanish: *blanco, rojo, amarillo, verde, azul.*

Any other kind of word-picture or word-word association cues can be readily created by both teachers and children. Class sessions devoted to the ways different children remember different things can be of lifelong benefit.

To Memorize or Not?

Memorization is something that is inherent in learning languages, in the opinion of many educators. The most recent views on memorization tend to stress "meaningful memorization." Perhaps this is a response to the overmemorization advocated by past methodologies, which required that almost every dialogue be memorized.

I tend to agree that some memorization has benefits for children on the **FLES*** level, particularly if it involves real-life situations, if it is *meaningful* to the children, if it is supported by some TPR activities, and if there is inherent value in the materials to be memorized (e.g., a famous short poem, proverbs, words to a song, etc.).

Error Correction

It is extremely helpful if students understand that they will make some errors while speaking, reading, and writing, and that they may not always understand what is being said, particularly in *Sequential FLES* and *FLEX* and early stages of *Immersion*. In *Immersion*, the language content and the subject-area content add to the natural anxiety about making mistakes, but as the students move ahead in the grade levels, there is less and less concern about the foreign language content because they use the language in their school activities.

Students ought to be made aware of different levels of proficiency: when 100 percent accuracy is required and when casual communication will permit some errors. This is a departure from the past, when there was only *one* correct answer to each exercise item in the text. Teachers may wish to elicit different answers and help the children see that one answer might be appropriate between friends, while another would be more suitable when communicating with an adult.

This is the teacher's responsibility—not to be the person who constantly red-pencils every attempt at written work and corrects every word uttered, but someone who clearly defines that ideas and concepts count and that communication must be suited to the situation, the people involved, and the level of expectation. This does not take away from the goal that students should be expected to learn how to use the foreign language correctly (in all four abilities) and that, for the most part, correct language is required in all test situations. But it is these nuances of language use that students need to learn, by explanation, by role-modeling, by suggestion, and by correction. Correction should be done in ways that will not suppress ideas and thinking skills. When many students make similar errors, the teacher will need to reteach specific elements or plan to teach concepts that may not have been reached as yet.

TEACHING TECHNIQUES FOR GIFTED LANGUAGE LEARNERS

Most teachers with many years of experience can easily identify the gifted language learners—those students who learn easily and who experience few difficulties in learning the four basic abilities of orally comprehending, speaking, reading, and writing in the language.

It is suggested here that teachers plan special ways to enrich these children's language abilities by having such students

- Serve as leaders of different kinds of class activities and games
- Work on independent projects of interest to them (e.g., poetry, computer programs)
- Use the foreign language in different types of impromptu situations
- Listen to recordings slightly above their level
- Make presentations before the class or other classes (choral, dramatic, etc.)
- Prepare special reports, riddles, etc., to be used with the rest of the class
- Create language games for the rest of the class
- Construct test items
- Give spot dictation
- Do research about the people who speak the foreign language
- Give model responses for the rest of the class or ask questions of other students
- Be leaders in small-group activities

Even on the elementary school level, differences in ability will be noted, and teachers should look for ways to stimulate gifted language learners. Although some research has been conducted in this field, there is no concrete evidence that only gifted students (in general) should study a foreign language. It is recommended that *all* students be offered the opportunity. However, there will always be some students who can listen carefully, who can pronounce the foreign language with accuracy and with very little effort, who seem to know how to get the gist of an utterance, and who do not experience great difficulty in writing the content of the language with accuracy. These are the students who require special attention and special encouragement, lest they become restless, bored, and, worst of all, "turned off" of foreign language learning.

This was one of the problems of **FLES*** in the 1960s, when the emphasis was on long sequences, rote learning, pattern practice, and memorization of dialogues, with rare opportunities for real-life situations and communication. This is not to say that repetition should be eliminated. Repetition is a necessary part of effective language learning, but youngsters need to perceive some end result of communication and need to feel the *power of language* through communicative experiences.

Children who have special talents in languages need special activities that will keep them interested and excited about using the language. Students in *Immersion* programs acquire this sense of power, but because they are involved in a long sequence, when they reach the preadolescent years, some may feel that they want to try something new. Unfortunately, in any long sequence, able and gifted students begin to think that the foreign language is old hat. That is why it is essential for teachers to be sensitive to these students and to plan effective ways of keeping them interested. Appealing to higher-order thinking skills by asking them to tell in the foreign language the similarities and differences between, for example, a hammer and a guitar, will perk up their powers of observation as well as their interest in the foreign language.

Using brainstorming techniques, in which there are no correct nor incorrect answers, can also provide challenges for children. Asking the class to suggest different uses for a paper clip, for example, or different uses for a half-cup of soda can provide additional stimulation for all children. Depending on the goals of the program, this can be done in the foreign language, within the limits of what the children have been taught. It can easily be done in *Immersion* programs and in grades 5 and 6 of a *Sequential FLES* program that began several years earlier.

SITUATION TECHNIQUES

Various real-life, natural, communicative situations can be introduced into the *Sequential FLES/FLEX/Immersion* class. They usually are very high in motivational appeal, and children are eager to participate. After motivating students to want to learn the new vocabulary, phrases, and idiomatic expressions needed for the situation, the teacher then presents the new items for repetition and practice. Situations could include some of the following:

- Going shopping
- Complaining about something
- Disagreeing about something
- Making up an excuse for some mistake
- Getting angry about something
- Feeling happy about something
- Apologizing for some offense

- Refusing to do something
- Inviting someone to do something
- Commending someone for an accomplishment

After the needed tools of communication have been developed (phrases, vocabulary, idiomatic expressions), the class and the teacher can create a conversation within the framework of the situation or theme. This conversation can then be practiced with partners and in small groups until the students are ready to try the conversation aloud. Later on, small groups of children will meet to find ways to vary the situation according to their own creative talents, using the dictionary and with the assistance of the teacher. These alternative situations can then be presented to the rest of the class on an impromptu basis. This procedure can also be very effective in evaluating student proficiency and/or in diagnosing the need for review, reteaching, or further drill and practice.

Many teachers ask about standards of accuracy for usage and pronunciation skills. That depends on the time of year, on the specific purpose of the proficiency activity, on what the instructions are, on the audience (if any), etc. If it is a more practiced activity, the teacher will want to take careful notes (and ask the students in the audience to do so as well) in order to suggest corrections. On the other hand, if this is the first attempt on the part of the children, as long as everyone understands what is being said (that is, as long as communication is taking place), the teacher may not want to stifle expression.

Here are additional suggestions for situations:

- Your dog has run away.
- You are eating at a friend's house and they serve something you dislike.
- Your friend has just broken your new toy.
- You are at the dentist's office with a terrible toothache, but you are frightened.
- You fall off your chair in a restaurant.
- You are introducing a new friend to your mother and you forget your friend's name.
- You spill your container of popcorn in the movies.
- You get lost at the airport.
- You get on the bus and discover that you do not have the correct change.
- You did not do your homework.
- You are at the zoo and you get sick.

The Situation Box

Keep a box (something like a treasure box) full of different situations. First, a model has to be presented by two, four, or five children. One child picks a situation out of the box and reads it aloud. Then the group decides how they will act out the situation, who is going to play which part, etc. Finally, they present their version of the situation for the whole class.

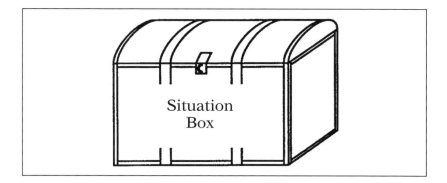

After several demonstrations of the process of preparing a situation, it is possible to have groups of children select a situation and work on it independently, provided that they have sufficient vocabulary and structures to handle it. Some teachers put difficult vocabulary on the actual situation card, so the children are not held back by vocabulary limitations.

Here are some suggested situations for the Situation Box:

- You deliver newspapers, and one of your customers has not paid or given you a tip. Try to persuade him or her to pay or to give you a tip.

- You and your friend were planning to go to the park, but you have just heard a weather forecast saying that it is going to rain. Call your friend and discuss what you will do.

- You have not finished some homework that was due today. Explain to your teacher why you did not finish it. Give some plausible reasons and then give some wild reasons.

- An "Options" Skit: Distribute the following cues to different groups:

  | Persons | Place | Time | Weather | Date | Problem |

  Each group is to invent a skit that includes information about the cues they received.

- Pretend that your group is the first group to land on the moon. Role-play your first steps on the moon.

- You and your friend are trying to sell Girl Scout cookies in a German-speaking community. Go to three houses and try to sell the cookies.
- You arrive six minutes late for your Russian class. Explain why you were late. Your teacher is very angry and gives you a special assignment! What is it? How will you do it?
- I am a present for _____. Tell the story of the present.

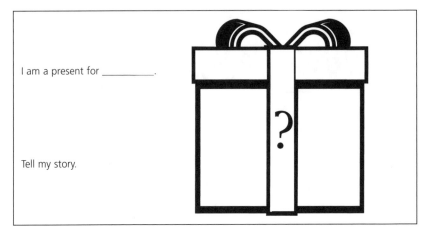

GROUP DECISIONS	SITUATIONS FOR ROLE-PLAYING
Who buys the present?	Buying the present
For what occasion?	Giving the present
For whom?	Returning the present

TECHNIQUES FOR TEACHING
LESS-MOTIVATED YOUNGSTERS

With the wide range of abilities of youngsters in *Sequential FLES*, *FLEX*, and *Immersion* classes, teachers need to consider special procedures for helping the less-motivated students to learn. Whatever the reasons for diminished motivation may be, teachers need to address such factors as inattention, restlessness, boredom, confusion, lack of understanding, frustration, and others. Following are some suggestions for helping to ameliorate difficult learning situations:

- Design each activity so that children will *want* to participate.
- Make certain that instructions are clear, understandable, and easy to follow.
- Teach by way of the "small increment approach," using familiar materials and adding on a small amount of new material.

- Review frequently, but use interesting and different formats.

- Alternate listening-speaking activities with reading or writing activities.

- Plan for five to seven different activities during one class session of approximately thirty minutes. If the class session is shorter or longer, make the necessary adjustments.

- Use a game format frequently for reinforcement of language learning.

- Make sure that all students follow classroom routines.

- Use abundant praise and encouragement.

- Keep the pace of the lesson rapid, but not too rushed.

- Stress routines and study skills as well as hints for remembering.

- Try to get at least one response *from each and every student* during each class session (but never force a response).

- Make certain from time to time to plan something that will surprise students.

- Try to incorporate the names of interesting and famous people, such as popular singers, TV personalities, sports heroes, etc.

- Try to guarantee some degree of success for *each* student.

- Make sure that the students understand. Students lose interest if they cannot understand what is being said and what is being asked of them. This means that English has to be used for very *brief* periods of time.

- Try to check youngsters' written work, because most students do not copy accurately. Check *all* written work. Use student helpers to assist.

- Be sure that students understand exactly what is expected of them. Not every vocabulary word or expression needs to be learned for active use (speaking and writing).

- Pay special attention to difficult words. Use cross-language contrasts, repetition, discussion of the configuration of the word, individual memory triggers, etc.

- Make certain that the content is appropriate for the students' level of instruction. Content should provide some challenge, but include sufficient familiar work to avoid frustration.

- When a number of children are restless (depending on the time of day, such as before or after lunch, right before dismissal time, etc.) it is time for a change-of-pace activity. Usually, a TPR activity will relieve the problem, provided that the class can settle down afterward.

- Plan to use simple questions with the less-motivated students so that they will experience success.

- Use partner practice (paired activities) frequently to capitalize on pupil-to-pupil help.

- Use cooperative learning activities so that students will get group encouragement and assistance, and also feel some group pressure for all students to contribute to the joint effort. (For more details about the cooperative learning approach, see Chapter Nine.)

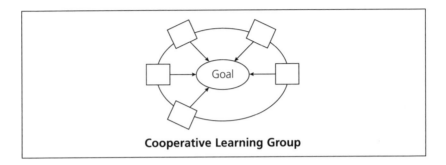

Cooperative Learning Group

PARTNER PRACTICE (PAIRED ACTIVITIES)

PURPOSES

1. Filling an opinion or information gap
2. Opportunities for using the FL
3. Drill
4. Remediation
5. Enrichment
6. Liberated communication
7. Other?

PROCESS

1. Teacher (or student) explanation to the class
2. Demonstration: two partners with flash cards (answers under a flap or on back)
3. Practice: Partner 1
   Check: Partner 2
4. Practice: Partner 2
   Check: Partner 1
5. Class: short initial partner practice (5 minutes)
6. Signals for turn-taking and for the end of practice period
7. Class and teacher evaluation of effectiveness of session

MATERIALS

Flash cards, game boards, worksheets, picture cues, printed cues, questions, answers, maps, charts, diagrams, culture cues, materials created by students, cartoons, etc.

SIMILARITIES BETWEEN **FLES*** METHODOLOGY AND SECONDARY SCHOOL METHODOLOGY

Use of English

Both methodologies tend to keep English to a minimum, with most instructions, directions, and explanations given in the target language, except at the very beginning. Use of real objects, gestures, pictures, and other visuals helps to convey meaning. When there is confusion, it might be better to give a *very brief* explanation in English. In *Immersion*, however, all content and explanations are given in the target language, with the exception of certain subjects, such as music, physical education, and art, in some *Partial Immersion* programs.

Functional Language

With the new emphasis on proficiency, elementary and secondary school methodologies have become closer in goals and content. Both are now concerned with functional situations and authentic utterances. Both do not always insist upon complete sentences, but mirror natural speech patterns. Both have a conversational approach based on real situations that are likely to occur. Vocabulary is taught in context, and all kinds of idiomatic phrases are included.

Opportunities for Use of the FL

At both **FLES*** and secondary levels, there are many opportunities to use the foreign language in meaningful situations. Both levels use paired activities, small-group learning, technology, etc. Secondary school programs generally have more sophisticated technology, however, in the form of more computer/video language laboratories, satellite dishes, and other forms of telecommunications.

Use of the Textbook

Although more emphasis is placed on the textbook or textbooks in secondary schools, both levels tend to use a variety of text materials, such as a basic text, periodicals, readers, and workbooks. Teachers at both levels need to know how to adapt their text materials to their requirements, giving students ample opportunities to use all four abilities and to gain an understanding of the cultural elements as well as the linguistic components.

Development of the Productive and Receptive Abilities

In both methodologies, the goals include the development of the four abilities. Depending upon the goals of the specific kind of **FLES*** program, the level of reading and writing skills may be considerably lower than in the secondary school program. This area is a point of departure for the two methodologies, although in *Sequential FLES* programs and *Immersion*, considerable amounts of reading and writing activities are an integral part of the program.

Development of Cultural Awareness

Both elementary and secondary school programs strive to develop cultural awareness through a variety of approaches and techniques. **FLES*** programs tend to compare both cultures from the point of view of the elementary and middle school child. Secondary school programs tend to develop cultural awareness from the point of view of the comparable secondary school student in the target culture.

FLES* Techniques Applicable to Secondary Schools and Beyond

- No one best way to teach foreign languages at any level
- Emphasis on topics of interest to students
- Student involvement
- Short segments to accommodate students' short attention span
- Use of four abilities and culture, depending on the goals
- Real-life situations, problems, and information gaps
- TPR
- Emphasis on communication
- Learner-centered focus using small groups and pairs
- Student-led activities
- Cooperative learning activities
- Higher-order thinking skills approach
- Role-playing and dramatics
- Humor approach

- Interdisciplinary approach—reaching out
- Variety of approaches, activities, and materials
- Adaptation of materials to suit the needs of learners
- Abundant use of student-made materials
- Words and expressions taught in context
- Avoidance of English
- Error correction and focus on accuracy
- Review, reentry, and reinforcement
- Language and culture intertwined
- Ongoing evaluation and assessment
- More "student-talk" than "teacher-talk"
- Special activities for gifted learners

USE OF TEXTBOOKS IN **FLES*** CLASSES

Textbooks and other instructional materials can be useful for implementing the **FLES*** curriculum. But a textbook is *not* the curriculum! Depending on the age and grade level of the students, the textbook helps reinforce learning through pictures, short labels, and sentences. At more advanced levels, if often contains puzzles, riddles, tongue twisters, and all kinds of motivational items. And if the pictures in the textbook are culturally authentic, they can provide much-needed real-life glimpses of the foreign culture.

Teachers need to look at their own scope and sequence and curriculum, and decide what they will teach in any given day, week, or month. They will be ready to look through the textbook to find ways in which they can use its material (and other materials) to support the topics they have already selected. This means skipping around, using some material more than once, but essentially, this approach uses the text as a tool, and *not* as the curriculum. For better articulation, it is important to inform secondary schools of the exact content covered.

When adapting a textbook or any other instructional materials, you might want to look for:

- The things that correlate well with your curriculum
- The things that are not related to your curriculum
- The topics you think are important
- The topics you will not cover
- The topics you think will not be of interest to your students

With this approach, you have the time to cover what is most important and what fits your curriculum. You also have more time, it is hoped, to include other spontaneous topics that occur in the classroom, material from other texts, etc.

It is true that some teachers get very uneasy using such an independent approach, even though they may have all kinds of concerns about their textbook. *This approach permits the teacher to be in charge*, to be in control of what is to be taught, based on the school or school district curriculum. If none exists, then the teacher must decide whether or not she or he will follow the text or adapt it to the needs of the class and what happens at more advanced levels.

HANDS-ON **FLES*** ACTIVITIES

1. Identify and label vocabulary.
2. Make a list of _____.
3. Role-play a skit.
4. Create a greeting card for _____.
5. Understand and respond to questions about _____.
6. Express preferences about _____.
7. Ask and answer questions about _____.
8. Describe familiar objects and persons.
9. Follow directions.
10. Match words and pictures.
11. Participate in language games.
12. Answer questions based on oral, picture, and written cues.
13. Complete sentences (oral or written).
14. Write a Cloze dictation; write a dictation.
15. Making a shopping list.
16. Write a meal plan for the day.
17. Participate in a treasure hunt for _____ in school, on the Internet, etc.
18. Make and label maps.
19. Make theme posters.
20. Record a message on an answering machine.
21. Write a letter to _____ about _____.
22. Tell how to do something (e.g., make, repair).
23. Make collages about _____.

24. Record ads for radio and TV.
25. Make announcements on the school public address system.
26. Create questions for a quiz or test.
27. Draw and label a cartoon about _____.
28. Take a written or oral quiz.
29. Create a written or oral test.
30. Create a Concentration game (or other games).
31. Plan, in groups, different aspects of a class celebration.
32. Prepare questions for a guest speaker.
33. Make a weather calendar.
34. Participate in a class store.
35. Sing authentic songs.
36. Draw the flag of a specific country.
37. Tell a folktale.
38. Create an ad for the school newspaper about FL study.
39. Plan a travel itinerary.
40. Design a menu.
41. Create the family tree of a famous family.

LIPTON'S NINE RULES FOR THE FLES* CLASSROOM

1. Real-life situations/problems/themes/information gaps are used—although they should be humorous, surprising, and interesting to students.
2. Students are not always working in the whole-class approach.
3. A variety of materials is used to make the situation(s) more realistic and challenging.
4. Not every error must be corrected at all times.
5. If your teaching is communication-/proficiency-oriented, your tests have to be communication-/proficiency-oriented.
6. Not every page in your textbook *has* to be covered. However, students need to learn the specific language components that will help them communicate in a functional situation.
7. It is essential that students show increasing ability in their functional use of the foreign language as they move from year to year.
8. More foreign language is used in the classroom by both students and teacher than ever before. The difference is that teachers do not

just talk *about* the language—students have opportunities to use the language functionally, in real-life situations.

9. We have to make sure that we occasionally bring some smiles and humor into the classroom—something to promote the *joy of learning another language and another culture!*

- There is no *one* best way to teach **FLES***!
- Encourage the active participation of students.
- Use a variety of approaches.
- Challenge students to find solutions to real problems or information gaps.
- Help students learn through their minds and their muscles.
- Relate content to the five C's of *Standards for Foreign Language Learning.*
- Use an integrated approach for weaving **FLES*** into the other aspects of the K–8 curriculum and the national FL standards.

🔖 FOR REFLECTION

Context is important: even if you are teaching on Mars, remember to always go from the known to the unknown.

DORA F. KENNEDY (PERSONAL COMMUNICATION, *10/7/96)*

National Standards for Foreign Language Learning and the Contextualized Focus of **FLES***

INTRODUCTION TO THE CONTEXTUALIZED FOCUS OF **FLES***

The delivery of foreign language instruction to children functions most effectively when there is a range of contexts that (1) are age-appropriate, (2) are of interest to children, (3) are capable of conveying cultural meanings either by themselves or with cross-cultural comparisons, and (4) involve educationally sound methodology for children.

This implies that **FLES*** methodology does not consist of isolated vocabulary and grammar or discrete cultural facts. The easiest way to provide contextualized **FLES*** is to provide a "setting" for activities in the classroom. Each setting may have an orientation following the five C goal areas: communication, cultures, connections, comparisons, and communities. Settings provide much-needed purposes(s) for language learning; e.g., in order to plan a class trip, we need travel vocabulary, map-reading abilities, knowledge of money conversions, courtesy questions and answers, and much more.

Sometimes settings are based on interdisciplinary topics and themes; sometimes they are based on information gaps; sometimes they involve activities on the local school or community levels. All settings should reflect real-life situations in the world of children.

A contextualized focus on **FLES*** gives the underpinnings for teaching and practicing the productive and receptive abilities, as we will discuss in this chapter. It also gives teachers opportunities to use various aspects of cultural components as they are linked with language learning.

Furthermore, this emphasis on context in **FLES*** helps teachers understand that students need to be taught (and need to practice) how to develop all kinds of language-learning strategies, such as (National Standards in Foreign Language Education Project 1996, 30):

1. Paraphrasing

2. Using circumlocution (particularly when students do not know or have forgotten a key word)

3. Making informed guesses

4. Getting meaning from the context of oral or written discourse

5. Learning how to get the gist without knowing every word

6. Using critical-thinking and problem-solving skills

7. Learning to recognize and use sociolinguistic features, such as gestures and nonverbal communication

8. Making inferences, generalizations, and predictions

9. Reflecting on the process and the product of language-learning activities

10. Drawing intelligent conclusions

11. Using graphic organizers (or webs) to organize content, stories, skits, and other materials

12. Using real-life (and real-culture) foreign language accurately and appropriately

TEACHING THE PRODUCTIVE ABILITIES: SPEAKING

The goal of most students, including elementary school language students, is to learn how to speak the language in real-life situations, according to Krashen and Terrell (1983). The companion ability, of course, is the ability to understand the foreign language. By definition, the speaking ability of youngsters is the ability to use the foreign language in natural situations, within the limits of the content they have been taught. Merely parroting lines of a dialogue (even if the pupil fully understands what he or she is saying) is not a demonstration of proficiency in speaking the foreign language. The youngster needs to be able to use the dialogue with some free variations and some accuracy of vocabulary, verb forms, idiomatic expressions, etc.

Also among the skills of speaking, the children need to pronounce accurately and have acceptable intonation patterns (phonology). Skills involved in the structure of the language (morphology) and the syntax (word order, negatives, etc.) are important aspects of successful oral communication.

FLES* programs rely, to a great extent, on the following guidelines:

• Speaking in the foreign language should be geared to real-life situations and contexts set within the limitations of vocabulary and structure previously taught to the children.

- Errors in pronunciation, structure, word order, etc., are to be expected, since children are urged to use the foreign language as much as possible.
- Vocabulary is taught in context.
- Numerous approaches are possible, such as the dialogue approach, the narrative approach, and others described in Chapter Nine.
- There is an interrelationship among the four abilities of listening, speaking, reading, and writing. No longer is a minimum waiting period recommended before the printed word is shown.
- Careful attention is paid to sound-letter correspondence so that pronunciation remains as accurate and authentic as possible, even after children begin to read the FL.
- Sometimes reading and writing abilities are used to enhance listening and speaking abilities; sometimes, it's the other way around. There is less rigidity in the teaching of abilities because of their interrelationship.
- Depending on the level and ability of the youngsters, grammar is taught either by modeling or by very brief explanation, as needed.
- For the most part, the speed of speaking, both by the teacher and by the children, is normal.
- Utterances may be complete sentences, groups of words, single words, etc., depending upon the nature of the communication activity or situation.
- In order to encourage the children to use the foreign language, English is very limited, used only by the teacher for clarification.
- Whether it is called the direct method, the audiolingual method, or the proficiency method, the best method for **FLES*** is involvement in real-life situations using the foreign language almost exclusively.
- Many of the approaches described in Chapter Nine are appropriate for teaching and developing speaking abilities in the FL.

Here are some speaking activities in the interpersonal mode:
- Giving TPR directions
- Answering and asking questions
- Complaining about a poor grade
- Describing a picture
- Role-playing a situation (going to a birthday party)
- Engaging in conversations about various topics
- Welcoming visitors to the classroom
- Asking questions about a train schedule
- Denying a fight in the school yard

- Insisting on being the leader of the game
- Suggesting that it would be better to play a different game
- Engaging in conversations (or dialogues) about various topics
- Introducing people

The following activities are in the presentational mode for the children who are presenting and in the interpretive mode for the children who are in the audience:

- Singing songs
- Performing impromptu situations from the Situation Box (which contains situation cards prepared in advance by the teacher and/or students)
- Telling a story
- Telling about a television program
- Role-playing a television program
- Role-playing the teacher and the class
- Narrating a pantomimed story
- Reciting poems
- Acting out a proverb
- Doing a puppet show
- Dramatizing famous events or current events
- Dramatizing going shopping or eating in a restaurant

Speaking in the Dialogue Approach

The dialogue approach is often used to practice the language and concepts in social studies, for example. A dialogue developed by the children to illustrate the discoveries of Cortés in Mexico would enhance important concepts in social studies.

The dialogue approach can also be applied to the development of higher-order thinking skills. For example, if the dialogue deals with taking a trip, students could be asked to categorize which articles they would take to travel, say, to Argentina in July. They could then be asked to contrast the type of clothing they would pack to travel to Spain in July.

A final word about the dialogue approach is essential at this point. Because many teachers in the past insisted that their students memorize every dialogue, memorizing is currently subject to some loss of acceptance. Here again I must stress that it is *not* necessary to discard effective practices because they may no longer be in vogue. Based on my experience and on the observation of hundreds of successful teachers, I am convinced that dialogues have value and should be included in the broad range of approaches used by the **FLES*** teacher, although each conversation or dialogue does not *have* to be memorized!

During the learning of the dialogue, teachers may wish to ask comprehension questions and/or personalized questions of the students (e.g., Do you like apples?) based on the likes and dislikes expressed in the dialogue. It is imperative that youngsters get a chance to ask questions, too, either of other students or of the teacher.

Children like to role-play or dramatize a dialogue when they feel comfortable with it. They particularly enjoy moving out of the original dialogue and shaping it according to their own imagination. This step is vital, so that students can learn how to say in the foreign language *their own ideas, humor, expressions*—within the limits of what they can

---

Communicative Interactions—N.L.K.T.
(Native Language Kid Talk)

1. What's your favorite subject in school?
2. What's your favorite CD-ROM?
3. Who's your favorite actress?
4. What's your favorite TV program?
5. How much time do you spend doing assignments?
6. What's your favorite place at school?
7. What's your favorite color?
8. What's your favorite dessert?
9. Which food(s) do you hate?
10. Where would you rather be right now?
11. Whose picture should be on a new stamp?
12. What time of day do you love the best?

Teacher ⇄ Student   Child ⇄ Child

absorb. They may want to go far afield, and the teacher has to narrow the range and simplify their expressions at early levels. Even if the amount of time devoted to the foreign language is limited, it is essential that children begin to feel the *power* of expressing their own thoughts and feelings in the foreign language in real-life situations of interest to them.

Teaching the Productive Abilities: Writing

In *FLEX* programs (those where limited time is devoted to foreign language instruction), writing activities are limited to brief captions, labels and simple sentences, greeting cards, and informal notes to friends and family. The writing activities are functional in nature.

In *Sequential FLES* programs, writing skills are developed in somewhat greater depth, and students are encouraged to keep a notebook or perform some of the functional writing activities that follow.

In *Immersion* programs, writing skills cover the content areas as well as spelling, accents, punctuation, structure, etc., in the language of instruction. The writing skills are developed as a direct outgrowth of the content-area instruction, and thus reinforce not only the foreign language, but also the concepts required by the content areas. In effective *Immersion* programs, writing skills in English are developed in increasing increments of time.

Role of Writing

Writing for different purposes can be developed at both early and later stages of *Sequential FLES* and *Immersion*. Writing is written communication in either the interpersonal mode or the presentational mode, as described in *Standards for Foreign Language Learning* (National Standards in Foreign Language Education Project 1996). *Casual writing* (a note to a friend) should be comprehensible, while more *formal writing* (a letter to a teacher and/or principal) should be comprehensible and thoroughly correct.

Writing is one of the abilities that should be developed with the primary goal of communication. Depending on the age of the learner, teachers find that some students need the support of reading and writing. Fifth and sixth graders are probably more dependent on reading and writing than are students in earlier grades. Thus, in developing writing abilities, the purpose, age, and individual student learning styles should be taken into consideration.

Some beginning writing activities might include copying, matching and copying, spot dictation, and word jumbles. Here are some examples:

Sample Word Puzzles (Spanish)

WORD JUMBLES (context is parts of the body)   (motivational)

CABO	ZIRAN
RODOL	NEDITE
PRUCEO	NOMA

COPYING (context is clothing)

Aquí está un sombrero.

— — — — — — — — — — — — — — — — — —.

SPOT DICTATION (context is friends)

1. Hoy es _____.
2. ¿Tienes un _____?
3. ¿Donde está la _____?
4. ¿_____ es?
5. _____ amigos.

MATCHING AND COPYING (context is food)

la leche	es rojo _____
la mantequilla	es blanca _____
el café	es amarilla _____
el vino	es negro _____

Writing Ideas and Activities (in Context)

Depending on the goals of the program and the grade level, students may write about the topics below. Writing activities may be in the interpersonal mode if the papers are shared with other students.

- Self-identification—pictures of things the student likes to do, eat, wear, etc.
- Minilogs about daily activities
- Family identification
- News events at home, at school, etc.
- Places the student visits
- Friends (similar to self-identification)
- Pet or pets
- Favorite TV program and stars

- Favorite movie stars
- Favorite sports figures
- Favorite hobbies
- Holidays the student likes—contrasted with holidays in a foreign culture
- Celebrating the student's birthday
- Favorite books
- Favorite magazines
- Favorite occupation(s)
- Cartoon(s) and captions
- Favorite recipes
- Favorite telephone numbers and pictures of friends/relatives
- Directions to the student's home, with pictures
- Résumé for a neighborhood job
- Poems
- Greeting cards for special occasions
- Puzzles
- Making a menu
- Creating a dialogue related to a learning scenario or unit/theme
- Calendar of events at home and/or school
- Invitations to a special event
- Simulated passport for a skit
- A class newspaper that compiles short items from *all* youngsters
- All kinds of puzzles and activities to stimulate higher-order thinking skills, such as:

  2 WORDS: one means life; one means death

  ANSWERS: poisson; poison (in French)

- Riddles:

  What do we have in December that appears in only one other month?

  ANSWER: the letter c (in Spanish and French)

- Word puzzles (brain teasers):

  10AC (Tennessee)

  mce, mce, mce (3 blind mice)

  knee / light (neon light [in English])

  ● de vue (point de vue [in French])

  s.o.c.k.s. (eso sí que es [in Spanish])

- Vocabulary in a meaningful picture or calligram (words written in the shape of the topic:

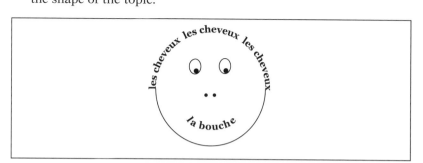

- Jigsaw puzzles with a hidden message:

These activities may fall into the interpretive and presentational modes:

- Creative creatures:

A cross between a rabbit and a turtle:

1. What is it? What's its name?
2. Name it.
3. Tell its story.
4. Invent another animal and its habitat.

- For more advanced students:

Create a story based on three cue words: e.g., "brown," "22," "uncertain" (in the foreign language). This gives students the opportunity to create a context for their stories.

- For the development of higher-order thinking skills:

  Write about the similarities and differences between an apple and an orange.

- Hidden words (hidden state and capital):

  Did Mary land as Anna polished cars? (Maryland—Annapolis [in English])

Many of the approaches described in Chapter Nine are appropriate for teaching and developing writing skills in the FL.

A final word about *dictation*. It is a writing activity, and a worth-while one. However, it is not solely a writing activity. Many teachers feel that it is a combination of listening comprehension, reading, and writing, and probably some silent speaking as well. It is useful to use dictation at the completion of a topic, unit, or any segment of learning. It can be used for testing, but it is extremely useful as a diagnostic tool for the teacher to determine what needs reteaching, who needs special assistance, and what the specific problems are. A dictation given two days in succession can also be very helpful. At the early stages of writing, the use of *spot dictations* is advisable. In a spot dictation, students write one or two missing words in a sentence or a short paragraph as the teacher reads the complete text. For example (in French):

1. Il fait _____ aujourd'hui.
2. C'est aujourd'hui _____, le _____ avril.

In the first sentence, students are to fill in *beau* as the teacher reads the complete sentence aloud. In the second sentence, students fill in *mardi* and *sept* as the teacher reads the complete sentence aloud.

Students then correct their papers (or turn them in to be corrected by the teacher). If students correct their own papers, the teacher must check carefully, because correcting (and proofreading skills) must be developed over a period of time. During an oral discussion with the students, the teacher might use the spot dictation as an opportunity to point out sound-letter correspondences in the foreign language.

Sample Integrated Writing Activity for FLES*, Grade 4 (French)

J'AI FAIM (context is food)

—J'ai faim. Qu'est-ce qu'on mange?

—Le _____.

—Mmm, j'aime le dindon. Et quoi encore?

—Les _____, _____ et _____.

—Et le dessert?

—Le _____.

—Oh, c'est _____!

MENU:

le pain	le dindon	les raisins
la pomme	le poulet	les fraises
le poisson	le gâteau	la glace
le fruit	la poire	le dessert

Sample Social Studies Activities (Spanish)

EL AVIÓN (context is South America)

- Vocabulario: ¿Qué es?

el anuncio	la compañía de aviación
el piloto	despegar
el avión	aterrizar
la pista	el vuelo
la salida	la puerta
el cinturón de seguridad	los billetes sencillos
el aeropuerto	los billetes de ida y vuelta
los pasajeros	las maletas
el equipaje	el clima

- Creating announcements in an airplane:

La compañía _____ _____ anuncia la _____ de su

_____ 201 destino Caracas. Los pasajeros pasan por la

_____ número 30. En el avión los pasajeros se abrocharán

el _____ _____ _____. El avión irá a la

_____ y _____. Muchas gracias y buen viaje.

- Creating a conversation between two passengers:

El hombre: _____

La mujer: _____

El hombre: _____

La mujer: _____

El hombre: _____

La mujer: _____

- Creating a Concentration game on South America:

Concentration Board

Under half of the numbered cards on the Concentration board is the name of a capital city of South America, and under the other half of the cards is the name of a South American country. Students attempt to match a capital with the appropriate country by taking turns selecting two numbered cards from the board. If a student guesses incorrectly, the cards are replaced; if a student guesses correctly, the cards are removed. For example, a correct match would be card number 11, Caracas, and card number 16, Venezuela. Play continues until all cards have been removed.

TEACHING THE RECEPTIVE ABILITIES: LISTENING

Contrasting FLES* Methodology and Comprehensible Input Methodology

FLES* methodology has its roots in the audiolingual approach to teaching foreign languages. Primarily, the emphasis is on listening and speaking abilities right from the start, although all four abilities are developed in varying degrees. There is stress on repetition, drills of all kinds, and manipulation of language—thus emphasis on input *and* output. The content is limited, but dialogue situations abound, particularly those of interest to young children.

With the comprehensible input approach, developed by Krashen and Terrell (1983), the most important element at the beginning is listening to get meaning, or comprehension. Students are not asked to repeat or drill or manipulate the language. They are encouraged to listen and understand, and then to demonstrate through actions that they have understood. Some research has shown that when speaking is delayed, the understanding mode builds up a background of language, and later, speech emerges without formal instruction. Here, the emphasis at the beginning is on input, and later, on input and output. Pressure on the students is minimized early on by delaying the time when they will be expected to produce language utterances. The content is limited, and real-life situations are extremely important.

Both approaches are useful in *Sequential FLES* and *FLEX* models. I strongly believe that a varied approach (in context) is essential. Whether one calls it an eclectic approach, or a "best of all worlds" model, it is important to hold fast to methods that show results and to vary *all* methods to keep motivation and interest high.

Children can be encouraged to participate in the following activities in order to give them extensive opportunities for refining the listening ability:

- TPR
- Discriminating between similar and dissimilar sounds
- Reacting physically in response to commands, new vocabulary, etc.
- Listening to a taped story (perhaps recorded by classmates)
- Listening to songs in the FL (records, cassettes, etc.)
- Listening to a skit on videotape
- Listening to a dialogue on film
- Taking a test on listening comprehension (spoken by the teacher or recorded on tape)
- Following instructions (folding papers, placing books, drawing a monster, etc.)
- Writing a spot dictation or full dictation
- Listening to a wide range of voices in the FL, in person and on tape
- Listening to radio weather forecasts, sports announcements, etc.
- Listening to different sounds on tape (familiar and unfamiliar)

A wide variety of activities can be devised that combine listening comprehension and motion or one or more of the other language skills. The teacher, however, will want to be alert to youngsters' listening comprehension skills and, if necessary, plan activities that foster more attentive listening skills, such as getting the gist of a story, paying attention to beginning sounds, listening for final sounds, etc.

Storytelling Activities

The most important reason for using the narrative, or story, approach for *Sequential FLES, FLEX,* and *Immersion* is that through this approach, the listening abilities are developed and enhanced. It gives the teacher many opportunities to read to the students and play recordings of stories so that the children hear different voices using the foreign language. It is not always necessary to complete the story in one class session. I used to read a story, and when I came to the most exciting part, I would stop and indicate that we would finish the story on the following day. This technique (used by radio and television producers!) works wonders for student motivation.

Guidelines for Teachers: Telling A Story

Teacher Preparation (at first, select a familiar story)
- Gather props and plan gestures.
- Be familiar with the story.

Telling the Story

- Coordinate props, gestures, and story. (Props may include pictures, transparencies, felt cutouts for the felt board, magnet cutouts for the magnet board, puppets, flip charts, pocket charts, toys, and the like.)
- Show enthusiasm as you tell the story.
- Include things for students to do during the story:
  Give students props to hold or wear.
  Ask simple questions that have easy answers.
  Ask students to act out part of the story.
  Include TPR activities, if possible.

Follow-up to the Story

- Ask students to draw a picture about the story.
- Ask students to dramatize the story as you narrate it.
- Ask students to change the ending of the story.
- Ask students (in cooperative groups) to dramatize different parts of the story.
- Retell the story using different props.
- Show sentence strips for different parts of the story.
- Ask students to put sentence strips in sequence.
- Ask students to create a web about the story.
- Ask students to create a rap about the story; make a "book" about the story; or create pictures, posters, puzzles, dioramas, a sequence time line, etc.

TEACHING THE RECEPTIVE ABILITIES: READING

In the 1960s, reading in **FLES*** programs consisted of reading labels, captions, and two- to three-line paragraphs geared to what the students were able to comprehend and say in the foreign language.

Today, that might be appropriate for *FLEX* programs that have limited time, limited goals, and a limited range of content to be covered during class sessions.

Sequential FLES programs and *Immersion* programs, on the other hand, have a broader scope for all language abilities, including reading. The content of the program will raise students' sights to the degree that they will attempt to read for meaning materials with both familiar and unfamiliar words and phrases. They will be taught many of the language arts skills of understanding through context, picture cues, reading between the lines, guessing, skimming, and others. Reading materials will provide a challenge to able students who can utilize higher-order thinking skills in their attempts to get meaning from the printed page.

Several Guiding Principles for Teaching Reading

- Reading skills are interrelated with the other language abilities.
- Reading-readiness activities and word-attack skills help students to get meaning from the printed page.
- The key steps in the development of reading abilities are reading readiness, reading familiar materials, reading recombined materials, controlled reading/comprehension checks, sound-letter analysis, and independent reading.

In grades 1 and 2, reading readiness consists of labeling objects around the classroom using familiar vocabulary and structures; labeling pictures, charts, and maps; and writing the date, weather, and attendance, as well as appropriate holiday sayings. Developing experience charts is appropriate for this level.

Hoy es viernes. Hace calor. Vamos a jugar y bailar en una fiesta de la primavera en el mes de mayo.

An experience chart dictated by the students in the foreign language.

In grade 3 and above (or earlier, depending on the class), reading consists of experience charts (material dictated by the students and written by the teacher on a large chart). The advantages of using experience charts are many, particularly since the students are encouraged to speak about what they are going to do or what they have experienced (and learned). There is a controversy about whether the teacher records statements made by the children, including errors, or whether the teacher takes the essential thought and writes it down correctly in the foreign language. It is my opinion that students should not be presented with incorrect patterns in the foreign language, and therefore I favor recording the *ideas*, but recording them correctly.

Use of the flannel board, flash cards, overhead transparencies, the computer, and many other devices is appropriate, too.

Steps in Teaching Reading

- Teacher motivates students by creating interest and presenting new vocabulary.
- Teacher reads material a paragraph at a time, asking questions to check comprehension.
- Teacher uses sentence strips (first in order, then out of order).
- Teacher uses phonics and other word-attack skills to help students deal with sound-letter correspondence.
- Teacher uses questions to help students frame key phrases.
- Teacher uses more sophisticated questions to help students learn how to make inferences from the reading materials.
- Teacher uses carefully composed questions to help students develop critical thinking skills (Wasserman 1987).
- Teacher challenges more able students to learn skills of comparing, describing similarities and differences, categorizing, etc., which help in developing higher-order thinking skills (Sternberg 1987).
- Teacher elicits summary of the materials in logical order of sequence.
- Teacher asks children to role-play or dramatize the material, if appropriate.
- Teacher may ask students to reinforce the reading with writing (depending on the goals of the program and the class).
- Teacher helps students develop word-attack skills by using sound-letter analysis.

Learning How to Use a Dictionary

An important aspect of the reading process is learning how to use a dictionary. Once this skill is learned, students will be able to read many varied materials independently, for the most part. Various components of dictionary use are presented over a series of lessons, with particular emphasis on pronunciation keys.

Learning to use a children's dictionary is important, but teachers should not expect children to be able to use adult dictionaries because they are too confusing (small pocket editions included). The best dictionaries for *Sequential FLES, FLEX,* and *Immersion* are picture dictionaries. Each entry with a picture conveys meaning and helps expand children's vocabulary in the foreign language if they learn to use the pronunciation keys. After learning to use picture dictionaries, children can move to a transitional, or intermediate, type of dictionary, which parallels the type used in language arts in English.

It should be remembered that word analysis, sound-symbol analysis, phonics, generalizations for word-attack skills, and correct pronunciation are often fused during any given lesson.

Finally, teachers are aware of the wide differences in the range of student reading abilities in the foreign language, and will make provision for them by providing suitable materials, partner practice, and group work, which help to reinforce learning. By following the developmental steps in reading, teachers will be able to incorporate a variety of reading strategies in planning foreign language lessons.

Developmental Steps in Reading

1. Reading readiness
2. Reading familiar materials
3. Reading recombined materials
4. Controlled text reading with comprehension checks
5. For some students, independent reading

In recent years, reading activities have been correlated with audio and visual supports, such as cassette recordings and video presentations. These, too, help students gain independence in reading and broaden their cognitive skills.

Here are some suggested reading activities (to be used in context):

- Reading aloud in chorus or individually
- Completing a sentence when a choice is given
- Reading to solve a riddle

- Choosing related items in a list of related and unrelated items
- Answering questions based on a short paragraph
- Making inferences based on a short paragraph
- Reading letters written by classmates
- Reading directions and following them (e.g., "Go to the door and open it.")
- Reading two advertisements from different stores and comparing prices
- Reading six random sentences about a story and putting them in the correct order
- Reading and understanding definitions in the dictionary (on students' own level)
- Reading the homework assignment on the chalkboard
- Reading a foreign language magazine (on students' own level)
- Reading a comic strip in the foreign language
- Reading a menu and deciding what to order
- Reading a recipe
- Reading the television schedule and deciding what to watch
- Reading a letter from a pen pal or key pal.

TEACHING CULTURE IN **FLES*** PROGRAMS

Cultures is one of the five C goal areas of the *Standards for Foreign Language Learning*. It also involves another goal area: comparisons. The content of cultural aspects is a vital segment of *Sequential FLES/FLEX/Immersion* programs. Language is a function of culture, and, as such, reflects the culture of the areas where the foreign language is spoken. Youngsters are fascinated by what youngsters their age do in the foreign culture—how it is similar to and how it is different from the ways we know in American culture. As Larew (1986) puts it, "The youngsters want to know how the Spanish-speaking people live and work; what they eat, dream, feel." Teaching these cultural components is not the memorization of isolated facts and figures. Rather, it is an attempt to help children understand a different way of life using another language of communication. Language, intonation, and gestures all convey aspects of the foreign culture.

Cultural awareness at the elementary-school level is *not*:

- "Flag waving"
- Facts to be memorized

- Stereotypes
- Generalities
- Outmoded concepts
- Only the unfamiliar and the differences
- Isolated concepts
- Any other procedures that do not promote greater understanding

Cultural Activities

Language *is* culture. Some examples are the use of *tu* and *vous* in French, intonation, gestures, songs, emotional exclamations, and so forth. Teachers will find many activities to integrate cultural components with linguistic aspects. Here are a number of suggestions:

1. Viewing media presentations (pictures, slides, videos, films, etc.)
2. Discussing current events in the FL-speaking country (countries)
3. Taking trips and excursions to neighborhood exhibits, restaurants, landmarks, bookshops, etc.
4. Looking at traveling exhibits that can be obtained for the classroom
5. Inviting guest speakers (NOTE: Speakers will be grateful if children prepare questions in advance.)
6. Looking at displays set up by the school and/or neighborhood specialist
7. Playing authentic games
8. Dancing authentic folk dances
9. Singing authentic songs
10. Learning and understanding authentic proverbs
11. Having pen pals or key pals from the foreign culture(s)
12. Examining realia from the foreign culture(s)
13. Recognizing famous places in the foreign culture(s)
14. Learning how to look at maps
15. Learning how to recognize street signs
16. Contrasting the appearance of public servants (e.g., police in Germany versus the United States)
17. Reading nonfiction books about the foreign culture
18. Looking through travel brochures and discussing them
19. Reading fiction books about the foreign culture in English (Advanced students, however, can do this in the foreign language.)
20. Contrasting meals, schools, homes, leisure activities

21. Discussing stereotyped reports in the media

22. Identifying "national characteristics," if any

23. Contrasting the concepts of time

24. Contrasting family relationships

25. Contrasting attitudes toward age

26. Discovering what the "new words" are in the foreign culture(s)

27. Understanding nonverbal communication in the foreign culture, such as gestures and kinesics

28. Understanding the influence of weather and geographical location on the foreign culture

29. Researching the country's heroes and heroines

30. Researching "What are the important holidays? How are they observed?"

31. Researching "What kind of money is used in the foreign culture? Does it reflect the culture?"

32. Finding out about the mealtime schedule in the foreign culture

33. Discussing favorite foods and which foods are taboo

34. Discussing what kind of schools they have; finding out how much homework the children get

35. Researching if things have changed in the last five years and why

Teachers and youngsters could most certainly continue this list from the questions the children ask and what is currently happening in the foreign culture(s). When a language is spoken in several different countries, it would be necessary for the children to understand that the language may differ from country to country. (The Spanish spoken in Argentina is slightly different from the Spanish spoken in Venezuela, for example.) Advertisements in the newspapers, magazines, and street signs give additional clues to the foreign culture.

Teachers, then, should *not* set aside ten minutes on Friday afternoons to "teach" culture, but should be alert for opportunities during the language lessons to present cultural information, urge the children to research and explore, display, encourage, explain—in short, make the cultural component an integral part of language learning.

Techniques for Teaching Culture

On those occasions when teachers wish to highlight cultural differences and/or similarities, they may try some of the following procedures:

CULTURAL ASSIMILATORS: A cross-cultural situation is stopped at a given point and the children are asked to select from a list of three or four possibilities the one choice they think would fit or follow the given situation. The most important part of this activity is the discussion of why one possibility is appropriate but the others are not.

CULTURE CAPSULE: Cross-cultural listing of a unit describing the foreign culture and American culture (descriptions of various aspects of the culture).

PSYCHOMOTOR UNIT OR THEME: Statements and actions demonstrating how an important activity in the foreign culture would be conducted and how it is conducted in the United States (e.g., going on a picnic, bringing different types of food, etc.).

TPR: Giving directions for actions in the foreign culture as contrasted with those for the U.S. culture (e.g., when buying food, first going to the butcher, then the grocery, etc., as contrasted with going to the supermarket in the United States). NOTE: Determine if in the last few years there *are* supermarkets in the target culture!

USING VOCABULARY TO CONTRAST DIFFERENT CULTURES: For example, using the words "home" and "house" and showing how people in the foreign culture have different concepts of these words as contrasted with the concepts held by Americans. What does a typical German house look like? Is it different in the city than in the country? Contrast this with a French house, a Spanish house, a house in the United States, etc.

Using activities and experiences with the foreign language, children can gain an insight into similar and dissimilar cultural patterns. Cultural concepts can be brought into the language lesson incidentally (such as different ways of shaking hands in greeting someone) or as a specific teaching concept, such as when to use the familiar and the formal "you" in the foreign language. Everyday topics are essential: food, dress, houses, dance, toys, family life, art, music, time, stories, folktales, customs, sports, leisure activities, famous personalities, holidays, word derivations, etc.

Suggestions for Teaching Culture

1. Use authentic materials, whenever possible
2. Simplify materials
3. Games
4. Puzzles

5. Riddles
6. Holidays and celebrations
7. Famous people
8. Research by children
9. Paired activities
10. Videos, videodiscs, pictures, cassette recordings, CD-ROMs and other technology
11. Guest speakers
12. Advertisements
13. Newspapers and magazines
14. Telephone books and catalogs
15. Current events and history
16. Maps and charts
17. Train and plane schedules
18. Contrasting customs
19. Songs and dances
20. Poetry
21. Developing a culture calendar
22. Proverbs
23. Tongue twisters
24. Role-playing
25. TPR
26. Culture capsules
27. Exploration of values
28. Food and recipes
29. Field trips

People-to-People Culture

- How do people in the target culture dress?
- What kinds of celebrations do they have?
- What do they eat? What do they eat at parties?
- What do they do in school? After school? When do they go to school? How do they get to school?
- What kinds of television programs do they watch?
- Do they have computers? Do they have video games?
- Do they celebrate the same holidays that we do?

What Kinds of Activities Are Appropriate for Teaching Culture?

- Hands-on approach
- Artifacts
- Role-playing
- Interviewing
- Comparing
- Breaking down stereotypes
- Examining a variety of cultures (e.g., in the francophone world)
- Avoiding "all" and "always"
- Examining American culture
- Making murals, collages, calendars
- Organizing a class trip to…
- Learning proverbs, rhymes, tongue twisters, etc. (see Appendix H)
- Planning a "culture freeze" (pantomiming a famous cultural event)

Finding Out About a Target Culture

What do children want to know about a culture?

- The people
- The things children do
- Family customs
- Schools
- National interests
- The things that are just like ours
- The things that are different
- Holidays and celebrations
- Food and drink
- Customs
- Famous people
- The arts
- The sciences
- Geography and history
- Current events: president, premier, leaders, recent events
- Other???

Specifics of Teaching Culture at the FLES* Level

How can anyone teach culture at the elementary-school level? "The children are too young…they do not have adequate language skills…they do not have the maturity to understand cross-cultural concepts…"

These are some of the excuses for *not* teaching culture to young children. While some of these reasons may be valid in some instances, there are many ways in which to help young people understand different cultures and appreciate the similarities and differences in other ways of life.

Of course, many dilemmas arise in dealing with the maturity levels of the children and their very limited knowledge of the target language. Unfortunately, it is easier to teach facts rather than values and sensitivities. But it *can* be done, if the teacher stresses comparisons between the target culture and our own, and if there is a curriculum for culture that progresses from one grade to another. Furthermore, it is best when culture permeates the language-learning lessons with a hands-on approach: let's explore; let's try out this idea; let's touch this article; let's role-play this event; let's research; etc.

Too often children get the idea that word-for-word translation is possible from English to French or from Russian to English. For example, if you are teaching about *le pain* and hold up a typical loaf of bread from the United States, which is sliced and cellophane-wrapped, you are missing an opportunity to also show a long loaf of French bread. Children need to draw the conclusion that even if they understand the word, they may not always know or understand the context in the foreign culture.

Some of the key concepts in teaching culture are:

- Don't indoctrinate!
- Encourage the children to ask questions.
- Compare and contrast.
- Talk about tendencies.
- Try "hypotheses."
- NEVER say "All…"
- Consult several sources.
- Evaluate the sources.
- Check the variables.
- Use authentic materials whenever possible.

It is often said that language is culture and culture is language. This profound statement, simply put, implies that when one is teaching language, the culture(s) of the language is intertwined with the linguistic components, and that when one attempts to teach the culture(s), this too is inextricably bound to the language.

Classroom Activities

Ongoing classroom activities may include some of the following:

- A cross-cultural center with books, magazines, recorded music, videos, and task sheets for information gathering (e.g., make a collage of people in the United States and Spain)

- A class cross-cultural mural or collage

- Research on the value of money and the rate of exchange in the target culture(s)

- Game boards in the form of maps, which can be used by paired groups practicing vocabulary, verbs, dialogues, situation rejoinders, historical events, etc.

- Small-group work dealing with different aspects of a learning module about Canada, for example. It could include questions, pictures, articles, places to write for information, etc.

- Plans for a pretend class trip to _____. The class could plan the logistics of the trip: what to do when we get there, what to do when we return home. After the pretend trip, depending on the age and maturity of the students, a real trip could be made to a country where the target language is spoken.

- Plans for a time capsule in the United States and in a foreign-language-speaking country.

- Make a suitcase and pack it with real objects or pictures for a trip:

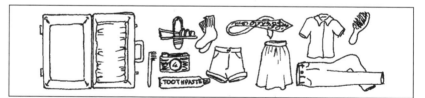

- Cultural components can be included in *every* **FLES*** lesson—such items as gestures, handshaking, advertisements, sports events, telephone books, catalogs, calendars with holidays, etc. These can be part of the content of the language-learning activities.

- A target-language cultural calendar is an interesting year-long class activity for children. Items that might be included are birthdays of famous people, holiday celebrations, historical events, special week-long celebrations, current happenings, etc., month by month.

- Learning about animals should also include the different sounds they make: e.g., in English-speaking cultures, dogs say "bow-wow" or "woof," and in French, dogs say "ouah-ouah"; cats say "meow" in English and "miaou" in French. A good question to encourage class discussion is: "Do American cats sound the same as French cats?"

- Typical recipes are always popular, whether they are cooked in the classroom or prepared at home to bring to a special class or school-wide celebration. Such items as mousse au chocolat, marguerites, quiche lorraine, soupe à l'oignon, consommé haïtien à l'orange, etc., can be easy to prepare in school and delightful to eat! Other languages, too, can provide recipes to enrich the curriculum.

- Proverbs and sayings reflect the foreign culture very well. Children may not understand every word, but if the proverbs are used frequently in the classroom, the children soon learn them without direct teaching and will often use them spontaneously. Teaching proverbs, tongue twisters, and rhymes helps students develop new insights into the target culture:

French Proverbs

Loin des yeux, loin du cœur.

Il n'y a pas de roses sans épines.

Il est bon comme le pain.

Spanish Proverbs

Más vale pájaro en mano que cien volando.

Perro que ladra no muerde.

No hay rosa sin espinas.

French Tongue Twisters

Un ver vert va vers un verre vert en verre.

Un chasseur sachant chasser chassait sans son chien de chasse.

Je crois que je vois trois oies dans le bois.

Spanish Tongue Twisters

En un plato de trigo comieron trigo tres tristes tigres.

Si Pancha plancha con cuatro planchas, ¿con cuántas planchas plancha Pancha?

German Tongue Twister

Fritz fischt frische Fische.

French Rhyme

Am stram gram

pic et pic et colégram

bourre et bourre

et ratatam

Am stram gram.

Spanish Rhyme

Pinto, pinto, gorgorito

¿Adónde vas tú tan bonito?

Por la acera verdadera

Pin, pon, afuera

- TPR (Total Physical Response) is an excellent way to have students incorporate learning through their muscles. For example, groups of children can be given task cards indicating a famous historical event. They then research the event and plan a group tableau, or "freeze," in which they demonstrate the event: for example, the beheading of Marie Antoinette is a favorite!

- A different type of interdisciplinary cultural unit can be developed when students are asked to invent a culture. This activity is highly empowering, because students, working in small groups, can use their imaginations to brainstorm their invented culture. This unit gives children opportunities to apply their interdisciplinary concepts to the creation of their invented culture as they examine the different elements that constitute a culture, such as name of country or culture; invented language, including basic vocabulary and basic expressions; people; values; holiday celebrations; flora and fauna; food; homes; water; air; clothing; occupations; transactions/business/money; government, officials, and flag; transportation; topography; geography; inventions; religion(s); and many other characteristics. By experimenting with an invented culture, students compare, contrast, and confirm what they know about their own culture and what they know about the culture(s) of the target language.

- All kinds of games, puzzles, and riddles appeal to children.

- Maps, charts, catalogs, and train and plane schedules help children compare and contrast; large mail-order catalogs are also interesting to children.

- Folk songs and dances help youngsters learn by doing.

- Field trips sometimes can help children see the reality of the foreign culture(s) in action (e.g., a trip to a local Japanese market).

- Cross-cultural understandings of the two cultures can often be accomplished by visuals:

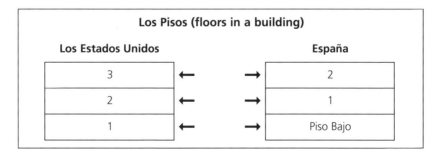

Los Pisos (floors in a building)			
Los Estados Unidos			**España**
3	←	→	2
2	←	→	1
1	←	→	Piso Bajo

- A learning module about (name of country). Include information, questions, pictures, puzzles, riddles, books, and other materials that will be helpful to read, to write for information, etc.

Teaching culture, then, is the twinning of culture and language so that youngsters gain insights, understandings, appreciations; they learn by exploration, by trying out ideas, by perhaps figuratively entering another way of life momentarily, and by wanting to learn more about the people!

💡 FOR REFLECTION

One way to ensure that language learning occurs in a meaningful context and that language processing goes beyond the level of the isolated sentence is to develop instructional models where language and content are closely intertwined.

ALICE OMAGGIO HADLEY (1993, 155)

Using Technology and Instructional Materials in **FLES*** Programs

USING TECHNOLOGY

Technology is making important changes in the lives of our students and their parents. It is reasonable to expect that technology does and will influence both the content and the delivery of foreign language instruction. Although budgets on the **FLES*** level do not permit a wide range of sophisticated equipment, there are many ways in which technology may play a significant role in **FLES*** programs.

According to *Standards for Foreign Language Learning* (National Standards in Foreign Language Education Project 1996, 31–32), technology "will help students strengthen linguistic skills, establish interactions with peers, and learn about contemporary culture and everyday life in the target country." This does not mean that print and audiovisual instructional materials such as texts, cassette recordings, authentic documents, dictionaries, newspapers, and magazines will be abandoned. Rather, the Standards document continues, "access to authentic sources of language, through high-tech or other means, helps establish the necessary knowledge base for language learners" (32).

Why Use Technology?

Many issues have been raised over the years about whether a machine can replace a teacher. This is an especially sensitive issue for the teaching of foreign language to children, because many educators think that young children need the personal, nurturing, and supportive attention of a teacher.

However, there are very few valid research studies about the effects of technology on foreign language instruction, and at the **FLES*** level in particular. Nevertheless, here are ten important reasons for teachers to include various aspects of technology in **FLES*** instruction:

1. Students are generally technology-literate and have become accustomed to using computers, videos, and other technology-based means of acquiring information.

2. Students learn at different rates and have different learning styles. The use of technology helps teachers reach all students in different ways.

3. Technology helps to relate the curriculum to life outside the classroom.

4. Technology helps to involve students in worthwhile, interactional activities, such as interpersonal exchanges, information gathering, and problem-solving projects.

5. Technology helps students to be active participants in the Information Age.

6. Using different aspects of technology helps to motivate students.

7. Technology adds many different dimensions of foreign language learning, particularly with the use of multimedia programs.

8. Technology helps to make the study of foreign languages very practical and significant in children's lives. If students can communicate readily through e-mail with children in a foreign country, it is unlikely that the teacher will hear them say, "But I'll never have a chance to really use Russian!"

9. Students are interested in and curious about the culture(s) of the foreign language they are studying, and technology can often bring that world directly into the classroom through satellite disks, and, ultimately, through virtual reality experiences.

10. Technology gives students opportunities to use their productive and receptive abilities for real purposes, such as publishing a newsletter or writing interactive journals.

It is difficult to believe that it was only in 1989 that Tim Berners-Lee proposed his idea about the World Wide Web, and that it has in such a short time become what many call a global phenomenon.

There are opposing views on the value of technology for educational purposes. Gates (1995, 66) discusses his belief in technology by stating: "Some fear that technology will dehumanize formal education. But anyone who has seen kids working together around a computer, the way my friends and I first did in 1968, or watched exchanges between students in classrooms separated by oceans, knows that technology can humanize the educational environment. The same technological forces that will make learning so necessary will also make it practical and enjoyable."

On the other hand, Talbott (343) has another point of view. He says that "we spend much time debating what manner of intelligence our machines are manifesting and toward what future goal they are evolving. But we are less inclined to ask toward what goal we are evolving. Perhaps we and our machines are converging upon the same goal...converging, that is, upon each other. Certainly if our computers are becoming ever more humanlike, then it goes without saying that we are becoming ever more computerlike. Who, we are well advised to ask, is doing the most changing?"

> Remember: The technology *must* be appropriate for the goals of the **FLES*** program!

Since technology is evolving rapidly, it is essential for **FLES*** practitioners, administrators, parents, and others to understand how the various technological advances can help the foreign-language-learning process. In my opinion (and that of others) young children (before the age of ten, the optimal time to introduce a foreign language) require interaction with a "live, human teacher." This is not to say that the **FLES*** teacher should avoid the use of technology! To the contrary, some aspects of technology often motivate and enhance the instructional program.

FLES* teachers should opt to use technology specifically when it:

- Is appropriate for the specific lesson
- Is age-appropriate
- Builds students' FL learning
- Provides authentic aspects of culture
- Demonstrates authentic cultural realia and documents
- Motivates students
- Is consistent with national FL standards
- Is appropriate for the local and state FL curriculum/framework
- Offers a better format for instruction
- Gives students opportunities to hear different speakers of the FL
- Gives students opportunities to interact with the program and with each other
- Gives the teacher a chance to observe students' reactions and performance
- Appeals to different students' learning styles and intelligences
- Meets the criteria for selection of instructional materials in this chapter
- Is user-friendly for the teacher and the students

Using Technology for Contemporary Culture

Teachers need to have access to current and accurate information about the target culture(s). These days, it is much easier than previously to get information about the current situation through the usual channels, such as newspapers, magazines, and other print materials; through audio and video cassettes; through TV programs (such as France 2 and France 5); and through the Internet and the World Wide Web. Teachers may also receive information through electronic mail, through comments on a discussion listserv, and through all the resources and search engines on the Web. The world is literally at the fingertips of both students and teachers!

Definitions of a Few Basic Terms

INTERNET: a worldwide computer network
   FRENCH: le Réseau
   SPANISH: el Internet, la Red

COMPUTER: for access to the Internet and electronic mail
   FRENCH: l'ordinateur
   SPANISH: la computadora

E-MAIL: electronic mail
   FRENCH: le courrier électronique
   SPANISH: el correo electrónico

MOUSE: used with the computer to access programs
   FRENCH: la souris
   SPANISH: el ratón

MODEM: telephone connection for the computer
   FRENCH: le modem
   SPANISH: el módem

For additional computer terms, see Gookin, Wang, et al., *Illustrated Computer Dictionary for Dummies.*

Computer on-line shorthand expressions:
   IMHO: in my humble opinion
   IMVHO: in my very humble opinion
   FAQ: frequently asked questions
   F2F: face to face, a meeting
   OTOH: on the other hand
   BTW: by the way
   WYSIWYG: what you see is what you get
   :-) happy
   :-(sad

;–) wink
:–* kiss

Teachers and students can create more of these shorthand expressions!

Suggestions for Using Technology in FLES* Programs

Teachers often ask, "How can I fit technology into my schedule? I have only twenty-minute sessions." Or they make excuses: "We don't have the equipment. "The equipment is broken." "The equipment is not at an appropriate level for my students." "Technology doesn't fit into my curriculum."

All of these concerns are valid, but **FLES*** teachers need to be aware that technology, in one form or another, is here to stay—and often changes rapidly. We use technology to make foreign language part of today's and tomorrow's world. We use technology to help students understand that "real people" speak the foreign language. And we use technology as a *significant* component of the **FLES*** curriculum—not as an add-on.

FLES* students are generally knowledgeable about technology... Are you?

There are many ways in which different aspects of technology can be used in **FLES*** programs. Using Print Shop Deluxe and other software programs:

- Students correspond with key pals through electronic mail. (These are the same as pen pals, but the means of communication is the computer, usually through e-mail.)

- Classes or groups of students correspond with video pals. (This is often a class exchange of videos with students in another class.)

- Students keep interactive journals. (Students write short entries into their electronic journal, and either the teacher and/or other students send reactions or comments about the journal.)

- Students do research on cultural projects, for example, by locating the Web sites for Le Louvre or El Prado. (They can simulate a visit to the museums and actually see some of the paintings and other works of art.)

- Students create class FL newsletters containing articles, comics, poetry, cultural notes, biographies, current news, and illustrations.

- Students compose a variety of written materials, such as letters, poetry, short articles, miniautobiographies, biographies of famous people in the foreign culture, etc. (They also have the opportunity to rewrite and correct their products with teacher assistance.)

- Students work on a treasure hunt on the Internet.

- Students create brochures, posters, and fliers about the importance of **FLES***.
- Students create graphic organizers for their autobiographies, for books they have read, for movie plots, etc.
- Students create bookmarks and placemats using FL expressions.
- Students create a **FLES*** cultural calendar, including dates of important events, birthdays of famous people, etc., in the foreign culture(s).
- Students, in groups, write the script for a skit to be presented in the auditorium for other classes, or for guests to the class or school.
- Students write letters to embassies, governmental agencies, etc., to gather information on a given topic or research the World Wide Web for Websites.
- Students interview various people both in and outside the school and write a summary of their interviews for a class newsletter.
- Students write reviews of books, movies, video games, and TV programs.
- Students go on a field trip and write a journal of their reactions.
- Students prepare questions to be asked of a foreign-language-speaking guest speaker.
- Students create a mapped itinerary for a real or pretend trip to a foreign-language-speaking country.
- Students keep records of sports events in a foreign country (e.g., the Tour de France).
- Students graph the weather in their own locality and compare it with the weather in a foreign-language-speaking country or countries.
- Students follow election results and the issues in a foreign-language-speaking country or countries.
- Students create their own study dictionary of expressions in the foreign language, with picture cues.
- Students (individually or in groups) write riddles and jokes in the foreign language.
- Students create an illustrated story or fairy tale in the foreign language for younger children.
- Students create a recipe book by compiling different kinds of recipes from the foreign culture(s).
- Students create greeting, birthday, and friendship cards in the foreign language for real people in their lives.
- Students make invitations, banners, and programs for school festivities in the foreign language, for festivals, miniOlympics, fashion shows, Grandparents' Day, National **FLES*** Day, etc.

- Students take pictures with a digital camera to record their classmates' presentation of a historical event in the foreign-language-speaking culture (e.g., the landing of Columbus in America).

Technology motivates and enhances student FL learning!

It is hoped that more and more **FLES*** students will have access to various types of technology, although where budgets are tight, this may not be possible. Whether students have access to computers, for example, in their schools, in their homes, at friends' homes, at computer stores, at recreation centers, etc., they are becoming computer literate and computer savvy. Therefore, one way or another, they will find a way to work on some of the activities suggested above. The students themselves will come up with new ideas and new applications for technology, often ahead of their teachers!

A few years ago, when a number of grant possibilities were available, some school districts invested in computer labs at the elementary school level. One such example is the Kansas City School District, which equipped nine magnet immersion schools. Other schools have been fortunate enough to equip a computer lab for schoolwide use in reading, social studies, science, and other areas. In such cases, **FLES*** teachers need to reserve the lab in order to provide their students with access to foreign language materials on the computer.

To summarize, then, here are the kinds of technology-based activities that may work successfully in **FLES*** classes:

- Correspondence with key pals, businesses, embassies, etc.
- Keeping interactive electronic journals
- Doing research on the World Wide Web
- Organizing creative projects
- Preparing skits for presentation
- Keeping records of all kinds with computers, cameras, etc.
- Creating a personal dictionary
- Compiling collections of recipes, fairy tales, poems, etc.
- Using Print Shop and other software
- Other activities developed at the local school

These suggestions represent the tip of the iceberg, because technological advances are occurring daily! (See Chapter Sixteen for futuristic predictions about **FLES***.)

Distance Learning

Administrators and parents often believe that distance learning will provide foreign language instruction for a great number of students. This approach can offer possibilities, provided that attention is paid to the following guidelines:

- The distance learning teacher has a high level of proficiency in the foreign language and has had extensive training in both **FLES*** methodology and distance learning techniques.

- The equipment used is interactive and gives students opportunities to use the productive skills of speaking and writing.

- There is a written curriculum stating the goals of the program for each year of instruction.

- The length and frequency of each session are sufficient to achieve the program goals.

- There are student materials (print, audio, computer, etc.) so that students have opportunities to practice using the foreign language.

- There is a foreign language teacher at each remote site to monitor the class and provide the necessary follow-up activities in accordance with the goals of the program.

- There is an assessment of each student's progress and there is provision for assessment of the program every year.

- There is provision to modify the program, as indicated, following valid assessment procedures.

Unfortunately, we have very few studies on distance learning for **FLES*** programs. We do know that young children need supportive and reassuring teachers. We also know that children often tire of educational distance learning, which is very different from their leisure-time TV and computer programs! Time will tell if there will be a sufficient number of carefully designed research studies that will provide directions for distance learning in **FLES*** programs. Until then, it would be wise to move slowly in planning **FLES*** programs using distance learning exclusively.

USING INSTRUCTIONAL MATERIALS IN **FLES*** PROGRAMS

The key word in the selection of materials for *Sequential FLES, FLEX,* and *Immersion* is *variety.* Young children, overstimulated by the rapid images of early television viewing, are easily bored by the use of the same kinds of materials, such as pictures and flash cards. On the other hand, children adore the use of a puppet or puppets with whom they can identify and empathize, and whom they can hug or chastise, according to the situations created by them and the teacher. Thus, teachers are dealing with two basic needs: the need for the new and exciting, and the need for the known and secure.

With the constantly evolving technology in instructional materials, and with publishers developing completely integrated packages with different kinds of components, one would think that there are sufficient materials of instruction. We are going to approach a satisfactory pool of materials within the next few years, but school districts and teachers need to be aware of some of the criteria for selection of appropriate materials. They also need to be reminded that because every class of students is different, a number of supplementary materials will always be needed, particularly if the goals of the program include group work and individualization of instruction, in order to appeal to different needs, learning styles, intelligences, and other student characteristics.

What Kinds of Easy-to-Obtain Materials Are Used in FLES*? (Selected)

Posters

Maps

Books, workbooks

Magazines

Pictures

Flash cards

Flip charts

Flannel board

Magnet board

Pocket charts

Records

Audiocassettes

All kinds of toys

Food, clothing, and other real objects

Greeting cards

Travel brochures

Computer games

Transparencies for overhead projector

Videocassettes

Films

Television schedules

Newspapers

Classroom objects and places in the school

Places in the neighborhood

Photographs (very effective if taken by students)

Teacher-made and student-made materials

Craft materials

Clocks

Beanbags

Board games

Computers, software, and disks

Maps

All kinds of balls

Flags

Toy telephones

Children's FL dictionaries

Materials for small-group projects

Calendars

Puzzles

Games

Advertisements

Catalogs

Telephone books

Globe

Charts

Train, plane schedules

Polaroid camera

Puppets, puppet stage

Magnetic cards for Language Master

Sentence strips and holder

What Are FLES* Authentic Materials? (Selected)

From the foreign culture:

Newspapers

Magazines

Advertisements

TV schedules

Train and plane schedules

Records, CD-ROMs

Videos

Greeting cards

Instructions for toys

Computer software

Mail-order catalogs

Money

Toys

Etc.

What Might Be on Your FLES* Equipment Wish List? (Selected)

Computers with CD-ROM drives, printers, and Internet access

Computer lab

Satellite dish

Overhead projector and screen

Audiocassette recorders

Videocassette recorders

Videodisc players

TV hooked up to satellite

Small TV/VCR with six earphones for a listening center

Distance learning classroom with fiber-optic system

Document camera, digital camera, digital video

Fax machine

Scanner

Laser disc equipment

Fiber-optic system

Electronic mail system

Connection to the World Wide Web

All kinds of multimedia and telecommunications

Materials Specifically for *Immersion* Programs

According to practitioners in the field, it is difficult to obtain appropriate materials for *Immersion* programs. Generally, materials are used from foreign sources (French materials from Canada and France; Spanish materials from Spain, Mexico, and Latin America; etc.). Most of these materials, however, need to be adapted for *Immersion* programs in U.S. schools, since they do not follow the guidelines for the U.S. elementary school curriculum in the various states.

For these reasons, materials for *Immersion* programs need to be supplemented by district-created guidelines and other support materials for teachers, students, and parents. Generally, curriculum materials used in such subjects as mathematics, science, and social studies are translated from the language used in the school/school district into the appropriate target language.

The Milwaukee *Immersion* program deemed the following materials or curriculum products necessary for their French program (these could be adapted to any language):

- Annotated list of publishers of French materials suitable for grades K–6
- Expressions in English and French
- Menus in French
- French vocabulary and expressions (classroom objects, clothing, classroom expressions)
- Useful French expressions
- Expressions in French for kindergarten
- Helping parents learn a second language with their children
- Vocabulary for physical education
- French first-grade reading units
- Penmanship—first grade
- Prereading unit
- Summer reading booklet—first grade
- Chart stories for first grade
- Short stories and activities
- Science unit on seeds
- Cursive writing unit—third grade
- How Do I Feel? and I Don't Feel Well
- French basic word list flash cards
- French vowel flash cards
- French phonics flash cards

These may be obtained at minimum cost from
    Curriculum Products
    Division of Curriculum and Instruction
    Milwaukee Public Schools, P.O. Drawer 10K
    Milwaukee, WI 53201-8210

Fortunately, there is a growing number of sources of effective materials for all types of **FLES*** programs. Currently, there are still too few *Immersion* materials produced in the United States, and too frequently foreign materials are not appropriate for U.S. students. This then necessitates much textbook adaptation and revision. It also necessitates much translation of curriculum materials that exist in English into the foreign language. Foreign materials sometimes include pictures and other types of supplementary materials that may not meet local school-district standards. It is hoped that more publishers will plan to produce effective materials for *Immersion* programs in social studies, mathematics, science, language arts, and other content areas.

Criteria for the Selection of FLES* Materials

The following criteria represent some of the points to be considered when selecting materials of instruction:

1. Do the materials satisfy the goals of the program?
2. Do the materials carry out the objectives for the grade level?
3. Are the materials developed in ways that can be easily adapted to the specific needs of a specific class?
4. Do the materials include a wide range of activities appealing to different learning modalities and styles?
5. Do the materials include a number of components that fit together well for the delivery of the goals of the program?
6. Are the materials of interest to children? Will they motivate the students to learn? Are they appropriate for the students' age group?
7. Are the materials attractive? Are the pictures important to the content? Do they have eye appeal?
8. Do the materials contain effective cultural components? Do they avoid stereotypes? Do the materials represent authentic culture?
9. Are the materials free from bias? Is a contrast made between standards in the United States and those in other countries?
10. Do the materials reflect sequential development? Are they articulated with middle school and secondary school materials?
11. Are concepts clearly delineated, illustrated, and highlighted?
12. Are all four abilities included in the plan of operation, depending on the grade level?
13. Is an evaluation plan included in the materials? Are there periodic checkpoints?
14. Do the materials include additional suggestions for the gifted student? The less able student? A variety of learning styles and intelligences? (found particularly in the teacher's manual)
15. Do the materials include activities for TPR as well as cognitive activities?
16. Do the materials appeal to the senses and emotions of young children as well as to their curiosity?
17. Does humor appear from time to time in the materials?
18. Do the materials suggest enrichment with computer programs, video, and other types of recent technology?

19. Do the materials indicate the type of program for which they are suitable (e.g., *Sequential FLES, FLEX, Immersion, Partial Immersion*)?

20. Are the materials doable? Is the content appropriate?

21. Are there suggestions for adapting the materials if the time schedule is severely curtailed or extended?

22. Are the strategies effective and worthwhile?

23. Is the pace satisfactory for the program and its goals?

24. Have the materials been field-tested? For what type of program? For what type of grade and class?

25. Is there an audio component? Are the voices native or near-native, clear, well paced?

26. Was the material planned for American students or foreign students? How important is this for the class(es)?

27. Are the materials easily used by an experienced teacher? By a beginning teacher? By a non-foreign-language teacher? By a volunteer?

28. Do the materials seem to follow any particular language-teaching philosophy? Does there seem to be an eclectic approach?

29. Do the materials fulfill the goals expressed by the author(s)?

30. Does an element of surprise appear in the materials from time to time?

31. Can the materials be used as a basic text, or are they considered supplementary?

32. Is there a teacher's manual? How helpful is it?

33. Is English included? How much? Too much?

34. Are there suggestions for follow-up and homework?

35. Are there explanations? Are they helpful?

36. Is there frequent review and reentry?

37. Is there variety of format? Language? Topics?

38. Do the materials reflect a prereading stage? A prespeaking stage?

39. Which other components are available? Will they enhance the learning?

40. Is the cultural material authentic and integrated with the linguistic elements?

41. Can the materials be adapted for use in several grades?

42. Are the materials in consonance with the national FL standards?

A Word About Teacher-Made Materials

Every effective teacher uses teacher-made materials to enrich learning, provide differentiated tasks for different types of learners, supplement inadequate commercial materials, and create activities that relate to the specific goals and objectives of the local program. As teachers gain experience and familiarity with the needs and interests of their students, they become adept at creating stimulating and interesting support materials in *FLES*, *FLEX*, and *Immersion*. For all the effort involved, however, teachers should exercise caution in the development of these "ditto sheets" by following these recommendations:

- Instructions should be clear.
- Copy should be legible—printed or typed.
- Worksheets should have eye appeal and be of interest to children.
- Content should be appropriate to the program goals and to the level and ability of the children.
- Materials should supplement, enrich, reinforce, and add variety to the program.
- Pictures and other visuals should accompany the written work.
- Usage of the foreign language should be correct and authentic.
- Complete sentences need not be expected of students at all times.
- Dialogues or conversations should be appropriate to real situations.
- Generally, worksheets should attempt to reinforce only *one* linguistic concept at early levels.
- Sentence structure should be parallel, and progress to more difficult patterns.
- Explanations should be brief, often accompanied by a clear diagram or visual.
- Every teacher-made sheet should have a specific purpose.
- Teachers should try to develop rapid means for both checking and student correction.
- Teachers should remember that students learn better through a variety of modalities. Therefore, some attempt should be made to correlate teacher-made materials with cassette recordings, visuals, and all kinds of TPR activities.

Selected Teaching Techniques and Materials for All Types of FLES* Programs

1. Question/answer communication
2. Lessons using:

- Transparencies
- Real objects or simulated objects
- Flash cards
- Flannel board and flannel cutouts
- Magnet board and cutouts with magnets
- Dolls, puppets, stick puppets, etc.
- Dioramas

3. Games
4. Group work, cooperative-learning groups
5. Videos and audiocassettes
6. Teacher-made, student-made materials
7. Advertisements, pictures from magazines, photographs, etc.
8. TPR—rhythms, chants, raps, etc.
9. Reading a story, poem, etc.
10. Telling about cultural patterns and contrasting with our own (with realia)
11. Dramatizations, skits, role-playing
12. Variety of props in a Prop Box for scenery, etc.
13. Use of globe, maps, charts, flags
14. Use of telephones, telephone books, train and plane schedules, calendars, travel brochures, menus, and other authentic materials
15. Use of Venn diagrams
16. Use of computers
17. Use of webs for many purposes
18. Use of all kinds of clothing in a Clothes Box
19. Use of a Future Box for contrasting present customs with those of the future
20. Use of interactive techniques, materials, activities
21. Language centers in the classroom: e.g., for games, video, newsletter, Internet treasure hunt

Easy-to-Make and Obtain FLES* Materials

1. Puppets (all kinds)
2. Flash cards and transparencies
3. Pictures (from coloring books, hand-drawn, etc.) grouped around different themes
4. Simulated objects (plastic food, animals, etc.) and games

5. Real objects

6. Posters

7. Flannel board, felt cutouts

8. Maps, globes, flags

9. Collages, dioramas

10. Stickers (student-created)

11. Calendars (dates, weather, birthdays, etc.)

12. Toy clocks with movable hands for all students

13. Bingo cards and other game cards

14. Menus (real and invented)

15. Balls and other toys

16. Toy telephones

17. Puppet theater, dollhouse, model of town, etc.

18. Greeting cards, invitations, letters, thank-you notes, etc.

19. Folders, notebooks, books, cookbooks, etc.

20. Advertisements, product wrappers, boxes, etc.

21. Postcards, bookmarks, etc.

22. Other items created by teachers and students

Suggested Sources of Materials for *Sequential FLES, FLEX,* and *Immersion* (Selected)

This is a selected list of publishers, just to get you started. Send for catalogs, make inquiries, do further research, and you will discover many other sources of materials for your program. The *s* preceding some entries indicates availability of software.

Addison-Wesley Longman Co.
10 Bank Street
White Plains, NY 10606

Adler's Foreign Books/Midwest
European Publications
915 Foster
Evanston, IL 60201

Aims International Books
7709 Hamilton Avenue
Cincinnati, OH 45231

AMSCO FL's
315 Hudson Street
New York, NY 10013

Applause Learning Resources
85 Fernwood Lane
Roslyn, NY 11576

Assn. for Childhood Education
   International
11501 Georgia Avenue
Wheaton, MD 20902

Audio Forum
96 Broad Street
Guilford, CT 06437

Barron's Educational Series
250 Wireless Boulevard
Hauppauge, NY 11788

Berlitz Publications
866 Third Avenue
New York, NY 10022

Bilingual Educational Services
2514 S. Grand Avenue
Los Angeles, CA 90007

Bilingual Review/Press
Hispanic Research Center
Arizona State University
P.O. Box 872702
Tempe, AZ 85287

Broderbund Software
500 Redwood Boulevard
Novato, CA 94948

Cambridge University Press
32 E. 57 Street
New York, NY 10022

Children's French Book Store
1486 Gainforth Avenue
Toronto, Ontario M4J IN5

Continental Books Co.
80-00 Cooper Avenue
Glendale, NY 11385

Editions Soleil
P.O. Box 890
Lewiston, NY 14092

ˢEducational Resources
1550 Executive Drive
P.O. Box 1900
Elgin, IL 60121

EMC Corp.
300 York Avenue
St. Paul, MN 55101

Europa Bookstore
3229 N. Clark Street
Chicago, IL 60657

ˢFairfield Language Technologies
122 S. Main Street
Harrisonburg, VA 22801

French and Spanish Book Corp.
115 Fifth Avenue
New York, NY 10003

French for Fun
4965 Hames Drive
Concord, CA 94521

ˢGlencoe Textbook Co.
P.O. Box 543
Blacklick, OH 43004

Goldsmith's Music Shop
301 E. Shore Road
Great Neck, NY 11023

Harper Collins
(Newbury House Division)
10 E. 53 Street
New York, NY 10022

Hatier-Didier
2805 M Street, NW
Washington, DC 20007

Iaconi Book Imports
970 Tennessee Street
San Francisco, CA 94107

Ideal Foreign Books
132–10 Hillside Avenue
Richmond Hill, NY 11418

Independent School Press
51 River Street
Wellesley Hills, MA 02181

In One Ear Publications
29481 Manzanita Drive
Campo, CA 91906

The Kiosk
19223 De Havilland Drive
Saratoga, CA 95020

Kraus Curriculum Development
  Library
Route 100
Millwood, NY 10546

Langenscheidt Publishers
46-35 54th Road
Maspeth, NY 11378

Languages for Kids
7403 Fifth Avenue
Brooklyn, NY 11209

Larousse
572 Fifth Avenue
New York, NY 10036

Lectorum Publications
137 W. 14 Street
New York, NY 10011

Librairie Dussault
8955 Boulevard St. Laurent
Montreal, Canada

sLingo Fun
P.O. Box 986
Westerville, OH 42881

sLinks-Lazos, Inc.
170-23 83rd Avenue
Jamaica Hills, NY 11432

Mac Warehouse/Micro
  Warehouse
47 Water Street
Norwalk, CT 06854

McGraw Hill Co.
1221 Avenue of the Americas
New York, NY 10020

sMED School Division
915 Foster Street
Evanston, IL 60201

Nana's Book Warehouse
848 Heber Avenue
Calexico, CA 92231

National Geographic Society
17th and M Street, NW
Washington, DC 20036

sNTC/Contemporary Publishing
  Company
4255 W. Touhy
Lincolnwood, IL 60646

Organization of American States
17th and Constitution Avenues
Washington, DC 20006

Polyglot Publications
P.O. Box 668
Cambridge, MA 02238-0668

Price Lab School
University of Northern Iowa
Cedar Falls, IA 50614

Rand McNally
P.O. Box 7600
Chicago, IL 60680

REI Materials
6355 N.W. 36 Street
Miami, FL 33166

Rizzoli Publications
712 Fifth Avenue
New York, NY 10019

Mary S. Rosenberg
100 W. 72 Street
New York, NY 10023

Scholastic Inc.
555 Broadway
New York, NY 10012

sScott Foresman-Addison Wesley
1900 E. Lake Avenue
Glenview, IL 60025

Silver Burdette Co.
250 James Street
Morristown, NJ 07960

Sing, Dance, Laugh and Eat
  Quiche
6945 Highway 14E
Janesville, WI 53546

Sky Oakes Publishers
P.O. Box 1102
Los Gatos, CA 95031

sSosnowski Associates
58 Sears Road
Wayland, MA 01778

sSumo
1005 Debra Lane
Madison, WI 53704

Teacher's Discovery
2741 Paldan Drive
Auburn Hill, MI 48326

Wible Language Institute
24 S. 8th Street
Allentown, PA 18105

World Press
100 Spartan Avenue
Staten Island, NY 10303

Other Sources

State departments of education in various states
Airlines
National airlines of the foreign country or countries
National railroads of the foreign country or countries
Cultural and commercial services of embassies of foreign countries
Foreign language bookstores
Department stores
Music and record stores
Public and university libraries
Computer stores
Travel agencies
Greeting card shops
Banks
Post offices
Other sources in the local area

Resources for Technology Activities

Software Programs for Students

It is not advisable to mention specific software programs at this writing, because the selection of programs is constantly changing, with new ones being added daily. Furthermore, there are many catalogs of software and CD-ROMs; many reviews in newsletters; many word-of-mouth recommendations; many sessions at national, regional, state, and local foreign language teachers' meetings, etc. The best advice for **FLES*** teachers is to read the reviews of software in the various newsletters, such as the *Tennessee Newsletter,* the *New Jersey Newsletter,* and the *Northeast Conference Newsletter,* and in the journals of language-specific national organizations, such as AATF, AATG, and AATSP. Also, teachers can get recommendations from colleagues on Internet foreign language discussion lists, such as FLTEACH (see Chapter Seven). Please consult the selected list of sources of **FLES*** materials in this chapter and request catalogs from those marked with an [s].

Software Programs for Teachers (A Sampling)

Print Shop Deluxe—clip art for making greeting cards, letterheads, etc.

Crossword Creator

Hyperstudio—for multimedia presentations

Making the Grade—a grade book program

Puzzleworks—many kinds of puzzles

Lipton's Favorite Bookmark Addresses on the Internet (A Sampling at This Writing)

FRENCH

Premiers Pas: http://www/imaginet.fr/momes/

FranceWeb: http://www/francenet.fr

Météo France: http://www.meteo.fr/

Le Louvre: http://web.culture.fr/louvre/francais/musee/collec.htm

AATF home page: http://www.utsa.edu/aatf/

Tennessee Bob's Famous French Links:
192.239.14.18/departments/french/french.html or
http://www.vtm.edu/departments/french/french.html

ITALIAN

Link to museums: http://www.mi.cnr.it/IGST/Musei.html

JAPANESE
Tokyo food: http://www.twics.com/~robbs/tokyofood.html

CLASSICS
American Classical League: http://www.umich.edu/~knudsvig/ACL.html

SPANISH
Elementary Spanish curriculum: http://www.veen.com/Veen/Leslie/
Curriculum

Spanish books K–8: http://www.mibibook.com/catalog/spholidy.html

Spain: http://www.uji.es/spain www.html

GERMAN
AATG home page: http://www/stolaf.edu/stolaf/depts/german/aatg/

OTHER
Agora Marketplace: http://agoralang.com/

Yahoo: http://www.yahoo.com/

Tenny's Education Page: http://www.mebbs.com/tenny/educate.html

FL Teachers' website: (to subscribe) FLTEACH

LISTSERV@UBVM.CC.BUFFALO.EDU

World Cultures: http://www.worldculture.com

GENERAL (NON-FL) WEBSITES
Teachers Helping Teachers: http://www.pacificnet.netl~mandel

Teacher's Edition Online: http://www.teachnet.com

Are You Technologically With It?

- Do you have an e-mail address?
- Do you correspond by e-mail with colleagues?
- Have you joined a LISTSERV, such as FLTEACH?
- Do your students have key pals?
- Do you explore the resources of the Internet?
- Do you have your personal list of favorite Internet addresses or bookmarks?
- Do you consult the home pages of FL organizations?
- Do you do research on the Internet?
- Do your students do research on the Internet?
- Are you ready and eager for the next technological innovation?

💡 FOR REFLECTION

The Network will enable teachers to share lessons and materials, so that the best educational practices can spread.

BILL GATES (1995, 66)

FLES* Evaluation and Assessment

GENERAL CONSIDERATIONS

In developing an evaluation design for *Sequential FLES/FLEX/Immersion* programs, a number of factors should be included, such as:

- The standards and progress indicators set forth in *Standards for Foreign Language Learning* (National Standards in Foreign Language Education Project 1996)

- Performance of students in the productive and receptive abilities and cultural awareness in the *foreign language* (for *Immersion* students, in addition to the above, progress in all aspects of the elementary school curriculum, including successful results on standardized tests in mathematics, reading, and language, in the foreign language, if valid tests exist)

- Attitudes of students toward foreign language study

- Reactions of parents

- Reactions of principals and administrators

- Reactions of classroom teachers (if they do not teach the FL)

- Reactions of classroom teachers (if they are also the FL teachers)

- Reactions of foreign language teachers

- Reactions of volunteers who provide instruction

- Other reactions

- Overall evaluation of the program

The central idea in planning any evaluation is the matching of the goals and objectives to the evaluation procedures. It is an unsound procedure to implement a program in the elementary schools and then, when it is time to evaluate the program, to administer a standardized *secondary school* foreign language examination (which may have no relationship to the local objectives) just because no other test exists! Educators would never dream of handling evaluation of other subject areas in this way. The problem derives from the fact that there are no valid standardized foreign language tests for the elementary school level as yet, but some are being developed. Even if one could locate such an examination, there would be no certainty that it measured what had been taught, since elementary school FL programs differ greatly from district to district, from school to school, etc.

For these reasons, as was indicated earlier, it is of great importance that during the planning and organizing stage a design for evaluation be developed that will be in consonance with local objectives and goals, and with the goals of the national FL standards.

Another crucial question to be determined at the local level is who will conduct the evaluation. Will it be one or more persons within the school district? Will it be an outside consultant or a team of consultants? Will it be a combination of both inside and outside people? Will it be someone who understands a foreign language program, or will it be a research specialist? This author would urge that at least one person on an evaluation team be a foreign language specialist, so that there would be input when there are deliberations on the analysis of data and interpretations to be derived from the data.

Finally, as with any educational undertaking, the goals and objectives of the evaluation procedures must be determined in advance, with an indication of the kinds of evaluation instruments that will be used and the kinds of evaluation instruments that will have to be developed. All of these functions, of course, should have been included in the planning budget for the program.

Evaluating **FLES*** Programs

Since evaluation of all types of **FLES*** programs is essential for success, there are a number of ways in which schools and school districts can plan for the assessment of their programs, using any or all of the following:

1. The **FLES*** Scale for the Evaluation of **FLES*** Programs, which can be found in Appendix A.
2. Self-evaluation using the **FLES*** Assessment Criteria List, which follows. This can serve as a guide for schools and school districts for improving their programs through comparison against four major categories: goals, administration, the instructional program, and evaluation procedures.
3. Assessment by outside evaluators
4. Evaluation by the **FLES*** advisory committee, by gathering all kinds of feedback from questionnaires, test scores, etc.
5. Other variations at the local level

The FLES* Assessment Criteria List

I. Goals

1. What are the goals of the program?
2. Is there an advisory/steering committee?
3. Have administrators, parents, and students been informed of the goals?
4. Does the instructional program reflect the goals?
5. Does the evaluation design reflect the goals?
6. How does the program fit in with the entire foreign language sequence? With the elementary school program?
7. Do the goals reflect the national FL standards?
8. Are there long-range goals for the program?

II. Administration of the Program

1. Does instruction occur during the school day? When? How often? Weekly time allotment? In consonance with the goals?
2. What kind of certification does each teacher have? Has the teacher had a **FLES*** methods course and student teaching?
3. What is the language proficiency of the teacher?
4. Is there a coordinator or supervisor of the program?
5. Does the teacher (or teachers) meet with secondary school FL teachers? How often? For what purpose?
6. Which materials are used for the program? How do they relate to the FL materials used in the secondary school?
7. In what grade does the program begin?
8. Are all students in a **FLES*** program?
9. What is the schedule (how many minutes per class, per grade; how many times a week)?
10. What is the teacher-student ratio? Is the teacher's total student load reasonable?
11. Which languages are taught? Which languages are taught in the secondary schools? What was the basis for the choice?
12. Is there a plan for articulation?
13. Is there a plan for changing or modifying the program?
14. How is the program perceived by parents, teachers, students, administrators, and others in the educational community?

III. Instructional Program

1. Are all four abilities presented in ways that are consistent with the goals, age, grade level, and abilities and interests of the students?

2. Are cultural components included in class sessions?

3. Is there variety of presentation?

4. Is there participation of *all* students?

5. Is there variety of materials? Are authentic materials used?

6. Is error correction handled appropriately?

7. Is each lesson carefully planned?

8. Is the foreign language used 90 to 99 percent of the time?

9. Do students get opportunities to use the language with partners or in small groups?

10. Do the children use the foreign language in real-life situations with fluency and ease, depending on the amount of time and intensity of exposure to the FL? How well do they use the FL, and how accurately?

11. At the conclusion of a lesson, do the children know that they have learned something?

12. At the conclusion of a lesson, do the children indicate that they are eager to come back for the next lesson?

13. Does the teacher include Total Physical Response or movement at all grade levels?

14. Do the students know the places in the world where the foreign language is spoken?

15. Are resource people from the community and from the consulates invited to class?

16. Are students from the secondary schools and native speakers invited to class?

17. Are elementary school students invited to participate in districtwide festivals, career activities, and other events with international themes?

18. Is there a scope and sequence, curriculum, or course of study for each year of the program?

19. Is a variety of media used in the program, including audio, visual, and computer?

20. Does the teacher assist individual students, both for remediation and for enrichment?

21. Do students understand why they are studying a foreign language?

22. Does the instructional program reflect the five C goal areas of the national FL standards?

IV. **Evaluation of the Program**

1. Is there ongoing evaluation in the classroom?

2. Is there an evaluation design for the program?

3. What kinds of instruments are used for evaluation? Are they formal or informal?

4. Are students graded for their foreign language work?

5. Is the program reviewed each year and evaluated formally every five to seven years?

6. Are changes made on the basis of the evaluation?

7. Is an outside consultant invited to assist in evaluation?

8. Are there ongoing procedures for feedback?

9. Does the advisory/steering committee contribute to the evaluation of the program?

10. Does the program reflect the five C goal areas of the national FL standards?

A School/School District Foreign Language Information Packet

Does your school/school district have a foreign language information packet? While a FLIP is most useful in promoting foreign language programs, it also plays an important role in providing data for the evaluation of the program.

A foreign language information packet might include the following items (and others that describe your program):

1. An explanation of the goals of the entire foreign language sequence, K–12, including the place of **FLES*** in the FL sequence

2. A description of the foreign language methodology at each stage, including provision for different abilities and learning styles plus small group, cooperative learning, and paired activities

3. For each stage of FL learning, a description and explanation of:

The implementation of the national standards and goals

The teacher's role

The student's role

Activities for in class and beyond

The parents' role

The design of assessment procedures, including alternative assessment tools

Grading policies

Articulation procedures

Student participation in competitions and contests at the local, state, and national levels

The level of success of students on national examinations, such as Advanced Placement Examinations and achievement tests

Students' use of the foreign language while participating in community activities

Anecdotal records of foreign language use in the community (newspaper clippings)

Anecdotal records of school/school district follow-up studies asking former FL students about the value of FL learning

Teachers' participation in courses, institutes, study-abroad programs, professional meetings, etc.

The use of the textbook and other instructional materials

The role of technology in the FL program

The implementation of the national FL standards

The results of research studies

An overview of the language-acquisition process

Plans for modifications to the FL program in the next five years and further into the future

Other factors of importance at the local level

Such descriptions provide an ongoing, detailed profile of the foreign language program: past, present, and future.

After Program Evaluation. . .Then What?

The whole point of program evaluation is to see how the program can be improved. After using The **FLES*** Scale for the Overall Assessment of **FLES*** Programs (see Appendix A) and working with the **FLES*** Assessment Criteria List (included in the chapter), members of the **FLES*** advisory committee can take a look at the results and pinpoint areas that need further development. If a program has been in existence for only two years, for example, the basic goals and outcomes should be clearly visible. If a program has been in operation for over five years, teachers probably need further in-service training and opportunities to attend professional meetings and institutes, among other activities.

Thus, program evaluation can reveal what is *excellent* about a **FLES*** program and what needs to be addressed, remedied, changed, or modified.

Obtaining Reactions of Parents, Principals and Administrators, Classroom Teachers, Foreign Language Teachers, and Volunteers

Probably the two most effective ways to discover the reactions of the above-mentioned persons would be through the use of questionnaires and person-to-person interviews. These should be geared to local goals.

Some of the questions that might be asked are:

1. What is your opinion, in general, of the program?
2. Do you think the children have made progress in their use of the foreign language?
3. Do you think they enjoy learning a foreign language?
4. Have you heard references to the foreign language outside of the foreign language class?
5. Are the children interested in continuing their study of a foreign language?
6. How would you rate the effectiveness of the teacher of the foreign language(s)?
7. Is sufficient time in the school day being devoted to the study of a foreign language? Too much?
8. What is your opinion of the materials used in the foreign language program?
9. Does there seem to be a relationship between the study of a foreign language and other subjects in the elementary school curriculum?
10. What is the basis of your information about the foreign language program (observation, discussion with child and/or children, etc.)?
11. What changes would you recommend for the foreign language program?
12. Is there a smooth transition from this program to the middle/junior high school?

The following is a sample questionnaire for obtaining reactions of principals:

A Sample Questionnaire for Principals of Elementary Schools That Offer Foreign Language (Rating: 1–5, with 5 being the highest)

1. Most of the children understand the foreign language. _____
2. Most of the children speak the foreign language. _____
3. Most of the children enjoy learning a foreign language. _____
4. The instructor enjoys teaching a foreign language. _____

   Parent volunteer _____

   High-school student _____

   Elementary school teacher _____

5. The classroom teacher is interested in the foreign language lesson. _____

6. The classroom has foreign language displays. _____
7. The time devoted to the foreign language has educational value. _____
8. Most of the parents enjoy the language program. _____

   This questionnaire could be adapted for parents, classroom teachers, students, etc.

Obtaining Reactions of Students

Reactions of students studying a foreign language can be obtained by questionnaires, person-to-person interviews, and observation of classes. The methods chosen depend on the ages and grade levels of the students.
   Some of the questions that might be asked are:

1. Do you enjoy learning a foreign language?
2. Would you like to continue to study the foreign language next year?
3. Would you like to read stories in the foreign language?
4. Would you like to have a pen pal from the foreign culture?
5. Do you think you will remember what you have learned?
6. Do you use the foreign language outside of the language class?
7. Do you come across articles and pictures about the foreign culture in newspapers and magazines?
8. Do you like the materials used in the foreign language class?
9. Is the foreign language connected to anything else you study at school?
10. Would you like to visit the foreign culture someday?
11. Is enough time devoted to the foreign language class?
12. What changes would you recommend for the foreign language program?
13. Do you want to continue your study of the foreign language in middle/junior high school?
14. What do you like best about the foreign language class?
15. Do you understand why you are studying a foreign language?

Obtaining Reactions of FLES* Classroom Teachers

There are three important ways of obtaining reactions from teachers of *FLES/FLEX/Immersion*. The use of a questionnaire is helpful, but a person-to-person interview is even better. Observation of the teacher in the foreign language class is still another way to get the teacher's point of view.

Some of the questions that might be asked are:

1. What is your opinion, in general, of the program?
2. Do you think the children have made progress in their use of the foreign language?
3. Do you think they enjoy learning a foreign language?
4. Do you enjoy teaching a foreign language to children?
5. Are the children interested in continuing their study of a foreign language?
6. Have the children complained about any aspect of their study of a foreign language?
7. Do the children bring in articles, objects, and pictures related to the foreign culture on their own?
8. Is sufficient time in the school day being devoted to the study of a foreign language? Too much?
9. What is your opinion of the materials used in the foreign language program?
10. Is there a relationship between the study of a foreign language and other subjects in the elementary school curriculum?
11. What happens to these children when they reach the middle/junior high school?
12. What changes would you recommend for the foreign language program?

ASSESSMENT OF STUDENT PROGRESS

In *Sequential FLES* and *FLEX* programs, the evaluation (both formal and informal) of student progress in all four abilities (listening, speaking, reading, writing) and culture should be ongoing. There should be listening checks for comprehension, and there should be oral tests for the ability to answer and ask questions and to respond in real-life situations. Depending on the goals of the program and the age of the students, there should also be reading and writing tests. There should be checks to highlight students' grasp of cross-cultural similarities and differences. We are beginning to see some formal tests created for this level, but they are still at the developmental stage.

In *Immersion* programs, the emphasis on evaluation is often on the content of the elementary school curriculum. This author believes that additional emphasis should be placed on foreign language evaluation in all four abilities (listening, speaking, reading, writing) and culture and that this evaluation should be ongoing.

Overview of Assessment of Student Progress

- Does the youngster understand the foreign language?
- Is the youngster communicating in the foreign language?
- Does the youngster get meaning from the printed page?
- Is the youngster communicating in writing?
- Does the youngster understand differences and similarities between the cultures?
- Does the youngster make connections and comparisons?
- Is the youngster able to use the foreign language in real-life, functional situations?

For all types of programs, we need to gather data on the following important questions:

- What are the short-term and longitudinal results of studying a foreign language in elementary school and the effect on English language skills and achievement in the different subject areas?
- What are the short-term and longitudinal results of studying a foreign language in elementary school and the formal achievement in the foreign language in all four abilities and culture?

Suggestions for the Assessment of Student Progress in the FL

Most assessment procedures for students involve locally prepared materials. There is a strong need for teachers to become familiar with the progress indicators identified in *Standards for Foreign Language Learning* and to develop appropriate assessment procedures at the local level.

First, here are some selected terms that will be helpful in the discussion of assessment.

Definitions of Selected Assessment Terms

ALTERNATIVE ASSESSMENT: other ways to assess what students know and can do in the foreign language

AUTHENTIC ASSESSMENT: assessment that is based on real-life experiences

CONTEXT IN ASSESSMENT: assessment that gives a context or setting for assessment, rather than assessment in isolation (contextualized assessment)

CULTURAL COMPETENCE ASSESSMENT: assessment of students' acquisition of cultural competence with respect to progress indicators

DISCRETE POINT TESTS: testing specific aspects of the language system in isolation

HOLISTIC SCORING: overall, or global, scoring

LEARNING SCENARIOS: situations described in *Standards for Foreign Language Learning* that help teachers during the transition to standards-based instruction

PERFORMANCE ASSESSMENT: the overall term for the various forms of assessment of student performance in the foreign language, based on practical and real-life experience, with respect to progress indicators for grades 4, 8, and 12

PORTFOLIO ASSESSMENT: evaluation based on the collection of a variety of examples of the student's work in the foreign language

PROGRESS INDICATORS: demonstrators of student progress in terms of the national FL standards at grades 4, 8, and 12 (but they are not standards themselves)

RUBRIC: a scoring guide that defines criteria for scoring

SELF-ASSESSMENT: giving students opportunities to assess their own progress in the use of the foreign language in accordance with guidelines or a rubric of some kind

For additional evaluation and assessment terms, see the *Standards for Foreign Language Learning* (National Standards in Foreign Language Education Project 1996).

Assessment in Context: Performance Assessment

If we consider the implications of the national FL standards for curriculum, for methodology, and for orientation, then we must consider the impact they have on assessment. *Standards for Foreign Language Learning* indicates that there needs to be a new focus on the teaching of foreign languages and that "knowledge of the linguistic system, its grammar, emerging vocabulary, phonology, pragmatic and discourse features undergirds the accuracy of communication" (38). It also says in this connection that "these elements are still important in the foreign language classroom, but the focus has shifted to knowing them in terms of the meanings they convey" (29).

Assessment of student progress now needs to be determined in terms of the five C goal areas of communication, cultures, connections, comparisons, and communities. It is the determination of "what students should know and be able to do, in grades four, eight, and twelve" (National Standards in Foreign Language Education Project 1996 , 13).

It also is a means of determining how well the students can perform in the foreign language according to the progress indicators for each of the aforementioned grades.

The new focus, then, is that curriculum is written for teaching in context, that teachers teach in context, and that student achievement is assessed in context. Contextualized assessment is distinct from discrete point testing. In discrete point testing (usually in quizzes), specific forms of the language system are tested in isolation. Contextualized performance assessment deals with the broad abilities of students to perform in the foreign language in real-life situations and experiences. Obviously, the discrete points of a language system have to be taught and assessed, but the reason for teaching them pursues a goal well beyond the mastery of vocabulary and verb endings.

Assessment of student progress is closely aligned with objectives, curriculum, methodology, and the five C's of the national FL standards. In other words, you test what you teach, and you test in the way you have taught! The progress indicators help to gauge how well students are achieving the five C goal areas of communication, cultures, connections, comparisons, and communities.

Sample Progress Indicators of the National FL Standards

As we saw in Chapter Eight, the "sample progress indicators for grades four, eight, and twelve define student progress in meeting the standards, but are not themselves standards. They are neither prescriptive nor exhaustive…they are measurable and assessable in numerous ways and are designed for use by states and individual districts to establish acceptable performance levels for their students" (National Standards in Foreign Language Education Project 1996, 23–24). In addition, the language-specific organizations are writing their own sample progress indicators that apply to the different languages.

It is important for **FLES*** teachers to become cognizant of the sample progress indicators and to recognize all aspects of the five C goal areas that contribute to their students' progress toward the standards. Let's analyze one of these:

> **STANDARD 1.1** Students engage in conversations, provide and obtain information, express feelings and emotions, and exchange opinions.

Sample Progress Indicators, Grade 4

- Students give and follow simple instructions in order to participate in age-appropriate classroom and/or cultural activities.
- Students ask and answer questions about topics such as family, school events, and celebrations in person or via letters, e-mail, audio, or video tapes.

- Students share likes and dislikes with each other and the class.

- Students exchange descriptions of people and tangible products of the culture, such as toys, dress, types of dwellings, and foods with each other and members of the class.

- Students exchange essential information such as greetings, leave-takings, and common classroom interactions using culturally appropriate gestures and oral expressions.

Several observations about these sample progress indicators may provide some insight into the philosophy behind the indicators and their implementation:

1. The sample progress indicators cover many aspects of the curriculum content of any form of **FLES*** program (*FLES, FLEX,* and *Immersion*).

2. The indicators suggest age-appropriate, real-life activities that children enjoy.

3. A great many contact hours in a continuum of learning are needed before children are able to perform the activities in the foreign language.

4. While the sample progress indicators are very broad in design, very specific elements need to be taught to enable students to perform the activities with fluency and accuracy. Knowledge of such things as questions and answers, vocabulary, structure, idiomatic expressions, grammar, and culture are required for children to be able to express themselves in the suggested real-life situations.

5. The sample progress indicators are not designed to be solely the basis for written tests. Rather, they are designed for children to demonstrate that they can use the foreign language in the specified types of situations and, in addition, to demonstrate how well they can use the foreign language.

6. Obviously, if we analyze the sample progress indicators for grades 8 and 12, we can see a progression of skills and abilities that demonstrate growth and maturity in the use of the foreign language and culture.

Probably the key to **FLES*** teachers' understanding and implementation of the sample progress indicators is for them to reflect on their planning and ask themselves: "For what purpose(s) am I teaching this particular topic to the students? How will they use this particular activity in real-life situations? How well will they be able to use the foreign language and how will I determine this?" (For more information about reflection techniques, see Chapter Ten and Appendix B.)

Aspects of Performance Assessment

The five major aspects of performance assessment are (1) authentic assessment, (2) alternative assessment, (3) portfolio assessment, (4) self-assessment, and (5) cultural competence assessment.

Authentic Assessment

Authentic assessment is the assessment of student performance in practical, real-life situations. Some examples of authentic assessment are:

- Present a conversation based on a theme
- Respond to questions based on different themes/situations
- Express preferences
- Ask questions about different themes/situations
- Describe familiar objects and persons
- Tell about an experience
- Describe a meal plan for one meal, for the whole day
- Design a menu
- Record a message
- Write a letter, a fax, a poem about…
- Tell how to do something
- Make announcements on the public address system
- Enter an e-mail message
- Create questions for a quiz
- Prepare questions for a guest speaker
- Tell a folktale
- Plan a travel itinerary (with maps)
- Write a dictation based on a theme
- Record ads for radio or TV
- Plan, in groups, for a party
- Go shopping in the classroom, in a simulated store, with a different department in each corner
- Sing authentic songs
- Create a personal family tree
- Create the family tree of a famous person
- Create directions for a treasure hunt
- Create greeting cards for special occasions
- Create and perform a cultural/historical skit
- Create a theme calendar (weather, sports, art, music, etc.)

Example of Criteria for Scoring

The following rubric can use a variety of criteria and may be adapted for all kinds of activities used in authentic assessment and alternative assessment:

	1	2	3	4
Communication	Very little; inappropriate	Fair; many errors	Good; few errors	Excellent; accurate for the most part
Pronunciation	Poor	Major problems	A few problems; no interference with communication	Very good
			Global Score	

Scoring may involve various components of the rubric as well as a global score.

Alternative Assessment

Alternative assessment gives teachers and students opportunities to assess student progress in a number of different ways, such as:

- Creating a story or poem
- Creating a foreign language game
- Researching a specific topic (an information gap)
- Making a presentation on a specific topic
- Creating a poster on a specific theme
- Collecting recipes from the foreign-language-speaking country or countries
- Preparing food representing the culture(s)
- Dialogue journals
- Role-plays
- Interviews
- Special projects for individuals or small groups
- Filling out forms

- Giving instructions, descriptions, or explanations
- Expressing personal attitudes, opinions, etc.
- Portfolio assessment

Criteria for Scoring

The rubric listed under "Authentic Assessment" may be used here, or a simpler one, such as the following, may be substituted:

0   Task not completed

1   Very little accomplished

2   Some parts accomplished

3   Fair amount accomplished

4   Good accomplishment

5   Excellent accomplishment

Portfolio Assessment

A portfolio is a collection of items that demonstrate what a student has been doing in the course of studying a foreign language. What goes into a student's portfolio may vary, but here is a list of ideas and products from which the teacher and students may choose:

ORAL ELEMENTS

- Recordings of presentations, storytelling, descriptions, how to do something, etc.
- Role-plays
- Poetry presentations
- Choral presentations
- Dances and songs
- Videos
- Written elements
- Journals, reports, poems, stories
- Cartoons
- Letters
- Surveys

PROJECTS

- Murals (pictures)
- Photographs

- Mobiles
- Greeting cards
- Posters
- Computer programs
- Student's reflections about items in his or her portfolio

Criteria for Assessing Portfolios

Select from the following list those criteria that are most appropriate to the individual situation:

- Range of experiences
- Variety
- Organization
- Significance
- Process used for selection
- Attractiveness
- Evidence of progress in the foreign language and culture
- Student's reflections

Self-Assessment

In self-assessment, students create their own records of their performance in whole-class, group, paired, and individual activities. For students to be successful at self-assessment, they need prior training by the teacher in the need for self-assessment, the opportunity it provides for taking responsibility for learning, and the ways in which both the student and the teacher will learn about the student's progress. On the following page is an example of a rubric for self-assessment:

How Am I Doing?

	Monday	Tuesday	Wednesday	Thursday	Friday
Did I volunteer?					
Did I ask a question?					
Did I follow directions?					
Did I answer a question?					
Did others understand me?					
Did my partner or teacher praise my work?					
Did I try my best?					
Did I use recombinations?					
Did I vary my responses?					
Did I express a preference?					
Did I contribute to the group?					
Did I do follow-up activities?					

Criteria for Scoring

Students will be asked to keep a journal or a portfolio to document some of the ratings that they include in the rubric. Teachers may then score the self-assessment scale and the accompanying documentation in accordance with some of the sample scoring suggestions mentioned previously.

Cultural Competence Assessment

There are few sources of assessment instruments and indicators of cultural competence. A major breakthrough is the reference manual developed for French by the Cultural Competence Commission of the American Association of Teachers of French (Singerman 1996).

In Chapter IV of this source, indicators are listed for the K–4 level and the K–8 level in the following categories: communication in cultural context, social patterns and conventions, social institutions, geography and the environment, history, literature and the arts. It also lists a second section of indicators for those K–8 programs that are "accelerated."

Teachers and administrators will find the reference manual a helpful source of ways to adapt materials to other languages and to make modifications in French for the needs and requirements of the French program.

Sources of Tests and Assessment Instruments

The best listing of sources of tests and assessment instruments appears in *K–8 Foreign Language Assessment: A Bibliography,* published by the ERIC Clearinghouse (1995). This compilation of assessment instruments and materials makes no attempt to evaluate the materials it lists, but it is helpful for those seeking models for assessment development on the local level.

Assessing the Productive Abilities (Speaking and Writing)

Speaking Ability: Can the Youngster Communicate in the FL?

A number of suggestions are listed below for assisting in the creation of quizzes at the local level, based on local goals, that test students' speaking ability:

- Answering direct questions, such as "How are you?"
- Asking students to ask someone something, such as "Ask Jack how old he is."
- Asking students to describe what they see in a picture
- Asking two students to perform an impromptu situation
- Showing students two types of food and asking them which one they would choose
- Asking students to take the part of the teacher for a class activity
- For more advanced students, showing a series of three pictures to be used in telling a story:

- Asking one student to perform a TPR activity and asking a second student to describe in the foreign language what the first student was doing

Determining how to rate items on a speaking test can sometimes be a problem. First, a decision must be made about which aspects of the responses are to be rated. For example, a rubric might have the following categories: appropriateness of response, pronunciation, fluency, accuracy, and comprehensibility of response. Each category would receive 1 point, for a maximum of 5 points on a global rating scale. Local areas may wish to list their own criteria for the grading of speaking proficiency.

Writing Ability: Can the Youngster Communicate in Writing in the FL?

A number of suggestions are listed below for assisting in the creation of quizzes at the local level, based on local goals, that test students' writing ability:

- Writing captions for pictures
- Taking a short dictation (or spot dictation)
- Writing answers to oral questions
- Writing answers or rejoinders to written questions or statements
- Rewriting a sentence (e.g., in the negative form) or beginning the sentence with "On July 4, _____."
- Rewriting a false statement (e.g., "Today it is snowing.")
- Writing a letter to a friend (guided composition), telling him or her about your school, your teacher, etc.
- Writing a letter to a friend (not guided)
- Writing a poem
- Writing a short composition based on a picture, a folk song, sounds in the street, etc.
- Writing an invitation to a party
- Completing sentences (e.g., "Because the weather is bad, we will not go fishing. We will _____.")

The rating of writing is quite similar to the rating of speaking. A decision must be made about which aspects of the responses are to be rated. For example, a rubric might have the following categories: appropriateness of response, fluency, accuracy, and comprehensibility. Each category would receive 1 point, for a maximum of 4 points on a global rating scale. Local areas may wish to list their own criteria for the grading of writing ability. Many school systems are using a global, or holistic, approach to grading writing ability in English. This can easily be adapted to grading written work in the foreign language.

Assessing the Receptive Abilities (Listening and Reading)

Listening Comprehension: Does the Youngster Understand the FL?

A number of suggestions are listed below for assisting in the creation of quizzes at the local level, based on local goals, that assess students' listening comprehension ability:

- The teacher may use TPR commands to see if students understand and perform the action(s).

- The teacher may use double or even triple TPR commands

- The teacher shows students two or more objects and asks them to circle the word the teacher says aloud. In the sample below, the teacher will say "the flag." Students will circle the picture that matches the utterance.

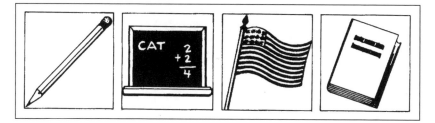

Sometimes the teacher may wish to prerecord the cues and play the tape during class. Instead of giving students drawings, the teacher may name an object and ask the children to draw it. (Students with artistic talents will not have an advantage on such a test because they will do well only if they understand what has been said in the FL.)

- An alternative to this type of test involves flash cards. Students are given answer sheets that say, for example, 1. a b c d. When the teacher holds up a series of flash cards and says the name of the object to be matched in the foreign language, students circle the appropriate letter on their answer sheets. For example, the teacher says "the chair" and then holds up each of the following pictures in turn:

- In another variation, students are given pictures about which the teacher makes true-false statements. For example, for the picture below, the teacher says, "There are three fish swimming in the lake." Students write "yes" or "no" on their papers:

In the upper grades (5 and 6), students could be required to correct the statement when they have written "no." This would then make it a combined listening comprehension and writing test item.

- Students listen to a short paragraph, then are asked a question, then hear a repetition of the short paragraph and the question. Students are given three or four possible answers on their answer sheet. They read all the possible answers and circle the one that seems best. For example:

    Teacher reads (in the FL): Mary is sick. She has a headache. She is going to her aunt's house with her father. Her aunt is a doctor. Her uncle is not home.

    Teacher asks: Who is a doctor?

The student reads on the answer sheet and circles one answer:

a. Mary's father is a doctor.

b. Mary is a doctor.

c. Mary's uncle is a doctor.

d. Mary's aunt is a doctor.

This, too, is not purely listening comprehension, because it combines listening comprehension and reading.

Reading Comprehension: Does the Youngster Get Meaning from the Printed Page?

A number of suggestions are listed below for assisting in the creating of quizzes at the local level, based on local goals, that test students' reading comprehension ability:

- Match pictures with words
- Match words with descriptions of the words
- Make columns of related words from a list of words
- Complete sentences or thoughts by choosing from three or four possibilities. For example:

    The weather is bad. _____

    a. The sun is shining.

    b. It is raining.

    c. The sky is blue.

- Read a short paragraph. Then answer a question by selecting from three or four choices. For example:

    Bob has three pets. He has a black cat, a green parrot, and a gold-fish. The parrot is singing. The cat is playing with a ball. The gold-fish, Carl, is swimming.

    What is the cat doing?

    a. It is singing.

    b. It is swimming.

    c. It is playing.

    d. Its name is Carl.

- Solve a riddle by choosing from several possible answers. For example:
  It is big. It is green and brown. It is not alive. What is it?
  a. A house
  b. A tree
  c. A chair
  d. A door

Informal Evaluation of Student Progress

The following was written by a sixth-grade girl after two months of studying Spanish:

YO AMOR ESPANOL Y USTED.

SOY NORTEAMERICANO.

AMOR,

MARÍA

How would you react to this note written by María? Does it convey meaning? Does it have errors that must be corrected immediately? Does it demonstrate that the student enjoys studying Spanish?

The matter of standards can often be controversial. Many teachers would regard the note above as very poor Spanish and would not encourage students to engage in writing until they were able to use the language correctly. On the other hand, some teachers feel that any attempt by students to *communicate* should be commended and encouraged, as long as the students understand that they must strive to learn how to express themselves correctly (both orally and in writing) so that their message will be understood.

As an early attempt at communicating in the foreign language, the message above seems to be clear. However, students must learn that they cannot remain at this primitive level. They must be motivated to reach a more standard level of communication (both orally and in writing). The mere fact that a student wanted to use the foreign language to express herself and her ideas speaks very well for her teacher's having motivated her to understand the *power* of the foreign language in communication.

Different Types of In-Class Evaluation Activities

1. Identify and label vocabulary.
2. Make a list of _____.
3. Role-play a skit.
4. Create a greeting card for _____.

5. Understand and respond to questions about _____.
6. Express preferences about _____.
7. Ask and answer questions about _____.
8. Describe familiar objects and persons.
9. Follow directions.
10. Match words and pictures.
11. Participate in language games.
12. Answer questions based on oral, picture, and written cues.
13. Complete sentences (oral and written).
14. Write a Cloze dictation; write a dictation.
15. Make a shopping list.
16. Write a meal plan for a day.
17. Participate in a treasure hunt for _____ in school, on the Internet, etc.
18. Make and label maps.
19. Make theme posters.
20. Record a message on an answering machine.
21. Write a letter to _____ about _____.
22. Tell how to do something (e.g., cook, sew, repair).
23. Make collages about _____.
24. Record ads for radio and TV.
25. Make announcements on the school public address system.
26. Create questions for a quiz or test.
27. Draw and label a cartoon about _____.
28. Take a written or oral quiz.
29. Create a written or oral test.
30. Play a Concentration game (or other games).
31. Plan, in groups, different aspects of a class celebration.
32. Prepare questions for a guest speaker.
33. Make a weather calendar.
34. Participate in a class store.
35. Sing authentic songs.
36. Draw a flag for a specific country.
37. Tell a folktale.
38. Create an ad for the school newspaper about foreign language study.
39. Plan a travel itinerary.

40. Design a menu.
41. Create the family tree of a famous family.

NOTE: **FLES*** classroom activities can often be modified into effective assessment activities.

After Student Progress Assessment...Then What?

The thrust of student progress evaluation is to match outcomes or accomplishments to the goals of the program. If, as a goal, it was stated that after one year students would be able to discuss the weather, using all four abilities and cultural components, the evaluation of student progress should demonstrate that students are indeed capable of performing this way in the foreign language. If they cannot demonstrate this, reteaching should occur. But teachers should ask themselves the following questions:

- Are the goals realistic?
- Is the class time sufficient to accomplish the goals?
- Do members of the class have some learning disabilities that require a different teaching approach?
- Have students responded in class?
- Have students done well on quizzes (both oral and written) in class? What are the students' major difficulties?
- Have students worked in small groups and pairs for practice and review?
- What different types of approaches should not be used to reteach the material?
- Have I discussed this with the students? Do they have any suggestions to offer for getting greater mastery of the context?
- Have we included activities from the five C goal areas of communication, cultures, connections, comparisons, and communities?
- Are we working toward reaching the levels of the progress indicators for grades 4 and 8?

⚲ FOR REFLECTION

It is time for evaluation of foreign language programs and students in order to point us in the right direction for the future . . .

Margaret Keefe Singer (1992, 10)

PR For **FLES**—
How to Get Publicity for Your Program

Effective Public Relations

Effective public relations can really help all kinds of **FLES*** programs by providing opportunities to explain the program, to publicize the goals and activities, and to demonstrate what the children have accomplished.

It pays to advertise. When you have a good product, it is important to let people know about it. Whether it is called **PR**, public relations, public awareness, or publicity, everyone concerned with the program needs to be involved in publicity, lest the program die a slow death because of nonexistence in the eyes of the public.

Who is this public? The public consists of the people in the community, in the school: students, teachers, principals and administrators, parents, guidance counselors, health personnel, food and janitorial staff, taxpayers of all kinds, and more.

There are some people who think that you do not publicize until the program has been running successfully for several years. This author does not agree with that philosophy. If the program has been very carefully planned, with input from many, many people, then the publicity will invite additional input from, perhaps, untouched sources, and that can only be a positive affirmation for the program.

There are others who feel that "hype" for a program, to use the vernacular, for developing public awareness, is not a professional activity, is unworthy of educational goals. This point of view is not valid in today's world of accountability and taxpayers' sense of economy. Obviously, programs that go unnoticed and unpublicized do not capture the attention of policymakers. The first and foremost premise is that the program *has* to be educationally sound and effective in terms of what the students are accomplishing. But a sound and effective program need not go unnoticed and unpublicized. As a matter of fact, having students demonstrate their achievements in the foreign language will help the program. It will also communicate to the students that they are, indeed, making great strides in their study of the foreign language.

Effective PR can really help *FLES/FLEX/Immersion* programs by giving opportunities to explain the program, publicize the goals and activities, and demonstrate what the children have accomplished. PR sells everything we come in contact with, so why not use it to help sell a *good* program?

Who is your public? These are some of the people who need to know about your program:

Students in the school and feeder schools	Former students
Parents	Scouts
Grandparents	Fraternal organizations
Members of the community	International organizations
Faculty of universities	Travel agencies
Teachers of other disciplines	Administrators
Taxpayer groups	Members of the school board
Business organizations	Guidance counselors
Senior citizens' groups	Other personnel in the schools
Educational associations	Local elected and appointed officials
Veterans' groups	Many others

Communicating with Parents

All of the following are good ways to communicate with parents about the program:

- Letters
- Brochures
- Events in school
- Conferences
- PTA meetings
- Open school week sessions, held periodically
- Awards to and achievements of students
- Awards to and achievements of teachers
- Comments by the FL advisory committee, which should include parents, teachers, students, university people, local businesspeople, etc.

The following are effective ways to communicate about individual students:

- Letters, telephone, fax, e-mail, etc.
- Samples of student work, tests in student portfolios
- Periodic anecdotal comments showing strengths as well as weaknesses
- Expressing student needs, such as tutorials, more study, more attention to details, homework, etc.
- Holding conferences with a focus on problem-solving
- Opportunities to find out more about individual students and their interests
- Enlisting parents' assistance with students and with the program

SUCCESSFUL PUBLIC AWARENESS

Getting Publicity for FLES* Programs

One of the most important aspects of public relations for **FLES*** is to know how to reach the media, be it radio, TV, newspapers, or whatever. Something as basic as writing a clear, legible, appealing press release is invaluable in helping to inform the public. The "WHO, WHAT, WHEN, WHERE, WHY, and HOW" approach tells it all!

Another important aspect of public relations that applies to **FLES*** (and to all other areas of the school program as well) deals with honesty about the program. It is appropriate to say, "I don't know about the problem you are discussing, but I will look into it and get back to you." Sometimes a "clearing-the-air" conference is necessary when complaints come from several parents and/or sources. The teacher and the administrator who understand all aspects of the program thus will be highly successful in responding to the public.

Consider these essential components of a successful public awareness program for *FLES, FLEX,* and *Immersion:*

- Organize a publicity committee (perhaps a subcommittee of the original advisory committee). Be sure to include the principal!
- Discuss these major questions:
  1. What is our objective?
  2. Who is our public (our audience)?
  3. What is our product? What is the specific event?
- Plan a long-range program that will be continuous and ongoing.
- Divide your audience into two segments: in the school and the school community, and beyond the school and the school community.
- Designate someone as the contact person.

A PR planning grid can be of assistance in planning a year-long sequential PR program.

PR Planning Grid

Steps	Date	Staff	Other Students	Parents	Guidance Counselors	County People	Other Educators	Press/ Media	Bd. of Ed. Members	Others
1										
2										
3										
4										
5										
6										

1. What is being done?
2. How effective are we?
3. What would we like the response to be?
4. What can we do to improve and change the response?

- Establish personal contacts with the media.
- Plan for publicity before, during, and after an event.
- Be scrupulously accurate with names, dates, places, etc.
- Show appreciation when you get publicity.
- Plan to take black-and-white glossy pictures that can be submitted after an event (be sure to get everyone's name). Show children in action!
- Write succinct press releases, one page if possible.
- Try to get specific information about deadlines and be sure to meet them.
- Give credit where it is due.
- Stick to the facts!
- Have everything and everyone ready when reporters and photographers come to the school.
- Don't be disappointed if you're turned down. Perhaps reporters will be able to come next time.

Stories that may be of interest to the media include:

- The follow-up success story of a student who started foreign language at the elementary school and is now in junior or senior high school
- Students who have done unusually well
- Students who have used foreign language to perform a community service
- New and interesting methods of instruction
- A project being carried out in an unusual fashion
- A resource person from the community or from the embassy making a presentation to a class
- The success story of a teacher
- Professional honors, awards, or grants earned by a student, teacher, or supervisor of foreign languages
- The unusual travel experience of a teacher or supervisor
- Reactions of students to a new program
- International students visiting the area
- Other local events

Getting Publicity for Special Events

Creating a Press Release

The basics of a press release for a special event are:

- What is happening (specifically)?
- What is the background (brief)?
- When is it happening?
- Who is involved? Who is sponsoring it?
- Who is invited to come?
- Is there a fee?
- Who is the contact person? Phone number?

Press releases, including a schedule of activities, should be sent to the education editor of local newspapers at least two weeks before a school event. A follow-up telephone call should be made three to four days in advance, giving further details and discussing the best time of day for action photographs. After the event, be sure to thank the newspaper office for their assistance, whether you have received extensive publicity or a three-line notice in the newspaper. Next time, maybe you will get better results!

Sample Press Release

ANNOUNCING
A FOREIGN LANGUAGE FESTIVAL

Saturday, March 31
at the
Belton Woods Elementary School

FOREIGN LANGUAGE FUN FOR
CHILDREN AND ADULTS!

11:00 A.M.–4:00 P.M.

There will be multicultural displays, minilessons in foreign languages, ethnic food booths, displays of student work and activities, skits, dances, and games.

You do not have to know a foreign language to attend and enjoy the festivities. The public is invited, and admission is free. For further information, call

Contact person _____

Telephone number _____

Best time to call _____

Suggestions for Celebrating National FLES* Day

1. Research your target audience: students, parents, other teachers, administrators, guidance counselors, secondary and college people, community and business people, etc.
2. Distribute a description of your program (aims, activities, student outcomes, etc.).
3. Plan events that demonstrate your students' achievements in the FL: skits, songs, conversations, etc.

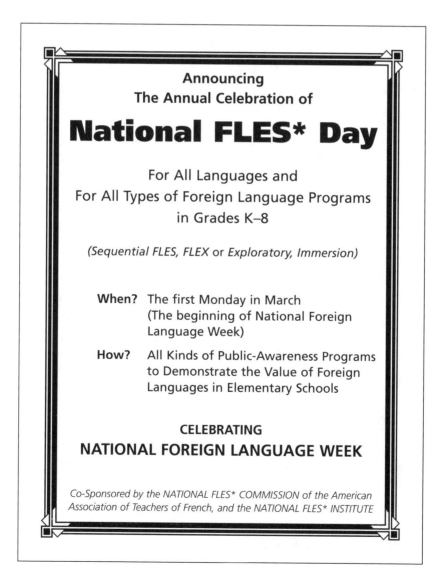

4. Plan an activity during which your students teach the FL to school visitors (a short poem, dialogue, joke, etc.).

5. Display students' work (posters, cultural pictures and drawings, videos, historical and geographical charts, maps, etc.).

6. Invite parents and grandparents for a special visitors' day.

7. Have students bring in different types of cultural cuisine for tasting by students, other teachers, administrators, etc.

8. Plan short skits in the FL for an assembly program or a meeting of parents, administrators, community groups, or educational and business leaders.

9. Exchange letters, e-mail, or faxes with other **FLES*** students and teachers.

10. Invite speakers of the FL into your classroom to show pictures and tell about their experiences as children in the foreign culture, speaking about family life, school, entertainment, etc.

11. Have an international festival in the school for the members of the community.

12. Have **FLES*** students teach miniconversations in the FL at libraries, Chamber of Commerce meetings, Board of Education meetings, department stores, etc.

13. Keep a **FLES*** visitors' book in which guests are asked to write comments

14. Present any activity that helps show the importance of the **FLES*** experience for young children.

Getting Publicity in School and in the School Community

There are a number of ways in which *Sequential FLES/FLEX/Immersion* teachers and students can make the foreign language program more visible. The very nature of the study of foreign languages is to use a language the other school and community members may not know. This connotes a certain exclusivity and aloofness from others. If the public is to become aware of the achievements of students involved in the study of a foreign language (be it *Sequential FLES, FLEX,* or *Immersion*), a number of procedures might be tried in order to bring foreign language into the basic curriculum for the elementary school. NOTE: Many of these suggestions may be used to celebrate National **FLES*** Day.

• As a homework assignment, have foreign language students teach non-foreign language students some basic greetings and phrases.

• Have cultural displays on bulletin boards and showcases.

• Prepare an assembly program on the language and culture, such as: Songs and dances

Skits showing how students learn the foreign language

Travel scenes in a foreign country

Skits at airports and train terminals

Humorous skits about lost baggage, lost passengers, etc.

Programs for special holidays, such as Pan American Day or July 14 (Bastille Day), held during the school year

Skits about famous people from the foreign culture, such as Louis Pasteur, Mozart, or Columbus

Challenges for the audience, such as riddles in the FL and/or charades

Skits showing famous historical and other important events as seen by the people in the foreign country, such as the landing on the moon, the election of a new president, or the baseball World Series

Minimusicals or operas presented by the FL class

Skits or puppet shows about fairy tales or children's stories

A special program about careers using foreign languages (children are interested even in elementary school)

- Designate a day to wear something from the foreign culture (hats, banners, iron-ons, etc.).
- Make a bilingual announcement over the loudspeaker. (This is a wonderful occasion for more advanced FL students to use their knowledge functionally.)
- Hold a foreign language spelling bee.
- Write letters to students in other language classes in the school (and to other classes in the school district).
- Have students contribute to a foreign language magazine or newspaper (and contribute articles to the school paper).
- Hold a poster contest in the school for FL and non-FL students.
- Make birthday cards and seasonal cards with foreign language poems and captions.
- Label different parts of the school building in the foreign language(s).
- Have a monthly bulletin board display.
- On special occasions, have the school menu devoted to the foreign culture or cultures (with printed menus).
- Teach folk dances from the culture to all students.
- Organize a mini-Olympics Day for the school with team names in the foreign language.
- Show travel films of the foreign culture.

Themes for French Bulletin Boards and Displays

It is very important to display the posters and projects of the French classes in the school corridors, on bulletin boards, and in display cases. The entire school community becomes aware of the French "joie de vivre" and the activities of the FL students. Contact your local library and request display space in either the library or the library window. The local city hall or shops or banks may also be available for displays at various times of the year. The following are themes that you might find successful:

Shake Hands with the World: Learn Another Language!
Let's Have a Frenchship!
Make Friends with French! (I used the theme of French fairy
    tales such as "Beauty and the Beast" and "Cinderella.")
Ring in the Year with French! (Use the idea of Quasimodo,
    Esmerelda, and the Gargoyles.)
Peace the World Together and Learn a Second Language!
If You Want to Mingle, Be Bilingual!
Kidding Around Paris!
Have Fun with French!
Don't Be Miserable, Speak French! (Use the theme of Les
    Miserables.)
Let's Make an Impression (bulletin board of Impressionist
    paintings designed by the students)
French Is the Language of Love (Valentine's Day theme)
Get Ahead of the Class! Speak French!

Reprinted with permission. Harriet Saxon, Rutherford, NJ.

- Describe a "mystery teacher" in the foreign language. Other students are to guess who it is.
- Send letters and newsletters home frequently about the program.
- Ask for feedback through questionnaires and at meetings.
- Have the principal develop a written proclamation that could be read over the loudspeaker on the occasion of Foreign Language Day or National Foreign Language Week.
- Have a bumper sticker contest about studying foreign languages, such as "Smile if You Speak a Foreign Language."
- Invite foreign language speakers to classes and to the school.
- Create banners (with the help of computers).

- Have a trivia contest about people and places in the FL culture.
- Hold an ID contest of famous people.
- Have a scavenger hunt (instructions in the FL).
- Distribute stickers, buttons, or bookmarks.
- Write foreign language slogans or proverbs on posters and bulletin boards.
- Have a display of books and magazines from the foreign culture in the classroom, the library, and the media center.
- Have students design and wear buttons and tee-shirts displaying brief expressions in the foreign language or about foreign languages, such as:

I FLIP FOR **FLES***

FRENCH IS FANTASTIQUE

SÍ FOR SPANISH

GÜTEN TAG IS TERRIFIC

- Develop an immersion day for foreign language students (perhaps over a weekend)—a camping trip, for example, at an outdoor recreation facility or park.
- Invite speakers from foreign embassies.
- Have local businesspeople visit the school to discuss job opportunities for students who speak a foreign language.
- Show the country of origin (on a large map of the world) of the school's teachers and administrators, perhaps going back several generations.
- Invite faculty members from a local college or university to speak at an assembly.
- Invite personnel from a local hospital or Red Cross unit to discuss their need to know a foreign language.
- Develop and distribute an attractive brochure about the program (*Sequential FLES, FLEX,* or *Immersion*) that gives information about the following:

Rationale for the program

Students who are eligible

Objectives of the program

Scheduling

Methodology

Results on standardized tests and FL tests

Materials of instruction

Transportation (if needed)

Recognition outside the school district (e.g., contests)

Articulation procedures

Quotes from students, parents, principals, etc.

Results of contests, spelling bees

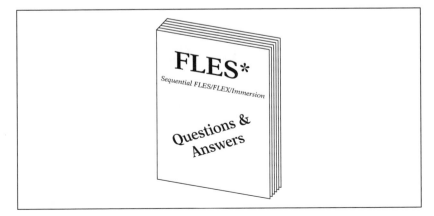

- Present awards to outstanding students and winners of various competitions (such as spelling bee, poster contest) like the samples below.

BELTON WOODS ELEMENTARY SCHOOL
FOREIGN LANGUAGE AWARD

Palma Nobilis   *Prix d'honneur*

Documento de Mérito   *Verdienst Bescheinigung*

_____
Name of student

_____

Language _____   *Teacher* _____

Date _____   Principal _____

CERTIFICATE
FOR
ITALIAN PROFICIENCY

THE FOREIGN LANGUAGE DEPARTMENT HEREBY RECOGNIZES

_____

FOR PROFICIENCY IN THE
ITALIAN LANGUAGE

ACHIEVEMENT AWARD

COORDINATOR OF FOREIGN LANGUAGE
Yonkers School District

April, 1998

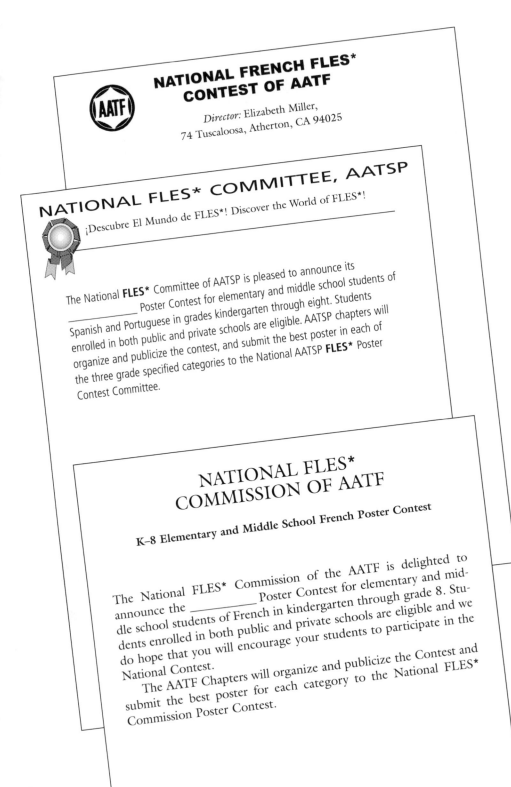

NATIONAL FRENCH FLES* CONTEST OF AATF

Director: Elizabeth Miller,
74 Tuscaloosa, Atherton, CA 94025

NATIONAL FLES* COMMITTEE, AATSP

¡Descubre El Mundo de FLES*! Discover the World of FLES*!

The National **FLES*** Committee of AATSP is pleased to announce its _____ Poster Contest for elementary and middle school students of Spanish and Portuguese in grades kindergarten through eight. Students enrolled in both public and private schools are eligible. AATSP chapters will organize and publicize the contest, and submit the best poster in each of the three grade specified categories to the National AATSP **FLES*** Poster Contest Committee.

NATIONAL FLES* COMMISSION OF AATF

K–8 Elementary and Middle School French Poster Contest

The National FLES* Commission of the AATF is delighted to announce the _____ Poster Contest for elementary and middle school students of French in kindergarten through grade 8. Students enrolled in both public and private schools are eligible and we do hope that you will encourage your students to participate in the National Contest.

The AATF Chapters will organize and publicize the Contest and submit the best poster for each category to the National FLES* Commission Poster Contest.

- Plan a balloon send-off with postcards attached, written in the foreign language. Offer prizes for the return of the postcard from the farthest location.
- Prepare articles for the PTA newsletter.
- Get air time at the local radio station to make a public announcement like the following:

  Visitors from many other lands come to this country. They bring with them their own language and culture, and they learn English. We need more Americans who can speak foreign languages, and we need to start children learning foreign languages early. Foreign languages in the elementary grades are important for the children, for the school, for the state, and for our country. Let's start foreign languages early!

- Offer mini-language lessons or songs for senior citizens' groups and other community groups.
- Organize an art exhibit with an international theme.
- Plan a piñata-making demonstration or contest.
- Hold a contest to guess the number of beans in a jar by writing the number in the foreign language.
- Organize a class trip to a restaurant that offers cuisine from the foreign culture. This requires careful planning ahead of time with the restaurant's management.
- Develop a booklet of recipes from around the world. Parents and grandparents like to help with a project of this kind.
- Plan projects with other teachers in the school on interdisciplinary aspects of the foreign culture (e.g., explorers in social studies, painters in art, composers in music).
- Develop many other activities on the local level, appropriate to the school and the school community.
- Celebrate National **FLES*** Day and National Foreign Language Week with all kinds of activities.
- Organize an essay contest or a poster contest or a computer software program contest on "Why Study Foreign Languages?"

Special Hints on Organizing a FLES Foreign Language Festival*

1. Get support from teachers, administrators, parents, and members of the community.
2. Get three to five people to assume leadership roles.
3. Tie the festival in with schoolwide competitions, such as a poster contest.
4. Make sure that you have chairpersons for the following key activities:

Publicity

Games

Decorations

Food

Cleanup

Entertainment

Printing

Buttons

Bumper stickers

Language-learning booths

Other ideas appropriate at the local level

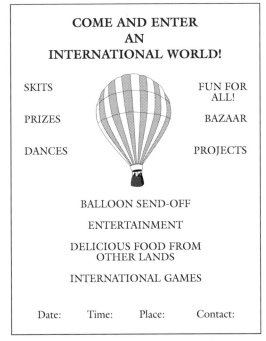

**COME AND ENTER
AN
INTERNATIONAL WORLD!**

SKITS

PRIZES

DANCES

FUN FOR ALL!

BAZAAR

PROJECTS

BALLOON SEND-OFF

ENTERTAINMENT

DELICIOUS FOOD FROM OTHER LANDS

INTERNATIONAL GAMES

Date:　　Time:　　Place:　　Contact:

Sample Flier for an International Fair

5. Two weeks before the festival, walk through the areas of the school with the key people.

6. Designate an area for coats.

7. Arrange for parking facilities.

8. Arrange for first aid, if necessary.

9. Designate an area for the festival headquarters.

10. The day before the festival, set up decorations.

11. Assign at least two people to be responsible for troubleshooting problems during the festival.

12. The day of the festival, ENJOY!

13. After the festival is over, clean up!

14. Thank everyone involved.

15. Hold a planning committee meeting to evaluate the success of the festival and to make plans and decisions about next year's festival.

This is an enormous undertaking, but it can run smoothly if each key person does his or her job with care and enthusiasm. It is important that all key people be informed of all plans and decisions, so that they do not work at cross-purposes. After a trial run at the school level, people on the planning committee may want to think in terms of a festival on a broader scale (districtwide and on all school levels). SPECIAL NOTE: If a foreign language festival is already in existence, *Sequential FLES/FLEX/Immersion* teachers, students, and parents may want to volunteer their services so that they can be included.

Promotion of FLES* Programs in Class: Some Basics

1. Give students something that happened in the FL class to talk about at the dinner table.
2. Give students a sense of accomplishment in the FL each day.
3. Appeal to students' personal interests.
4. Help students learn! Appeal to multiple intelligences.
5. From time to time, give students a homework assignment to teach some communicative aspects of the FL to another person.
6. Integrate the **FLES*** program with the rest of the school curriculum, if possible.
7. Integrate the **FLES*** program with other activities and events in the school and the community.
8. Do something memorable!
9. Find ways to bring the school community to your **FLES*** classroom.
10. Evaluate student performance frequently so youngsters (and you) will know how they are doing and that they are making significant progress.

REMEMBER: Your students are the ones who will talk about foreign languages to their friends and siblings!

Getting Publicity Beyond the School

Going beyond the school and the school community requires collaboration with foreign language teachers and others at secondary school levels. Activities for a wider audience require more elaborate planning and more enthusiastic people. Some of the activities for a districtwide public-awareness program on all school levels might include the following:

- Planning a districtwide foreign language festival that includes **FLES*** students

- Planning a districtwide camping experience during which the foreign language is used as much as possible. This type of activity can also be used as a motivational device. For example, at the University of Maryland, Baltimore County, an international language camp has been in operation for several years, with the goal of exposing nine- to eleven-year-olds to a different language and culture *each day*. Words and phrases, customs, songs, dances, and guest speakers form the language content. This "Language a Day" concept can be incorporated into camps on the local level, along with the usual swimming, outdoor games, and dramatic activities.

- Placing posters and student project displays in local stores, libraries, museums, and other public places

- Having students teach the foreign language to shoppers at a shopping mall or at a large department store or at a county education fair. Some of the dialogues that could be taught briefly at such an activity could be adapted from the samples that follow:

French

SPEAKER 1: Bonjour! Je m'appelle _____.

SPEAKER 2: Bonjour! Je m'appelle _____.

SPEAKER 1: Vous parlez très bien le français.

SPEAKER 2: Merci. Vous êtes un bon professeur.

SPEAKER 1: Merci, j'aime parler français.

SPEAKER 2: Au revoir.

SPEAKER 1: À bientôt.

German

SPEAKER 1: Tag! Ich heisse _____.

SPEAKER 2: Güten Tag! Ich heisse _____.

SPEAKER 1: Sie sprechen Deutsch sehr gut.

SPEAKER 2: Danke schön. Sie sind eine gute Lehrerin.

SPEAKER 1: Danke, ich spreche gerne Deutsch.

SPEAKER 2: Auf Wiedersehen!

SPEAKER 1: Tschüss!

Spanish

SPEAKER 1: ¡Hola! Me llamo _____.

SPEAKER 2: ¡Hola! Me llamo _____.

SPEAKER 1: Usted habla muy bien el español.

SPEAKER 2: Gracias. Usted es un buen profesor.

SPEAKER 1: Gracias. Me gusta hablar español.

SPEAKER 2: Adiós.

SPEAKER 1: Hasta luego.

- Organize a districtwide or citywide language week, such as the French language week organized in New York City several years ago. Special events, proclamations by the mayor, buttons, stickers, bumper stickers, guest speakers, events at the local universities, etc., were all geared to emphasize the foreign language programs in the schools and universities to parents, school administrators, and the general public.

- Enlarge the scope of many of the suggestions listed above under the category of the school and the school community.

- Plan with local associations of teachers of French, Spanish, German, Italian, etc., so that joint efforts can be organized.

- Obtain materials on public relations for specific languages. Many regional and state associations of foreign language teachers as well as the AATF, AATG, AATI, AATSP, etc., have written materials, slide/sound presentations, and videos.

Parent Support in the Promotion of FLES* Programs

If you have an effective, creative **FLES*** program in which children are learning and excited about the foreign language, parents will be enormously supportive.

As mentioned in Chapter Six, there are many ways in which parents may be involved in helping with the **FLES*** program. They may also be

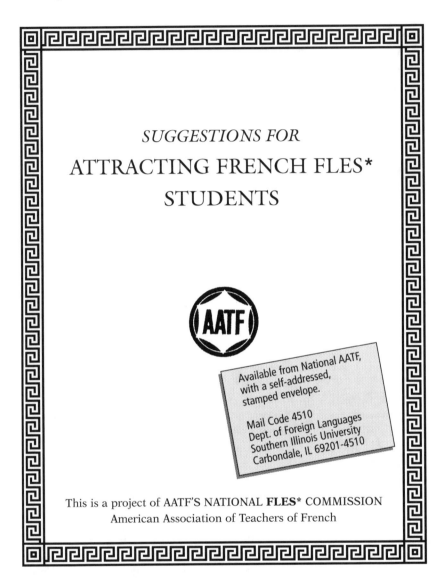

SUGGESTIONS FOR

ATTRACTING FRENCH FLES*
STUDENTS

Available from National AATF,
with a self-addressed,
stamped envelope.

Mail Code 4510
Dept. of Foreign Languages
Southern Illinois University
Carbondale, IL 69201-4510

This is a project of AATF'S NATIONAL **FLES*** COMMISSION
American Association of Teachers of French

helpful in promoting the program. They can often be counted on as communicators of satisfaction. They may write letters of support or appear at hearings to provide testimonials for **FLES***. They may be interviewed by local news people, and they may work through their local, state, and national parent organizations to issue strong statements in support of **FLES*** programs and the study of foreign languages.

For example, Georgia parent groups worked together to pass a state PTA resolution on foreign languages. Their text and procedures could serve as a model for other local and state PTAs. Contact Lynne Bryan at Macon College, Georgia, for additional information.

Georgia Congress of Parents and Teachers
114 Baker Street, NE, Atlanta, Georgia 30308

RESOLUTION

Foreign Language Programs

1) Whereas, Children have the ability to learn and excel in the pronunciation and comprehension of a foreign language; and

2) Whereas, Children who have studied a foreign language in elementary school achieve expected gains and even have higher scores on standardized tests in reading, language arts and mathematics than those who have not; and

3) Whereas, Children who have studied a foreign language show greater flexibility, creativity, divergent thinking and higher order thinking skills; and

4) Whereas, Children who have studied a foreign language develop a sense of cultural pluralism (openness to and appreciation of other cultures); and

5) Whereas, Children studying a foreign language have an improved self-concept and sense of achievement in school; and

6) Whereas, Elementary foreign language study has a favorable effect on foreign language study later on in high school and college; and

7) Whereas, The possession of foreign language skills and the ability communicate across cultures, both within the United States and abroad, enhances the employability of our citizens and their career success; and

8) Whereas, The possession of foreign language skills enhances the ability of United States citizens to do business in a global economy, and

9) Whereas, The ability to use foreign languages in the sociopolitical arena is critical in promoting a democratic way of life; now, therefore be it

Resolved, That the National PTA and its constituent bodies support the inclusion of foreign language programs in our elementary (K–5) and middle schools, and be it further

Resolved, That the National PTA and constituent bodies encourage the implementation of these foreign language programs to begin as early as possible and provide the longest possible sequence of instruction; and be it further

Resolved, That the National PTA and its constituent bodies promote articulated foreign language study from early childhood through high school, college and university levels.

Adopted by the Georgia PTA Board of Managers
April 29, 1994

THE FLES* PUBLIC RELATIONS (ADVOCACY) KIT

AATF. "Suggestions for Attracting French **FLES*** Students." Carbondale, IL: AATF, Mail Code 4510, Dept. of Foreign Languages, Southern Illinois University 62901

AATSP. 1996. "Planning Effective Spanish **FLES*** Programs." Greeley, CO: AATSP, Frasier Hall, University of North Colorado 80639.

Cribari, S. 1993. "**FLES***—It's Elementary, My Dear Watson!" *Collaborare* 8, 3 (June): 1–3.

Curtain, H., and C. Pesola. 1994. *Language and Children: Making the Match.* 2nd ed. Reading, MA: Addison-Wesley.

FLES* *Programs in Action Video* and *Study Guide.* **National FLES* Institute.** 1991. G. Lipton, project director. Baltimore, MD: National **FLES*** Institute, University of Maryland, Baltimore County 21250.

Lipton, G. 1992. *Elementary Foreign Language Programs (FLES*): An Administrator's Handbook.* Lincolnwood, IL: National Textbook Co.

———. 1996. "The Many Benefits of All Types of **FLES*** Programs." *Northeast Conference Newsletter* (Fall): 56–57.

———. 1998. *Practical Handbook to Elementary Foreign Language Programs Including FLES, FLEX, and Immersion Programs.* 3rd ed. Lincolnwood, IL: NTC/Contemporary Publishing Company.

Lipton, G., ed. 1998. *A Celebration of FLES*.* Lincolnwood, IL: NTC/Contemporary Publishing Company.

———. 1996. "Focus on **FLES***: A Position Paper." Baltimore, MD: University of Maryland, Baltimore County 21250.

———. 1997. "Advocacy for **FLES*** Packet." Baltimore, MD: National **FLES*** Institute, University of Maryland, Baltimore County 21250.

Rafferty, E. 1986. *Second Language Study and Basic Skills in Louisiana.* Baton Rouge, LA: Louisiana Department of Education.

Rehorick, S., and V. Edwards. 1992. *French Immersion: Process, Product and Perspectives.* Welland, Ontario, Canada: Canadian Modern Language Review.

"Why **FLES***?" 1994. Brochure available from AATSP, University of Northern Colorado, Greeley, CO 80639, or AATF, Mail Code 4510, Dept. of Foreign Languages, Southern Illinois University, Carbondale, IL 62901-4510.

Locally Prepared Materials

A school district foreign language information packet (FLIP) is an essential tool for presenting the FL program to the public. For a detailed description of a FLIP, see Chapter Thirteen. Other useful materials include:

- A brochure describing the local **FLES*** program, including the rationale and goals of the program

- A display of photos showing the program in action in the classroom
- Copies of the **FLES*** curriculum
- Appropriate signs and directions in the foreign language throughout the school and administrative offices
- School newsletters to parents that include news about the **FLES*** program
- A list of the members of the **FLES*** advisory committee
- Other ideas generated at the local level

The FLES*
Public Relations
Kit

Advocacy

In planning a public-awareness program, one should deal with the "who," the "what," the "when," the "where," and the "how" of advocacy. There should be short-term as well as long-range goals and strategies for implementation.

WHO IS INVOLVED IN ADVOCACY?

Almost everybody involved in the school community should be involved in a comprehensive advocacy program, including administrators, teachers, parents, supervisors, university people, civic and business leaders, and other representatives. Actually, one should consider two aspects of involvement: those who develop the advocacy program and those who are part of the target audience (or, in most cases, audiences).

EXACTLY WHAT CONSTITUTES AN ADVOCACY PROGRAM?

After making decisions about the rationale, the needs, and the goals of a **FLES*** program, another important consideration should be the development of an ongoing advocacy program. Learning about research is highly significant, since the school community is always interested in the findings of valid research as the basis for support for a program. Two "must-have" documents can be obtained from The National **FLES*** Insti-

tute (University of Maryland, Baltimore County, Baltimore, MD 21250):
the "**FLES*** Research Packet" and the "Advocacy for **FLES*** Packet."

IS ADVOCACY A ONE-TIME EFFORT?

If one views advocacy as a process of communication and feedback, it
is essential to plan an ongoing program. This means that there will be
two-way communication to and from those in charge of the **FLES*** program and to and from the various audiences in the school community.
Think of it as something that must be included before and during the
implementation of all kinds of **FLES*** programs.

IS THE SCHOOL SITE THE ONLY PLACE FOR ADVOCACY?

Obviously, the most important factor in any successful advocacy program is a successful and effective **FLES*** program! When that is evi-
dent, advocacy for it can take place almost anywhere: at PTA meetings,
at soccer games, at FL song festivals, in chat rooms and discussion lists,
on radio, TV, etc. Those who are in charge of the advocacy program
should be prepared to spring into action, promotional materials in
hand, almost anywhere, anyplace, and anytime!

HOW DOES ADVOCACY WORK?

There is no limit to the creative techniques enthusiastic people can use
to make an advocacy program successful. Here are a few examples, in
addition to the others found in this chapter:

- Attractive presentations by students
- All kinds of correspondence (pen pals, key pals, etc.)
- Activities in the classroom that are memorable
- Informational displays of student work
- Development of a school-based advocacy portfolio that contains
  brochures, pictures, student-made materials, photographs, fliers, etc.
- Foreign language fairs, bake sales, festivals, etc.
- Events at civic offices
- Celebrations of National **FLES*** Day and National Foreign Lan-
  guage Week
- Award ceremonies for students who have participated in local, state,
  regional, and national competitions
- Distribution of brochures, such as the "Why **FLES***?" brochure dis-
  tributed by AATF and AATSP

- Assemblies where students perform and where videos about **FLES*** programs are shown (e.g., **FLES*** *Programs in Action,* available from the National **FLES*** Institute).
- Organizing all kinds of international games, such as soccer matches and mini-Olympics
- Inviting members of the press to all kinds of **FLES*** events, performances, and celebrations
- Developing a summer **FLES*** camp, where the usual camp activities are included along with extensive use of the foreign language(s). A **FLES*** camp newsletter with student work is very effective in communicating the successes of students.
- Creating a **FLES*** "happening" as an annual event
- Inviting elected officials, civic leaders, and others in the community to school **FLES*** events
- Creating a school-based plan of advocacy, year-round, with specific events happening each month

Are You a FLES* Advocate?

1. Am I a strong advocate for the **FLES*** program?
2. Have I explained, orally and in writing, the rationale for the program? Have I distributed the "Why **FLES***?" brochure?
3. Have I encouraged the hiring of exciting, dynamic teachers with excellent foreign language skills for the program?
4. Have I given input to the schedule so that it is reasonable and cost-effective?
5. Have I kept the school community informed about the **FLES*** program on a regular basis?
6. Have I asked to visit other classes in the **FLES*** program?
7. Have I suggested appropriate materials of instruction for purchase? Have I kept up with the new materials being offered?
8. Have I helped non-**FLES*** teachers understand the importance of foreign languages for young students?
9. Have I attended in-service opportunities for **FLES*** teachers? For foreign language teachers?
10. Do I participate in regular faculty meetings as well as in foreign language department meetings?
11. Do I actively seek opportunities to network with other **FLES*** teachers?
12. Have I joined professional foreign language associations?

13. Has a **FLES*** curriculum been developed? Does it show progression of skills from year to year? Does it articulate well with the secondary school foreign language curriculum?

14. Do parents know about the program and do they praise it? Are they involved in the program?

15. Do the students greet me by using the foreign language?

16. Have I encouraged administrators to greet teachers and students and to make a few announcements over the public-address system in the foreign language?

17. Have I informed colleges and universities of the continuing need for training for **FLES*** teachers? Have I encouraged administrators to be in touch with foundations and embassies for additional assistance?

18. Have I indicated to administrators that the **FLES*** program needs to be evaluated formally and periodically, and has this been included in the budget? Have I encouraged the publication of the results of research?

19. Have I given input to the **FLES*** advisory committee on an ongoing basis?

20. Have I encouraged feedback about the program from students and parents?

21. Have I been in touch with former students to see how they have done at advanced foreign language levels?

22. Have I invited school board members, administrators, parents, grandparents, and members of the **FLES*** advisory committee to visit my classes?

23. Have I volunteered to make exciting displays in the school, showing **FLES*** students in action?

24. Have I contacted the media when special **FLES*** events will take place in the school or elsewhere?

25. Have I provided all kinds of visibility for the **FLES*** program?

Sample Bookmark to Promote FLES*

FLES* FOR KIDS **✱ FOREIGN LANGUAGES IN K–8 ✱** FLES* FOR KIDS

Could include name of school, art by students, several expressions in the foreign language, etc.

Reaching FLES* Decision-Makers:
The Top Ten Best Ways to Get Community Support

1. Assess community language needs. (For example, which languages are offered at the high school level?)
2. Involve community members in the planning process.
3. Develop doable goals and outcomes.
4. Deliver what you have promised.
5. Assess the program and documents that you have delivered—what you have promised in the goals and outcomes in terms of what students are able to do in the FL and how well they do it.
6. Be sure to use alternative procedures for assessment (contests, activities in the community, etc.).
7. Have an ongoing public relations program stressing the successful aspects of the program (newspapers, radio, TV, cable, etc.).
8. Plan numerous open-school events.
9. Involve community members in the evaluation process.
10. If there are concerns, check on and try to remedy them; then publicize the new procedures, etc.

NATIONAL BROCHURE AVAILABLE
WHY FLES*? FOR KIDS

This is a new brochure, *in color,* indicating the important reasons for an early start in the study of a foreign language. This brochure includes:

- Rationale for all types of **FLES*** programs for all children
- Definitions of programs *(Sequential FLES, FLEX* [*or Exploratory*], *Immersion)*
- Testimonials from administrators, parents, teachers
- Sponsorship by National **FLES*** Commission of the American Association of Teachers of French and the National **FLES*** Committee of the American Association of Teachers of Spanish and Portuguese

HOW TO USE THIS NEW BROCHURE

- Planning new **FLES*** programs; maintaining programs
- Distribution at local, state, and national parents' meetings
- Distribution at local, state, and national administrators' and guidance counselors' meetings
- Distribution at local, state, and national teachers' meetings

- Distribution at local, state, regional, and national FL meetings
- Discussion in foreign language methods courses and institutes
- Distribution to funding agencies; local, state, and national business agencies; civic associations; elected officials; etc.
- Distribution to and discussion by other interested groups

Available from:

AATSP   OR   AATF
Frasier Hall   Mail Code 4510
University of North Colorado   Dept. of Foreign Languages
Greeley, CO 80639   Southern Illinois University
                                       Carbondale, IL 62901

Brochures are $1.00 each. Quantity orders: 10–99 copies, $.65 each; 100–199 copies, $.50 each; 200+ copies, $.25 each.

FOR REFLECTION

By conjoining the foreign language with another discipline, the teacher enriches the foreign language classroom and helps to reveal the differences between the native and the target cultures.

LENA LUCIETTO (1994, 7)

Selected Strategies, Games, and Activities for **FLES***

INTRODUCTION

Learning a foreign language can be enhanced, enriched, and reinforced by a wide range of approaches and activities. Since youngsters are interested in the new, the exciting, the challenging, the competitive, and the enjoyable, teachers may wish to broaden their repertoire of activities for presenting and reinforcing foreign language content.

When planning for different types of activities, it should be remembered that

- The emphasis is on some aspect of learning language and culture.
- The instructions should be clear and well thought out.
- The activity may be used for presentation, reinforcement, a change of pace, review, or even testing.
- The activity should not require elaborate preparation.
- The activity should be uncomplicated and permit variations in order to be useful for a number of linguistic concepts.
- The classroom climate should be within acceptable limits before, during, and after the activity.
- The activity may involve listening, speaking, reading, writing, culture, TPR gestures, and other types of communication.
- For the children, an activity that has a "game" approach is fun; for the teacher, it is primarily a learning activity.
- If an activity is repeated, it should always have a new twist or surprise.
- Both the teacher and the children should think that the activity is both worthwhile and fun.

Many types of learning activities can be used in the **FLES*** classroom. They can be categorized and grouped, but essentially

- The content of the activity can be varied (one time on clothing, another time on rivers, another time on food).
- If it is a competitive activity, the manner of team composition and scoring can be varied (boys versus girls, people born in the spring versus people born in winter, baseball scoring format, etc.).

Among the most commonly used activities with a "game" approach are:

Bingo-type games (all kinds of activities with cards)

Listening activities

Team games (answering questions of all kinds)

Guessing activities and riddles

TPR activities (such as Simon Says)

Add-on activities

Word activities (such as scrambled sentences, matching, spelling bees)

Number games (such as Buzz and variations)

Wheel games (for numbers, vocabulary, verbs, etc.)

Singing games (for hot or cold)

Charades (for animals, careers)

Prop games (such as Telephone, Restaurant, etc.)

Geography and history games

Board games

Simulations

Problem-solving activities

Other activities and games created by teachers and students

SELECTED STRATEGIES FOR FLES*

The ABCs of FLES* Strategies

A	Activate the learning.
B	Boggle the minds of your students.
C	"Con" your students by motivating them to learn.
D	Dramatize the learning.
E	Evaluate progress.
F	Facilitate the learning.
G	Gauge what works.
H	Use Humor.

I   Invigorate your lessons.

J   Put Joy in your lessons.

K   Use a Kinesthetic approach (appeal to all the senses).

L   Liberate your students to be able to speak the FL.

M   Employ Motivational techniques.

N   Look under your Nose for ideas!

O   Be Open to new ideas.

P   Praise!

Q   Everyone should know how to ask Questions.

R   Be Realistic.

S   Use a variety of real-life Situations.

T   Let them TALK!

U   Have Upbeat lessons.

V   Variety is crucial.

W   It takes a lot of Work.

X   Xercise—Move—TPR.

Z   Sometimes it feels like a Zoo! But it involves active learning!

Super Strategies for FLES*

1. Let's Exaggerate! (with adjectives)
2. Where Are All the Animals? (Who's your favorite?)
3. What Is It? (an invented animal!)
4. Praise—Praise—Praise—and More Praise!
5. Two by Two (find someone who shares your preferences)
6. The five C's of the national FL standards: communication, cultures, connections, comparisons, and communities
7. Let's Line Up! (according to favorite desserts)
8. Let's Make a Place Mat! (practice while we eat)
9. Back to Back (describe one another) and other TPR activities
10. What's Your Message? (jigsaw puzzle communication)
11. A Present Pour Moi? (No, it's for...)
12. Two Circles Are Better than One! (for conversation)
13. Venn Do We Categorize? (using Venn diagrams)
14. Culture Alive! (dramatizing cultural events)
15. Who's Very Hungry? (the caterpillar, of course, and other children's stories)
16. Riddles and jokes

17. Surprises

18. Unusual props

19. Change: seats, format of class, pairs, groups, materials, etc.

20. Let's reach them all!

SELECTED GAMES FOR *SEQUENTIAL FLES, FLEX,* AND *IMMERSION*

Games for Younger Children

TAP. One child taps rapidly on the desk. Others are called on to tell (in the foreign language) how many taps were heard.

HELLO. One child stands with her or his back to the class. Another child (selected by the teacher) says in the foreign language "Hello, _____. How are you?" The first child replies, "Hello. I'm fine. Your name is _____."

DUCK, DUCK, GOOSE. Students sit in a circle, holding items (or pictures of items). "It" taps each student on the head and names the item the student is holding. When "It" doesn't tap, but says *"Canard"* or some other cue, the student has to catch "It" before "It" reaches his or her seat in the circle.

Any of the games played in grades K–2 may be adapted to the FL classroom, based on themes and topics that are appropriate for younger children.

All Kinds of Team Games

BEFORE/AFTER. Members of each team are expected to answer, at first, what comes after the picture cue (e.g., if picture cue is 21, the answer would be 22). This could be used for days of the week, months, historical events, holidays, etc. Then, children would be asked to answer what comes before. In the sample, the number would be 20. For more advanced classes, children would be asked to say what comes both before and after.

SPELLING BEE. Two teams compete for vocabulary spelling review.

RELAY RACES. Two teams race to touch, draw, erase, etc., the correct word on a wall or the chalkboard. Good for review of vocabulary, numbers, shapes, etc.

FLY SWATTER GAME. This is a relay race with two teams, but each member of each team touches the cue on the board with a fly swatter. A variation would be to use baseball mitts in place of fly swatters.

BASEBALL. Two teams respond to cues, but following the procedures of baseball. Good for vocabulary, numbers, famous people from the target culture, etc.

JEOPARDY. Two teams make up questions that correspond to answer cues (using a buzzer when they know the questions). Team members may discuss an answer, but the response, in question form, must be given by the end of the specified time limit.

BRAINSTORMING. Two teams work on getting the most ideas in response to a cue, such as the many uses of a paper clip, using the FL.

RABBIT. Two teams complete the drawing of a team rabbit on the board. Individual members must first answer a question correctly before drawing a part of the rabbit.

TRUE/FALSE CHAIRS. If a statement is true, the first student to sit in the true chair (or if false, in the false chair) wins.

MONSTER DRAWING. A monster is drawn according to directions given by the teacher or another student.

Guessing Games

The teacher (or a child) describes a child in the class (hair color, clothing, etc.). The rest of the class guesses who it is.

WHAT'S IN THE BOX (PAPER BAG, ETC.)? Students guess what the teacher has hidden in a box. Good for vocabulary review.

I AM THINKING OF. . . Students try to guess what object the person is thinking about. A variation is The Date of My Birthday Is...

TWENTY QUESTIONS. Students may ask up to twenty questions to get clues about a secret person, place, or thing. (Use fewer questions for younger students.)

TPR Games

REVERSE SIMON SAYS. Instead of acting on a command when they hear "Simon says," children are expected to follow a command when they *do not* hear "Simon says" and *not* to follow a command when they hear "Simon says."

CHARADES (PROFESSIONS AND CAREERS). One child is called on to pantomime the profession listed on a card she or he has picked. The rest of the class tries to guess the profession or career as acted out by the first child.

WHAT WAS STOLEN? A student looks at fifteen to twenty articles or pictures of articles displayed on a tray. He or she leaves the room and one item is removed. The student returns and tries to identify the stolen article. Use fewer or more articles depending on the grade level and ability of the class.

COLOR MAGIC. The teacher agrees with a student helper that the chosen object will be the one immediately after the teacher names a blue object. The class chooses an object, and then the teacher points to a number of objects, asking "Is it the pen?" and so on. The helper knows to say it is the object only when it is the next one after the teacher has pointed out a blue object. Colors can be changed in subsequent games.

GROUP LETTER. The teacher distributes a sheet of paper to each group of five students. The first student writes a sentence and folds the paper over so the sentence cannot be read. The other students in the group in turn do the same. When all members of the group have written their sentences, one student reads all the sentences to the class. Sometimes students may wish to send these amusing letters to a sick classmate.

IT'S MINE! The student who is "It" walks around the room and stops near another student and touches an article of clothing or an object on the desk. "It" then says, "It's my [pen]," but does not use the correct name of the object. The student who is seated says, "No, it's my [pencil]." If the seated student cannot identify the object correctly, he or she becomes "It."

PIN THE TAIL ON THE _____. A picture of a large animal is displayed on a corkboard. The teacher or leader gives various instructions (some of them humorous), about pinning body parts to the animal and calls on students from each team to follow the instructions. There should be a collection of tails, ears, eyes, paws, hats, etc., available.

MEMORY GAME. After discussing (in the foreign language) some of the children's food preferences, the teacher asks: "Who likes bananas?"

"Who hates green beans?" After several times, the children will listen more carefully and will make an association between the food and the person.

FALSE ACCUSATION (GRADES 5 AND 6). The teacher (or a student) prepares cards such as "I went to Paris" or "I went to the bullfight" or "I went to the opera." Students on one team, in turn, try to guess what students on the other team have done. For example, a student might guess that Helen went to Paris. Helen, on the opposite team, replies, "Yes, I went to Paris" or "No, I did not go to Paris," according to the card she is holding. The team with the greatest number of correct guesses wins.

GROWING, GROWING (GRADES 5 AND 6). One student says a word. The next student has to add another word or phrase, and so on, until the sentence has become so long that no one can say the whole sentence in order to add something else on. This can be played in teams. A variation is to pack a suitcase for a trip, with each child saying what has been packed and adding another item.

BALL OF YARN PLUS SINGING (OR TELLING A STORY). Students pass a ball of yarn (with knots in it), giving answers to questions. When a student has a knot, he or she must recite a poem, or give three excuses for not doing homework, or...(like Hot Potato game). (Seen on FLTEACH.)

Games for All Children

MUSIC WITH MOTION. Singing songs with all types of motions. Aerobics to music, following directions. Singing musical chairs.

STORIES WITH MOTION. Using motions for different parts of a story. Story sequencing.
Imitations. Students pretend to be a favorite animal, various modes of transportation, etc.

OPINION POLLS. Students walk around the class to gather other students' opinions and preferences on different topics.

"GUESS WHO" PARTIES. The teacher pins the name of a different famous person on the back of each student. Students then walk around the class, asking questions and trying to guess their secret identity.

SIMON SAYS. Use the usual rules, but vary the cues by making them funny or unexpected.

FOUR CORNERS. Assign themes to the corners, such as the four seasons. Students go to their favorite season, or to the season in which their birthday occurs. Vary the number of corners and themes.

LINE-UPS. Students line up according to their birth dates, the first letter of their first name, their favorite holiday, their favorite dessert, capitals of countries, the first number of their telephone number, etc.

RELAY RACES (see above). Students form teams and race to touch, or draw, or erase, etc., the correct word on the wall or board (e.g., vocabulary, numbers, shapes, etc.). (Sometimes played with one fly swatter per team.)

CULTURE IN MOTION. Groups of students reenact a famous cultural event, such as the landing of Columbus in America.

CIRCLES FOR CONVERSATION (SOMETIMES CALLED INSIDE/OUTSIDE CIRCLES). Students are in two circles, moving in different directions. On the command (or when the music stops), students engage in conversation on a given topic (weather, health, favorite movie, etc.).

MATCH THE PAIRS. Some students are given a card with the name of a famous person. Others have an event, or a date, etc., that matches this person. Students walk around, asking questions in the FL, to try to match their cards.

JAZZ CHANTS (RAPS). Groups of students create a rap and then present it to the class. The entire class is encouraged to participate in walking around the room, clapping hands, etc.

LIVE TIC-TAC-TOE. Two teams compete, using a tic-tac-toe diagram on the floor (drawn either with chalk or with masking tape). After correctly answering questions in the target language, individual students strategically place themselves where the usual X's and O's would go. The first team to place three students across, down, or diagonally wins.

LIVE SENTENCE BINGO. Two teams compete to be the first to form a complete sentence. Taking turns, a student from each team may pick a word from a hat after correctly answering a question. Each team chooses words from its own hat, but the words in each hat are the same. The first team to draw all the words and unscramble them into a full sentence wins.

TWISTER AND THE KNOT. In Twister, students stand on colors or numbers on the floor or mat. In The Knot, students hold hands and form a knot by weaving in and out of the formation. Then they try to unravel the knot without dropping hands.

DANCING WITH MOTION AND MUSIC. Chicken Dance, Macarena, Aux Champs-Élysées, Hokey Pokey, etc.

EXCHANGE. Students sit in a circle with one child in the center. Assign names of fruits, animals, numbers, etc., to children, making sure that the same item is assigned to two different children. When the child in the center calls an item, the two students who have it try to exchange seats, but the child in the center may try to get into a seat before the others.

HOT/COLD. One student leaves the room and an object is hidden. When the student returns and approaches the object, the class calls out, claps, or sings louder than before.

CATCH AND RESPOND. Students catch a regular ball or Koosh ball and respond to a question, give the answer to a mathematics problem, give the capital of a country, etc. Then they throw the ball to someone else.

SELECTED ACTIVITIES

Group Projects

- Students have a fashion show.
- Students invent an animal and its habitat.
- Students invent a culture and its language.
- Students make a literary poster or place mat showing the characters and time sequences of a story.
- Students write Haiku poetry:

    Line 1: one word—the subject

    Line 2: two words—describe the subject

    Line 3: three words—express feelings

    Line 4: four words—describe actions

    Line 5: one word—refer to the subject
- Students create puzzles.
- Students create concrete poetry (in the shape of the topic).
- Students create a "Gouin' series" (e.g., going to the movies, etc.).

- Students work on three skits about giving a present to somebody: buying the present, giving the present, returning the present.
- Students create a *Michelin Guide* for the school, their home, the imaginary home of a famous person, etc.
- Students work on "Magic Eye" pictures while the teacher or another student records their comments and frustrations.
- Students create sponge activities (short activities to use when there is a little extra time left for class), such as "Catch and Answer" or "Culture Quiz."
- Students do a theme-related Venn diagram (e.g., July 14 in France and July 4 in the United States).

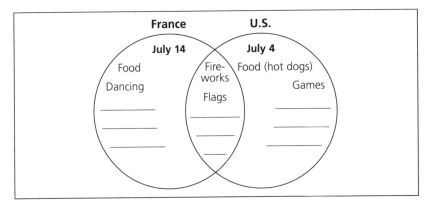

- Students create a theme-related name grid:
(Spanish)

Categories	L	I	P	T	O	N
Fruits						naranja
Vegetables						
Desserts			postre			
Beverages				té		

- Students create games like Concentration and Jeopardy.
- Students make topical wheels showing clothing and seasons:

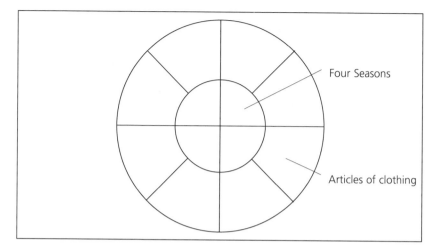

- Students create a skit about eating in a restaurant (or going to the dentist, etc.).
- Students create a small recipe book.

Class Projects

- Make a class mural.
- Create a class newsletter, including such categories as news about people, puzzles, jokes, and cultural information.
- Make a cultural calendar, showing dates of famous events and information about famous people of the culture.
- Create a theme-related graffiti wall.
- Create a "Guess Who?" bulletin board of baby pictures.
- Create a story using paper folds, similar to Mad Libs.
- Create a mini shopping mall in the classroom.
- Plan a pretend trip to the foreign country.
- Participate in a treasure (scavenger) hunt in class and outside of class.

Individual Projects

- Students make a place mat with thematic expressions, such as greetings, health, etc.
- Students interview other students, the teacher, other teachers, etc., and present the person to the class, making a "YOU" web.
- Students make an accordion book or a pop-up book.
- Students make bookmarks about the foreign culture.

- Students make a "Me" web, or a timeline of their lives, or write an autobiography.
- Students make silhouettes about themselves, including name, date of birth, family members, preferences, what they will be doing in ten years, etc.
- Students create all kinds of graphic organizers (e.g., webs) that connect different themes.
- Students create greeting cards, invitations, and thank-you cards.
- Students write letters, poetry, letters to the editor, etc.
- Students create puzzles and riddles.
- Students make passports.
- Students keep journals (age-appropriate) of their activities. (Younger students make drawings or collect pictures.)
- Students make masks for Mardi Gras.
- Students make sock or paper-bag puppets.
- Students create their own business cards.
- Students create brainteasers.
- Students create a new creature.

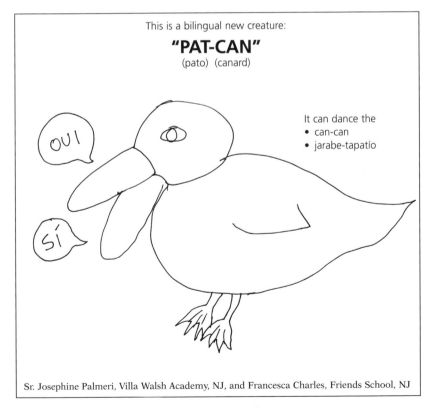

This is a bilingual new creature:

"PAT-CAN"

(pato) (canard)

It can dance the
- can-can
- jarabe-tapatío

Sr. Josephine Palmeri, Villa Walsh Academy, NJ, and Francesca Charles, Friends School, NJ

- Students write a letter to Santa Claus.
- Students make New Year's resolutions.
- Students correspond with pen pals and key pals.
- Students keep a weather record locally and in the target culture(s).
- Students make mini-dictionaries.
- Students create postcards from the foreign culture.

NOTE: Almost any game or activity played on the playground or other activities at school may be adapted for **FLES*** classes.

SELECTED SOURCES FOR ACTIVITIES AND GAMES

Allen, E., and R. Valette. 1977. *Modern Language Classroom Techniques.* 2nd ed. New York: Harcourt Brace Jovanovich.

Curtain, H., and C. Pesola. 1994. *Language and Children: Making the Match.* 2nd ed. Reading, MA: Addison-Wesley.

Danesi, Marcel. 1986. *Puzzles and Games in Language Teaching.* Lincolnwood, IL: National Textbook Co.

Dorry, G. 1966. *Games for Second Language Learning.* New York: McGraw-Hill.

Figueroa, Minerva. 1985. *Spanish Resources and Activities.* Lincolnwood, IL: National Textbook Co.

FLTEACH electronic listserv (see Chapter 7).

Lipton, G., ed. 1987. *A FLES Sampler: Learning Activities for FLES, FLEX, Immersion.* Champaign, IL: FLES Commission Report to AATF.

Macdonald, M., and S. Rogers-Gordon. 1984. *Action Plans.* Rowley, MA: Newbury House.

MacRae, M. 1960. *Teaching Spanish in the Grades.* Boston: Houghton Mifflin.

Moskowitz, G. 1978. *Caring and Sharing in the Foreign Language Class.* Rowley, MA: Newbury House.

Omaggio, A. 1978. *Games and Simulations in the Foreign Language Classroom.* Arlington, VA: Center for Applied Linguistics.

Sadow, S. 1982. *Idea Bank: Creative Activities for the Language Class.* Rowley, MA: Newbury House.

Schmidt, E. 1977. *Let's Play Games in German.* Lincolnwood, IL: National Textbook Co.

Taylor, M. 1975. *Jeux Culturels, Jeux Faciles, Amusons-Nous.* Lincolnwood, IL: National Textbook Co.

Wright, A., et al. 1984. *Games for Language Learning.* 2nd ed. Cambridge: Cambridge University Press.

NOTE: Additional strategies, games, and activities can be found in Chapters Nine, Ten, and Eleven.

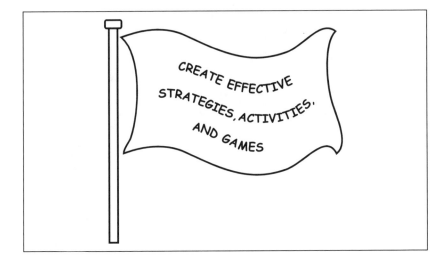

💡 FOR REFLECTION

Every day of French class must be a new experience in which each student feels a special importance and relationship between himself or herself and the French teacher. You must be ALIVE, VIBRANT, SCINTILLATING, and SPARKLING!

HARRIET SAXON (1994, 37)

What's in the Future for **FLES***?

OVERVIEW

This generation is often called the "S and N" generation...those children who grew up playing with Sega and Nintendo and Super Mario and his adventures in computerized games. Since the computer evolved, every generation of children will be associated with different cartoon characters, and one cannot predict which one will hold their attention in the future.

In thinking about futuristic **FLES***, it is important to remember the rapid changes that have occurred in technology, in language acquisition, in research studies, in the advent of *Standards for Foreign Language Learning* (National Standards in Foreign Language Education Project 1996), in **FLES*** teacher preparation, and in the nature of elementary school education. Even today, the teaching of foreign languages to young children is in the mainstream, and its position in elementary education is probably as secure as it ever will be. **FLES*** programs will, of necessity, undergo many changes, depending on a number of factors: needs and learning styles of children, needs of society, the role of languages in a global society, greater understanding of different approaches to teaching **FLES***, and the many characteristics of individual students, such as abilities, interests, multiple intelligences, short-term and long-term language needs, strengths, challenges, and other factors.

Charting a course for the future of **FLES*** will indeed take careful planning, and the National Foreign Language Standards Project is a good beginning. There must be provision for different expectations and needs at different local levels, encouraging, as the national standards do, modifications and adaptations in accordance to varying local needs and interests. Following are some guidelines that may be helpful in planning **FLES*** programs in the next decade:

1. Reaffirm the importance of early language learning for elementary school children.

2. State objectives in general terms that can serve as an umbrella accommodating all kinds of programs at the regional, state, and local levels.

3. Recognize that not all programs can fit predetermined dimensions, and that all types of programs can contribute, in different ways, to achieving high levels of proficiency in the long haul.

4. Encourage preservice elementary school teachers to obtain training in a foreign language. They are and will be important players in planning for the future.

5. Encourage parents to become actively involved in the planning, implementation, and evaluation stages.

6. Involve administrators and guidance counselors in planning the most effective programs possible so that decisions are not made on the basis of dollars alone.

7. Conduct future planning with contributions from all sectors of the school community (parents, administrators, teachers, etc.), and build consensus by accommodating the varying opinions of the different groups who are involved.

8. Recognize in the process of future planning the importance of valid research studies. Future planners must dismiss biased studies, studies that contain contaminating factors, studies that have predetermined assumptions, etc. Conduct further research on the importance of early "wiring of a child's brain" to languages.

9. Make provision for periodic modifications in future planning, in accordance with the new demands of society and new information from valid language-acquisition studies. Future plans should not be "set in stone," impervious to changing times.

10. Reach for the stars, but be flexible about how and when the destination(s) will be reached.

Predictions About FLES* for the Year 2500

- Children will continue to outperform adolescents and adults in language acquisition in pronunciation skills.

- Parents will continue to press for **FLES*** programs for their children.

- Children will continue to need nurturing adults: parents and teachers.

- Computers will become ever smaller and more portable, in the form of helmets, wristwatches, bracelets, and wallets, which will greatly increase opportunities for language learning.

- Computers will become voice-activated and no longer require typing.

- Opportunities for travel will increase dramatically, and travel time will be significantly reduced, thus enabling all foreign language students to participate in foreign culture(s) for varying lengths of time.

- Through the technology of virtual reality and global imaging, many students will visit the target culture(s) and begin to feel at home there without ever leaving their own homes.

- There will be more opportunities for participation in global language-specific organizations and worldwide meetings, such as the Fédération Internationale des Professeurs de Français.

- Technology will enable students to access appropriate materials of instruction, with all kinds of adaptations for individual differences and learning styles, in a variety of learning locations.

- Technology will enable children, adolescents, and adults to refine their abilities in one language and/or to start another language as their needs and work/life requirements change.

- *Standards for Foreign Language Learning* will continue to serve as a guide for **FLES*** programs, and they will be modified periodically, as needed.

- Technology will facilitate more effective ways to train **FLES*** teachers, appealing to different modalities of learning.

- Technology will greatly facilitate the networking of **FLES*** teachers. No longer will they feel isolated and out of touch with others.

- Because technology will enhance the attractiveness of foreign language programs, children will eagerly spend hours upon hours learning a foreign language, and enjoying it!

- Technology will facilitate more valid research studies on language acquisition by children.

- By the twenty-sixth century, the software will finally catch up to the hardware!

- By the twenty-sixth century, people will still be trying to "humanize" technology.

- The future will be exciting for **FLES*** teachers and for foreign language teachers on all levels. The momentum will continue...and the need for **FLES*** advocacy will continue too!

💡 FOR REFLECTION

Humanistic techniques help create a warmer, more accepting climate, and a feeling of greater closeness among students.

GERTRUDE MOSKOWITZ *(1978, 17)*

The **FLES*** Scale for the Evaluation of **FLES*** Programs

1. All students have access to **FLES*** programs.
2. There is a foreign language advisory committee for K–12 programs.
3. The goals of the **FLES*** program are clearly stated.
4. There is provision for articulation with upper schools.
5. There is provision for ongoing informal feedback and formal evaluation (every five to seven years).
6. There is assurance that there is a continuing supply of appropriate **FLES*** materials.
7. There is assurance that there is a continuing supply of well-prepared and trained **FLES*** teachers.
8. There is documentation of the short-term and longitudinal results of studying **FLES*** and the effect on English language skills and achievement in other curriculum areas.
9. There is a written **FLES*** curriculum that indicates progress, based on national standards, in linguistic, cultural, and interdisciplinary approaches.
10. Students demonstrate their progress in **FLES*** (K–8) in a variety of ways, including progress indicators suggested by national FL standards committees.
11. The **FLES*** instructional program in class reflects the goals of the program through the curriculum content and the methods.
12. There is enthusiasm for the **FLES*** program on the part of students, parents, administrators, school board members, guidance counselors, and other members of the school/school district community.
13. There is more than one foreign language offered at the **FLES*** level (K–8), depending on the size of the school and the school community.

Be a Reflective **FLES*** Teacher: A Self-Evaluation Checklist

How do you know when you've taught an effective foreign language lesson? Ask yourself the following questions:

1. Are all students actively participating in the foreign language, either individually, in small groups, or in whole-class activities?
2. Are the youngsters given the opportunity to use the foreign language in functional situations during the lesson?
3. Are students able to use the language (depending on the goals of the program) in all four abilities of listening, speaking, reading, and writing? For higher-order thinking skills activities?
4. Have I planned a variety of activities in short segments?
5. Do I plan review and reinforcement activities as well as the presentation of new work in each lesson?
6. Do I use a wide variety of auditory and visual materials of interest to young children? Do I sometimes plan a surprise?
7. Do I try to motivate each lesson and each part of the lesson?
8. Is there ongoing evaluation for purposes of diagnosis of problems as well as for grouping?
9. Are cultural topics woven into each foreign language lesson?
10. Is the textbook adapted and modified to suit the curriculum and the ability of the students?
11. Do I have effective classroom routines so that everyone is on task during the entire lesson? Is every minute used?
12. Do I explain the new homework clearly? Do I check the homework (if any) each class session?
13. Do the students and I use the foreign language? Do I only very briefly explain something in English (and only when necessary)?
14. Do my students appear to look forward to the next FL lesson?
15. Do I look forward to the next FL lesson?

Reaching All
FLES* Students

1. Honestly believe that ALL children can learn...some in different ways.
2. Explore different ways to reach ALL students.
3. Find ways to appeal to all the senses, if possible.
4. Discover ways to appeal to the different intelligences of children.
5. Use topics of interest to children—things children talk about at home, at recess, on the playground—the N.L.K.T. approach.
6. Use real-life situations and scenarios...for teaching and for assessment of student progress.
7. Provide more to do for gifted students (challenging projects, appeals to higher-order thinking skills, service projects for other classmates and for children in other classes and grades).
8. Explore alternative ways to review, reteach, and practice (e.g., different visuals, different classroom organization, using partners and small groups).
9. Sneak in all kinds of review by recombining themes (e.g., weather and clothing, clothing and colors, interdisciplinary science activities and mathematics and sports).
10. Use TPR and rhythm activities in different ways, because children learn through their muscles!
11. Create a "joy in learning" classroom that is both nonthreatening and challenging.
12. Listen carefully to children's comments...there's a lot of wisdom in young minds!

Suggested *FLEX* Lesson Plan Format (for a 30-Minute Class)

I. Opening routine (5 minutes)
   A. Roll call (in foreign language)
   B. Review of items previously taught, such as:
      1. What day is today?
      2. What is the date?
      3. What is the weather like today?
      4. How old are you?
      5. What are you wearing?
      6. Etc.

II. Introduction of new material (10 minutes)
   A. Direct instruction of new concept (always include visuals, manipulatives, audio when possible)
   B. Practice/check for understanding with whole class
   C. Individual student response activity

III. Reinforcement of new concept (10 minutes)
   This should be in the form of a game, song, or other enjoyable activity that involves multisensory strategies.

IV. Closure (5 minutes)
   A. Brief discussion about what students learned
      1. What did we do/learn today?
      2. What did you like best?
      3. How is the new concept like or different from English/our culture?
      4. Etc.
   B. Plans for follow-up, what you'll be doing next time
   C. Closing routines

NOTE: For longer time frames, add an extra "fun" activity to reinforce the new concept.

Reprinted with permission. Anne Arundel County Public Schools, Foreign Language Office.

Sample Lesson Plans for *Sequential FLES, FLEX,* and *Immersion*

SAMPLE FLEX LESSON (FRENCH)

CONTEXT: Learning scenario, unit plan, or other

GOAL AREA(S) OF THE FIVE C'S:

FL STANDARDS NUMBER(S):

(To be conducted in French)

1. Opening
   Comment t'appelles-tu?

2. New presentation—colors
   Blanc, rouge, bleu, vert, jaune, orange, noir

3. Label colors
   Match the color with the written form.

4. Game
   Who can find something in the room that is *rouge*?
   Who is wearing something *vert*?

5. Culture
   Show flag of France.
   Which colors are in the French flag?

6. Follow-up
   Find out which colors are in the flags of Canada and Martinique.

7. Reflection about the lesson

SAMPLE *FLEX* LESSON (SPANISH)

CONTEXT: Learning scenario, unit plan, or other
GOAL AREA(S) OF THE FIVE C's:
FL STANDARDS NUMBER(S):
   (To be conducted in Spanish)

1. Opening
   ¿Cómo te llamas?

2. New presentation—colors
   blanco, rojo, azul, verde, amarillo, anaranjado, negro

3. Label colors
   Match the color with the written form.

4. Game
   Who can find something in the room that is *rojo*?
   Who is wearing something *verde*?

5. Culture
   Show flag of Spain.
   Which colors are in the Spanish flag?

6. Follow-up
   Find out which colors are in the flags of Mexico and Argentina.

7. Reflection about the lesson

Notes for FLEX Lessons in French and Spanish

- Future follow-up lessons review colors and apply them to new vocabulary about food, clothing, objects in the room and at home, etc.

- This lesson (in French *or* Spanish) could be used in grades 2 or 3; it also could be expanded to include more reading and some writing for grades 4–6 (20 to 30 minutes).

- In grades 5 and 6, some social studies applications could be included, such as colors on a map, etc.

- In *FLEX* in elementary school or *Exploratory* in middle school, there might be a joint French/Spanish lesson that would permit language comparison, so students begin to see the similarities and differences of languages.

SAMPLE *FLEX* LESSON (MULTILANGUAGE) (GRADES 4–6)

CONTEXT: Learning scenario, unit plan, or other

GOAL AREA(S) OF THE FIVE C'S:

FL STANDARDS NUMBER(S):

(To be conducted in English)

1. Introduction to many languages

   Demonstration of places in the world as each "hello" is presented and repeated by the class:

Bonjour (France)	*Güten Tag* (Germany)
Buon giorno (Italy)	*Kalimera* (Greece)
Buenos días (Spain, Mexico, etc.)	*Konnichiwa* (Japan)
God morgon (Sweden)	*Shalom* (Israel)
	Zdrastvuytye (Russia)

2. Design international greeting cards, using some or all of the greetings

3. Follow-up

   Ask students to locate the following information about one or more of the countries:

   • Location of the country
   • Type of government
   • Capital, flag
   • Name of president, prime minister
   • Special products from the country
   • World-famous people from the country
   • Other interesting information

   Another assignment might be to create a poem incorporating some or all of the greetings introduced.

4. Reflection about the lesson

SAMPLE SEQUENTIAL *FLES* OR *FLEX* LESSON
(GRADES K–3)

CONTEXT: Learning scenario, unit plan, or other

GOAL AREA(S) OF THE FIVE C'S:

FL STANDARDS NUMBER(S):

(To be conducted in the FL)

1. Warm-up (topics previously learned)

2. Show me _____ (various objects in the room).

3. Review numbers.

4. New work
   - Teach days of the week.
   - Teach today's date.
   - Teach possession (e.g., Robert's desk).

5. TPR activity
   Go to the chalkboard.

   > window.
   > door.
   > desk.
   > Marcia's desk.
   > Richard's chair.

6. Review days of the week

7. Sing song (previously learned).

8. Follow-up
   - Children bring in a calendar for the month.
   - Children begin making a foreign language calendar.

9. Reflection about the lesson

SAMPLE *SEQUENTIAL FLES, FLEX,* OR *IMMERSION* LESSON(GRADES 5–6)

(The class is divided into two groups—one group for reading, the other group for oral skills practice.)

CONTEXT: Learning scenario, unit plan, or other

GOAL AREA(S) OF THE FIVE C'S:

FL STANDARDS NUMBER(S):

(To be conducted in the FL)

1. Warm-up (whole class)

   Review numbers, colors, weather.

2. New work (whole class)
   * Listening to a story about months of year, seasons
   * Repetition of vocabulary
   * Questions and answers

3. Group work

   Group 1: Prepare an oral description of pictures with partners.

   Work with teacher on oral descriptions.

   Group 2: Follow-up of story covered by whole class

   Read story.

   Write riddles.

   Do a crossword puzzle.

4. Summary (whole class)

   Group 1: Students present oral descriptions of pictures.

   Group 2: Students present riddles.

5. Follow-up
   * Find pictures of the four seasons and label them.
   * Some groups or pairs may wish to change the ending of the story.

6. Reflection (teacher with whole class): How did the group work go today? What did you learn today? How did you contribute to group progress?

SAMPLE CONTENT-BASED LESSON IN SCIENCE
(GRADES 1–4)

CONTEXT: Learning scenario, unit plan, or other

GOAL AREA(S) OF THE FIVE C'S:

FL STANDARDS NUMBER(S):

(To be conducted in the foreign language)

1. Aim(s)
   - To give students opportunities to discover which substances are attracted to magnets
   - To give students practice in the specific method of "Let's Find Out"
   - To develop record-keeping skills

   Materials:

   Coins, feathers, balloons, fabric, keys, clips, pencils, jar covers, buttons, and other objects, plus small magnets distributed to pairs of students

2. Procedures
   - Teacher presents (and reviews) the vocabulary for the different objects and the terms for "is attracted to magnets" and "is not attracted to magnets."
   - Pairs of students test various objects.
   - Pairs of students record their observations on a chart.
   - The class discusses findings, including conflicting reports, such as "some keys are not attracted to magnets." Why?
   - The class creates a chart with generalizations from the students.

3. Cultural contrasts

   Students test foreign coins and other objects of realia from the foreign culture.

4. Reflection on the lesson

5. Follow-up
   - Students test objects at home and make a chart showing which objects are attracted to magnets and which are not.
   - At more advanced levels, the teacher and students may go into the uses of magnetism in daily life and in science.

Sample Interdisciplinary Lesson (French) (Grades 4–6)

A follow-up interdisciplinary lesson (FL, social studies, music, science; to extend over several lessons)

Context: Learning scenario, unit plan, or other
Goal area(s) of the five C's:
FL standards number(s):
  (To be conducted in French)

1. Aims
   * To learn directions in the foreign language and practice them in dialogues, narratives, and TPR
   * To explore street names based on names of composers, scientists, and other historical figures

Materials:
  Large map of the area, with labels that will be taught
  Individual map provided for each student
  Large floor map (on newsprint) for TPR activities
  Street name signs

2. Procedures
   * Warm-up
   * Teach the vocabulary of locations and directions, using a blank map; add streets: *avenue Bizet, avenue Marie Curie*, etc.
   * Label the large map; children label their maps. (See sample map.)
   * Teach a dialogue about two children going to various places in the city, looking at street signs.
   * Have groups of children write a narrative or conversation about the names of people on the street signs.
   * Label the map on the floor. Have children follow directions, such as, "Put your right foot on the school and your left foot on Robert's house," or "Start at the hospital. Go north on *avenue le Louvre* to *avenue Bizet*. Then go west to the garden."
   * Groups of children research the composers and scientists whose names are on streets, and report to the class.
   * Partner practice with maps

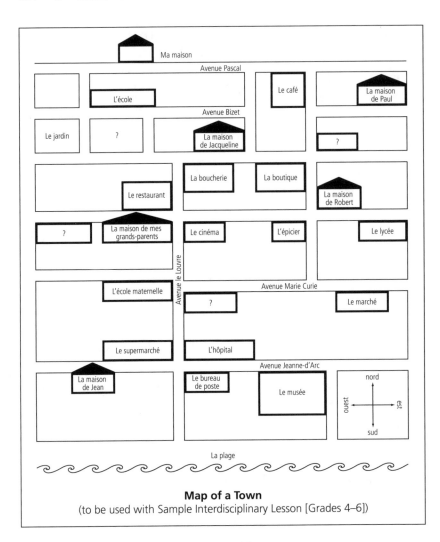

Map of a Town
(to be used with Sample Interdisciplinary Lesson [Grades 4–6])

3. Cultural contrasts

- What does a city look like in the foreign (target) culture? Similarities to cities in the United States? Differences? Compare names of streets.

- What are the differences between an American market and *l'épicier*? Between an American market and *le supermarché*? Between an American high school and *le lycée*?

4. Assessment and follow-up

- Check to see how well children can follow directions.

- Ask the children to create another map of an invented town with different locations and different streets named after composers, scientists, etc.

- Have one group of children create a test on locations and directions.

5. Reflection about the lesson

6. Follow-up in other lessons

   Teach additional vocabulary to be placed on the map, including additional streets named after composers, scientists, artists, historical figures, etc.

Reminders About Group Work

GUIDELINES FOR GROUP WORK

1. Know students.
2. Have a specific purpose.
3. Prepare students, space, materials, and equipment.
4. Arrange the room effectively.
5. Train assistants (if available): students, student teachers, etc.
6. Define routines.
7. Prepare charts of "More to Do" when students are finished with tasks.
8. Try group work for short periods (at first, five minutes).
9. Establish the standards for attention to task.
10. Build flexibility into groups. Have groups based on needs, talents, interests, weaknesses, absence, enrichment, friendship, sociometric indications.
11. Evaluate with each group the effectiveness of the session.
12. Evaluate with the whole class the effectiveness of the class session.

FLES* Teacher Competencies

The following revision of **FLES*** Teacher Competencies are recommended by the 1996 National **FLES*** Commission of AATF:

I. Language competency

  1. Foreign language competency

    • Functional proficiency (oral and written) for *Sequential FLES* and *FLEX*

    • Near-native proficiency (oral and written) for *Immersion* programs

  2. English language competency

    • For all three program models, functional proficiency (oral and written)

II. Knowledge/skills regarding

  1. Rationale for **FLES***, and the ability to communicate this to members of the school community

  2. **FLES*** methodology for all three program models

  3. National FL standards and their implementation

  4. State and local FL frameworks and standards

  5. General elementary school (K–8) curriculum and methodology

  6. Target culture(s) and how to teach culture

  7. The American elementary school (K–8) setting

  8. Multiple intelligences of children

III. Understanding language acquisition by children in terms of

  1. **FLES*** methodology

  2. Research studies on **FLES***

  3. National FL standards

  4. Assessing student progress

  5. Evaluation of **FLES*** programs

  6. Implications of first and second language acquisition principles

7. Appropriate children's literature (in the target language and in English)

8. Implications of child psychology and child development

9. Principles of applied linguistics

IV. Professional competence/skills

1. Multiethnic, multicultural sensitivity

2. Ability to work effectively with children

3. Ability to teach to the different learning styles of children

4. Ability to establish rapport with children, colleagues, parents, administrators, and others in the school community

5. Knowledge of technology appropriate for this age level

6. Skill in involving parents in the **FLES*** program

7. Skill in classroom management and conflict resolution

8. Ability to make connections with other disciplines (interdisciplinary) and other languages and cultures

9. Conversant with resources for age-appropriate **FLES*** materials

10. Aware of contemporary trends in foreign languages (e.g., membership in FL associations and attendance at FL conferences)

Tips on Being a Resourceful **FLES*** Teacher

- Locate materials in unexpected places.
- Learn how to adapt materials from all levels.
- Think "creative" and "inexpensive."
- Dramatize everything!
- Publicize everything!
- When you get a "no," it means you have to be more resourceful.
- Keep cheerful and optimistic.
- Invent different methods of repetition and reinforcement.
- Make friends with a computer guru, a secretary, a kindergarten teacher, a secondary school FL teacher, a custodian, a number of parents, a student teacher, a number of classroom elementary school teachers, an artistic student, a parent, etc.
- Think of different ways to use old catalogs, greeting cards, advertisements, dolls, puppets, etc.
- Know where you can get assistance.
- Attend FL conferences on the local, state, and national levels.
- Speak/write to publishers and tell them what you need.
- Join FL organizations and tell them what you need.
- Tell administrators what you need (politely).
- Discover *new* ways to use books, audiovisual materials, computers, e-mail, catalogs, wallpaper books, shoe boxes and cartons, etc.
- Be resourceful and creative, and enjoy!

FLES* Benefits to Children

Children should leave all types of **FLES*** programs having developed, to varying degrees, the following skills and positive attitudes. Children should...

- Enjoy studying a foreign language and culture
- Acquire linguistic abilities (and others) in accordance with the performance indicators for the five C's of *Standards for Foreign Language Learning* (National Standards in Foreign Language Education Project 1996)
- Acquire cultural insights about the people(s) who speak the foreign language
- Experience the success of foreign language learning
- Demonstrate achievement of the linguistic and cultural goals of their programs
- Develop an awareness of and sensitivity to people from different cultures who speak a foreign language
- Be prepared to continue their study of the foreign language, and be ready for new challenges in their continued study of foreign languages
- Display near-native pronunciation of the FL, if they started before the age of ten
- Recognize the importance of knowing a foreign language in today's and tomorrow's world
- Develop listening and speaking abilities in the foreign language in real-life situations
- Display reading and writing abilities in the foreign language
- Know how to follow directions in the FL and perform different tasks in the classroom
- Develop good study habits for all aspects of foreign language learning
- Understand the need for accuracy in the foreign language
- Experience integrated foreign language learning through an interdisciplinary approach

- Participate in foreign language learning activities through partnered and small-group cooperative-learning activities
- Have a sense of the power of using a foreign language to express one's thoughts and wishes
- Have an openness to people from other cultures who speak other languages
- Be ready for new challenges in learning foreign languages

  All children deserve the opportunity to study a foreign language before the age of ten. No child should be deprived access to the world of languages and cultures!

Adapted from Lipton, G. 1996. "The Many Benefits of All Types of **FLES*** Programs." *Northeast Conference Newsletter* (Fall): 56–57.

Focus on **FLES***

PLANNING AND IMPLEMENTING **FLES*** PROGRAMS

(Foreign Languages in Elementary Schools)

Gladys C. Lipton,
Director, National **FLES*** Institute

Why FLES*?

All types of **FLES*** programs can be highly beneficial to children. Research tells us that an early introduction to foreign languages provides many advantages for them, as follows:

1. Children have the ability to learn and excel in the pronunciation of a foreign language.
2. Children who have studied a foreign language in elementary school achieve expected gains and even have higher scores on standardized tests in reading, language arts and mathematics than those who have not.
3. Children who have studied a foreign language show greater cognitive development in such areas as mental flexibility, creativity, divergent thinking, and higher-order thinking skills.
4. Children who have studied a foreign language develop a sense of cultural pluralism (openness to and appreciation of other cultures).
5. Children studying a foreign language have an improved self-concept and sense of achievement in school.
6. Brain surgeons question why foreign language is not initiated before the age of ten, since that period of time is optimum for learning a foreign language.
7. Positive AP/**FLES*** results.

FLES* (pronounced "flestar") is the umbrella term for all types of elementary-school (K–8) foreign language programs, including *Sequential FLES, FLEX,* and *Immersion.*

Choice of Program Models

There are three basic types of **FLES*** program models. A definition of terms can help to clarify these different program models, based on the "Why **FLES***?" brochure.

FLES* is the overall, or "umbrella," term for all types of elementary school foreign language programs in grades K–8. All three program models have the potential for continuing FL study.

Sequential FLES is an introduction to one foreign language for two or more years, with a systematic development of language skills (listening, speaking, reading, writing, and culture) within the parameters of themes and functional topics. Good theme-related fluency is expected if scheduled five times a week, thirty minutes or more a day, for four or more years. All children can be served by this type of program.

FLEX-Exploratory is an introduction to one or more foreign languages, with limited foreign language skills expected. There may be limited fluency with a once- or twice-a-week program that emphasizes functional language and cultural awareness. All children can be served by this type of program.

Immersion (also *Partial Immersion, Content-Based*) programs include the use of the foreign language throughout the school day by teachers and students. Because of the shortage of qualified teachers, it is difficult to serve many students in this type of program. Its major goal is to provide the basic elementary school program through the foreign language. Good fluency in the foreign language is expected after four or more years in the program.

Which One Is Best?

It is impossible to say which program model is best without identifying the context of the educational community. So much depends on the needs of the school/school community, the budgetary resources, the desired student outcomes, the continuing supply of teachers, and many other important factors. The greatest overall consideration, however, should be equity: that all students have access to some type of elementary school foreign language program. It may be that a fairly large school district can afford to schedule one or more than one type of **FLES*** program model, depending on what they have decided to be their goals and student outcomes.

The following issues must be examined, preferably by a school or school district Foreign Language Advisory Committee, looking at the various options for a foreign language sequence:

1. long-range planning, commitment, and funding
2. development of a broad base of support from different members of the school or school district community, including parents and others, in the creation of a Foreign Language Advisory Committee

3. development of goals and student outcomes for the program

4. availability of fluent, trained teachers

5. development of a realistic curriculum

6. availability of age-appropriate materials of instruction

7. development of an evaluation design of the program, based on the goals and student outcomes

8. development of the rationale for the program, articulation plans, decisions concerning beginning grade, students, schedule, and other administrative concerns

9. provision for flexibility and opportunities for modification of the program, as an evaluation of the program indicates (every three to five years).

Basis for Decisions

Decisions must be made within the constraints of time, budgets, goals, equity of access, and student outcomes in consonance with national foreign language standards. Many foreign language leaders, parents, and administrators on school and university levels have supported the following guidelines for the implementation of K–8 **FLES*** programs:

1. All K–8 elementary school students should have the opportunity to start the study of a foreign language, before the age of ten.

2. All three program models *(Sequential FLES, FLEX-Exploratory,* and *Immersion)* are valid foreign language programs, provided that they fulfill their goals.

3. There is no one best way to provide **FLES*** instruction, nor is there only one best method of **FLES*** instruction.

4. All program models contribute to a K–12 foreign language sequence.

References

Boyer, E. L. 1995. *The Basic School: A Community for Learning.* Princeton, NJ: The Carnegie Foundation for the Advancement of Teaching.

Curtain, H., and C. Pesola. 1994. *Language and Children: Making the Match.* 2nd ed. Reading, MA: Addison-Wesley.

Kennedy, D., and W. DeLorenzo. 1985. *Complete Guide to Exploratory Foreign Language Programs.* Lincolnwood, IL: National Textbook Co.

Lipton, G. 1992. *Elementary Foreign Language Programs (FLES*): An Administrator's Handbook.* Lincolnwood, IL: National Textbook Co.

———. 1994. "**FLES*** Programs Today: Options and Opportunities." *French Review* 65, 1 (Oct.): 7–10.

————. 1995. "The High School Chair's Relation to the Local **FLES*** Program." In *Managing the High School Foreign Language Department,* ed. R. Klein and S. Slick. Lincolnwood, IL: National Textbook Co.

————. 1998. *Practical Handbook to Elementary Foreign Language Programs Including FLES, FLEX and Immersion.* 3rd ed. Lincolnwood, IL: NTC/Contemporary Publishing Company.

Lipton, G., ed. 1992. *Evaluating **FLES*** Programs.* Champaign, IL: Report of the **FLES*** Commission of AATF.

National **FLES*** Institute. 1991. ***FLES**** *Programs in Action Video* and *Study Guide.* G. Lipton, project director. Baltimore, MD: National **FLES*** Institute, University of Maryland, Baltimore County 21250.

Rafferty, E. 1986. *Second Language Study and Basic Skills in Louisiana.* Baton Rouge, LA: Louisiana Department of Education.

Rehorick, S., and V. Edwards. 1992. *French Immersion: Process, Product and Perspectives.* Welland, Ontario, Canada: Canadian Modern Language Review.

"Why **FLES***?" 1994. Brochure available from AATSP, University of Northern Colorado, Greeley, CO 80639, or AATF, Mail Code 4510, Dept. of Foreign Languages, Southern Illinois University, Carbondale, IL 62901.

For additional information, contact Dr. Gladys Lipton, Director, The National **FLES*** Institute, University of Maryland, Baltimore County, Baltimore, MD 21250. FAX: 301-230-2652.

Sample Interdisciplinary Webs

HATS

Science

What are hats used for?

Temperature

Weather

Different fabrics (natural and invented)

Social Studies

Hats around the world

Ceremonial hats

Customs (tipping one's hat...)

Courtesy about hats

Language Arts

Expressions (throwing one's hat in..., hats off...)

Fairy tales in which one of the characters wears a distinctive hat (e.g., Robin Hood, Little Red Riding Hood, etc.)

Creative poetry and compositions about hats

Reading stories in which hats are involved

Music

"My Hat Has Three Corners"

"Sur le pont d'Avignon"

Other songs?

Art

Making a class collage of different hats

Physical Education

Mexican hat dance
Other dances in which hats are involved

Mathematics

Counting hats by twos, by the dozen, etc.
Hat sizes in United States and in the foreign country
Cost of hats

INSECTS

Language Arts

Identification of insects: ant, bee, butterfly, mosquito, spider, etc.
Poems and stories about insects
Classification of insects
Writing stories, poems, haiku in cooperative groups
Fable about the grasshopper and the ant

Science

Size, shape, number of wings, etc.
Protective coloring
Where insects live
What insects need to live

Art

Weaving, string art
Bark painting
Collage of pictures of insects

Music

Songs about insects

Famous compositions about insects ("Flight of the Bumble Bee")

Social Studies

Are insects helpful or harmful to humans?

Using maps to show areas where different insects live

Learning about bee societies, ant colonies, etc.

Physical Education

Invent a dance about different insects

Act out the "lady bug" chant

Invent a "crossed" insect and tell its story (two or more creatures)

Math

Problems using sixes and eights

Simple math operations using sixes and eights

Play Buzz by sixes

Effective **FLES*** Practitioners

1. Are memorable!
2. Are sensitive to interests and needs of children
3. Plan and implement effective **FLES*** programs
4. Use exciting instructional materials
5. Make assessment part of every lesson
6. Plan an ongoing evaluation of the **FLES*** program
7. Use reflection techniques effectively
8. Plan and implement an effective public-awareness program
9. Make use of a wide variety of school, parent, and community resources
10. Strive to be an essential component of the total elementary school program
11. Reach out to students, teachers, counselors, and administrators on all levels
12. Refine and renew their perspectives about teaching

Selected Sources of **FLES*** Curriculum *(Sequential FLES, FLEX, Immersion)*

Sequential FLES*

Breckenridge Public Schools, CO

Broward County Public Schools, FL

Bryn Mawr School, Baltimore, MD

Ferndale Public Schools, MI

Flint Public Schools, MI

Glastonbury Public Schools, CT

Hinsdale Public Schools, IL

Hockaday School, TX

Lexington Public Schools, MA

Louisiana State Department of Education

Lower Merion School District, PA

Newman School, LA

Pinellas County Schools, FL

Savannah-Chatham County Schools, GA

Shawnee Mission Public Schools, KS

Simsbury Public Schools, CT

Springfield Public Schools, MA

FLEX

Anne Arundel County Public Schools, MD

Harford County Public Schools, MD

Prince Georges County Public Schools, MD

Rockingham County Public Schools, VA

South Orange-Maplewood Public Schools, NJ

U.S. Virgin Islands Public Schools, USVI

Immersion

Arlington Public Schools, VA

Culver City Schools, CA

Fairfax County Public Schools, VA

Fort Worth Independent School District, TX

Kansas City Public Schools, MO

Montgomery County Public Schools, MD

Prince Georges County Public Schools, MD

Selected **FLES***
Bibliography

ACTFL. 1990. *Foreign Languages in the Elementary School: A Summary.* New York, NY: ACTFL.

Alcorn, C. 1987. "College Language Students in the Elementary School Classroom." *Language Association Bulletin* 37 Jan.: 9–10.

Allen, E., and R. Valette. 1977. *Modern Language Classroom Techniques.* 2nd ed. New York: Harcourt Brace Jovanovich.

Allen, V. 1979. "If Reading—How?" In *Teaching Foreign Languages to the Very Young,* ed. R. Freudenstein, pp. 53–60. Oxford: Pergamon Press.

Andersson, T. 1969. *Foreign Language in the Elementary School: A Struggle Against Mediocrity.* Austin: University of Texas Press.

———. 1980. "Parents, Wake Up! Why Deprive Your Child of a Superior Education?" *Hispania* 63 (May): 391–393.

Andersson, T. A. 1981. *Guide to Family Reading in Two Languages: The Preschool Years.* Roslyn, VA: National Clearinghouse for Bilingual Education.

Angiolillo, P. 1942. "French for the Feebleminded: An Experiment." *Modern Language Journal* 26 (April): 266–271.

Anne Arundel County Public Schools. 1982. *Everything You Always Wanted to Know about Foreign Languages: A Handbook on How to Be a Successful Foreign Language Student.* Annapolis, MD: Anne Arundel County Public Schools.

Armstrong, E. 1998. "Summer Language Immersion Day Camps." In *A Celebration of FLES*,* ed. G. Lipton. Lincolnwood, IL: NTC/Contemporary Publishing Company.

Armstrong, K., and C. Yetter-Vassat. 1994. "Transforming Teaching Through Technology." *FL Annals* 27, 4.

Asher, J. 1982. *Learning Another Language Through Actions.* 2nd ed. Los Gatos, CA: Sky Oakes Publications.

———. 1988. *Brainswitching: A Skill for the 21st Century.* Los Gatos, CA: Sky Oakes Publications.

Asher, J., and R. Garcia. 1982. "The Optimal Age to Learn a Foreign Language." In *Child-Adult Differences in Second Language Acquisition,* ed. S. Krashen et al., pp. 3–12. Rowley, MA: Newbury House.

Astley, H. 1985. *Get the Message.* New York: Cambridge University Press.

Bachia, A., V. Díaz, and M. Gavilán. 1992. "Saludos! An Innovative Program Developed by Broward County Public Schools in Florida." *Hispania* 75 (March): 188–196.

Bagg, G., M. Oates, and G. Zucker. 1984. "Building Community Support Through a Spanish FLES Program." *Hispania* 67 (Mar.): 105–108.

Balanz, L., and W. Teetor. 1970. *German for Elementary Schools.* Albany, NY: New York State Education Department.

Baldauf, S. 1997. "Children Say 'Oui' to Foreign Languages." *Christian Science Monitor* (June 13): 1, 10.

Baranick, W., and P. Markham. 1986. "Attitudes of Elementary School Principals toward Foreign Language Instruction." *FL Annals* 19 (Dec.): 481–489.

Barnett, H. 1970. "Let's Harness FLES Enthusiasm." *Hispania* 53 (Dec.): 979–982.

———. 1973. "Peer Teaching: FLES Programs." *Hispania* 56 (Sept.): 635–638.

———. 1986. "Foreign Languages for Younger Students and Foreign Languages for ALL Students: A Perfect Marriage." *Language Association Bulletin* (Jan.): 5.

Bartz, W. 1979. *Testing Oral Communication in the Foreign Language Classroom.* Washington, DC: Center for Applied Linguistics.

Begley, S. 1996. "Your Child's Brain." *Newsweek* (Feb. 19): 55–61.

Bellevue Public Schools. 1987. "Bellevue Spanish Immersion Program: A Description for Parents." Bellevue, WA: Bellevue Public Schools.

Bennett, R. 1990. "Authentic Materials for the **FLES*** Class." *Hispania* (Mar.): 259–261.

Bennett, W. 1988. *James Madison Elementary School. A Curriculum for American Students.* Washington, DC: U.S. Dept. of Education.

Bernhardt, E. 1992. *Life in Language Immersion Classrooms.* Great Britain: Clevedon.

Birckbichler, D. 1982. *Creative Activities for the Second Language Classroom.* Washington, DC: Center for Applied Linguistics.

Birckbichler, D., and A. Omaggio. 1978. "Diagnosing and Responding to Individual Learner Needs." *Modern Language Journal* 62 (Nov.): 336–345.

Black, S. 1993. "Learning Languages." *Executive Educator* (Mar.): 33–36.

———. 1997. "Branches of Knowledge." *American School Board Journal* (Aug.): 35–37.

Blackmon, C., and L. Pagcaliwagan. 1997. "Small World Language and Culture for Children: FLEX and the New Standards." In *Addressing the Standards for Foreign Language Learning,* ed. R. Terry, 99–114. Valdosta, GA: SCOLT.

Bourque, J., and L. Chehy. 1976. "Exploratory Language and Culture: A Unique Program." *FL Annals* 9 (Feb.): 10–16.

Boyer, E.L. 1995. *The Basic School: A Community for Learning.* Princeton, NJ: The Carnegie Foundation for the Advancement of Teaching.

Bragaw, D., H. Zimmer-Lowe, et al. 1985. "Social Studies and Foreign Languages: A Partnership." *Social Education* (Feb.): 92–96.

Brooks, N. 1964. *Language and Language Learning.* New York: Harcourt, Brace and World.

Brown, C. 1989. "The People Factor in the Glastonbury Public Schools." In *The People Factor in FLES* Programs,* ed. G Lipton, 71–78. Champaign, IL: Report of the National **FLES*** Commission of AATF.

———. 1997. "A Case for Foreign Languages: The Glastonbury Language Program." *Learning Languages* 2, 2: 3–8.

Brubacher, J., C. Case, et al. 1994. *Becoming a Reflective Educator.* Thousand Oaks, CA: Corwin Press.

Bruer, J. 1997. "The Science of Learning." *American School Board Journal* (Feb.): 24–27.

Buckby, M. 1976. "Is Primary Foreign Language Really in the Balance?" *Modern Language Journal* 60 (Nov.): 340–346.

Bush, M., and R. Terry, eds. 1996. *Technology-Enhanced Language Learning.* Lincolnwood, IL: National Textbook Co.

Canadian Association of Immersion Teachers. 1995. *Introducing English Language Arts & Early French Immersion.* Canadian Association of Immersion Teachers.

Carle, E. 1994. *La Oruga Muy Hambrienta.* Cleveland: World Publishing Co.

Carpenter, J., and J. Torney. 1974. "Beyond the Melting Pot." In *Childhood and Intercultural Education,* ed. P. Markum, 14–23. Wheaton, MD: Association for Childhood Education International.

Center for Applied Linguistics. 1992. *Elementary School K–8 Foreign Language Teacher Education Curriculum.* Washington, DC: Center for Applied Linguistics.

———. 1995. "Total and Partial Immersion Language Programs in U.S. Schools." Washington, DC: Center for Applied Linguistics.

Chapman, M., E. Grob, and M. Haas. 1989. "The Ages and Learning Stages of Children and Their Implications for Foreign Language Learning." In *Languages in Elementary Schools,* ed. K. Muller, 27–42. New York: American Forum.

Chase, C. 1986. "An Hispanic Tale for the Second Language Elementary Classroom." *Hispania* 69 (May): 395–398.

Cheney, L. 1990. *Tyrannical Machines.* Washington, DC: National Endowment for the Humanities.

Cohen, A. 1974. "The Culver City Spanish Immersion Program." *Modern Language Journal* 58 (Mar.): 95–103.

Collet, E. 1987. "Teaching French to the Very Young." *AATF National Bulletin* 12 (Jan.): 8.

Connecticut Council of Language Teachers. 1994. "Second Language Learning in the Elementary School: A Position Paper." Connecticut Council of Language Teachers.

Connor-Linton, J. 1996. "The Arlington Curriculum Development Model." *FL Annals* 29, 2: 139–151.

Cooper, T.C. 1987. "Foreign Language Study and SAT Verbal Scores." *Modern Language Journal* 71, IV: 381–387.

Covey, S. 1994. *First Things First.* NY: Simon and Schuster.

Cribari, S. 1993. "**FLES***—It's Elementary, My Dear Watson!" *Collaborare* 8, 3 (June): 1–3.

Curtain, H., and C. Pesola. 1994. *Language and Children: Making the Match.* 2nd ed. Reading, MA: Addison-Wesley.

Damen, L. 1987. *Culture Learning: The Fifth Dimension in the Language Classroom. Reading,* MA: Addison-Wesley.

Darling-Hammond, L. 1997. *The Right to Learn: A Blueprint for School Reform.* San Francisco: Jossey-Bass.

DeBuhr, A. 1993. "**FLES*** Learning Centers." In *Expanding **FLES*** Horizons,* ed. G Lipton, 24–31. Champaign, IL: AATF.

De López, M., and M. Montalvo. 1986. "Developing Public Support for Community Language Programs: A Working Model." *FL Annals* 19 (Sept.): 529–531.

De Pietro, R. 1980. "Filling the Elementary School Curriculum with Languages: What Are the Effects?" *FL Annals* 13 (April): 115–123.

De Sauzé, E. 1929. *The Cleveland Plan for the Teaching of Modern Languages.* Philadelphia: Winston Co.

Dismuke, D. 1987. "Learning Foreign Languages Is 'In' at All Levels." *NEA Today* 5 (April): 4–5.

Donato, R., and R. Terry, eds. 1995. *Foreign Language Learning: The Journey of a Lifetime.* Lincolnwood, IL: National Textbook Co.

Donoghue, M. 1968. *Foreign Languages and the Elementary School Child.* Dubuque, IA: William C. Brown.

———. 1978. "Presenting the Cultural Component during FLES." *Hispania* 61 (Mar.): 124–126.

Donoghue, M., and J. Kunkle. 1979. *Second Languages in Primary Education.* Rowley, MA: Newbury House.

Dulay, H., M. Burt, and S. Krashen. 1982. *Language Two.* New York: Oxford University Press.

Duncan, G. 1988–1989. "Administrators and Counselors: Essential Partners to FLES." *FLESNEWS* 2, 2 (Winter): 1,6.

Dunkel, H., and R. Pillett. 1962. *French in the Elementary School.* Chicago: University of Chicago Press.

Dunlea, A. 1985. *How Do We Learn Languages?* New York: Cambridge University Press.

Easley, J. 1995. "Stimulating Oral Production." *Hispania* 78, 4: 864–865.

Eddy, P. 1980. "Foreign Language in the USA: A National Survey of American Attitudes and Experience." *Modern Language Journal* 64 (Spring): 58–63.

Ehrlich, M. 1987. "Parents: The Child's Most Important Teachers." In *The Language Teacher: Commitment and Collaboration,* ed. J. Darcy, 97–110. Middlebury, VT: Northeast Conference on the Teaching of Foreign Language.

Eisenhardt, M. 1991. "FLEX: Administrative Practices...Problems Encountered in a Required FLEX Program." In *Implementing **FLES*** Programs,* ed. G. Lipton, 51–56. Champaign, IL: AATF.

"Elementary School Foreign Language." 1983. In *Foreign Languages: Key Links in the Chain in Learning,* ed. R. Mead, 11–23. Middlebury, VT: Northeast Conference on the Teaching of Foreign Languages.

ERIC Clearinghouse. 1995. *K–8 Foreign Language Assessment: A Bibliography.* Washington, DC: ERIC Clearinghouse.

"Evaluation des Programes d'Etude de Québec." 1992. In *Evaluating **FLES*** *Programs,* ed. G. Lipton, 59–77. Champaign, IL: AATF.

Fathman, A. 1982. "The Relationship between Age and Second Language Productive Ability." In *Child-Adult Differences in Second Language Acquisition,* ed. S. Krashen et al., 115–122. Rowley, MA: Newbury House.

Feindler, J. 1981. "Whatever Happened to the Joy of Foreign Language Teaching?" *Language Association Bulletin* 32 (May): 10.

Felder, R., and E. Henriques. 1995. "Learning and Teaching Styles in Foreign and Second Language Education." *FL Annals* 28, 1: 21–31.

Finnemann, M. 1996. "The World Wide Web and Foreign Language Teaching." *ERIC/CLL News Bulletin* (Sept.): 1, 6–8.

Finocchiaro, M. 1964. *Teaching Children Foreign Languages.* New York: McGraw-Hill.

Fiske, E. 1983. "Foreign Languages in Early Grades." *Baltimore Sun.* June 10.

Flaitz, J. 1983. "Building the Basic Skills through Foreign Language in the Elementary School." *Language Association Bulletin* 24 (May): 1–3.

Foreign Language Technology Activities Guide. 1995. Denver, CO: University of Denver.

Forsythe, T. 1980. "Soaking It Up in Milwaukee." *American Education* 17 (July): 21–25.

Fortune, T., and H. Jorstad. 1996. "U.S. Immersion Programs: A National Survey." *FL Annals* 29, 2 (Summer): 163–190.

Foster, K., and C. Reeves. 1989. "FLES Improves Cognitive Skills." *FLESNEWS* (Spring): 4, 5.

Fountain, A. 1996. "Articulating Literature: Concerns and Considerations." *Hispania,* 79 (Sept.): 538–542.

Freudenstein, R., ed. 1979. *Teaching Foreign Languages to the Very Young.* Oxford: Pergamon Press.

Fuchsen, M. 1989. "Starting Language Early: A Rationale." *FLESNEWS* (Spring): 1, 6.

Gahala, E., and D. Lange. 1997. "Multiple Intelligences: Multiple Ways to Help Students Learn Foreign Languages." *Northeast Conference Newsletter* 41: 29–34.

Gaies, S., and R. Bowers. 1990. "Clinical Supervision of Language Teaching: The Supervisor as Trainer and Educator." In *Second Language Teacher Education,* ed. J. Richards and D. Nunan, 167–181. New York: Cambridge University Press.

García, P. 1990a. "Five Easy Pieces: Consideration of the Inservice Needs of **FLES*** Teachers." In *Innovations in **FLES*** *Programs,* ed. G. Lipton, 23–32. Champaign, IL: Report of the National **FLES*** Commission of AATF.

————. 1990b. "Adelante! The Spanish Immersion Program of the Kansas City, Missouri, Schools." *Hispania* 73 (Dec.): 1130–1133.

————. 1991. "Allegro Sostenuto: A Baker's Dozen of Concerns for the Immersion Educator." In *Implementing FLES* Programs*, ed. G. Lipton, 92–103. Champaign, IL: Report of the National FLES* Commission of AATF.

Gardner, H. 1993. *Multiple Intelligences: The Theory in Practice*. New York: Basic Books.

Garfinkel, A., and K. Tabor. 1991. "Elementary School of Foreign Languages and English Reading Achievement." *FL Annals* 24, 5 (Oct.): 375–382.

Garnett, N. 1987. "Establishing a Primary Level School of Spanish." *Hispania* 70 (Mar.): 167–170.

Garza, T. 1995–1996. "The Imagination and CD-ROM: Multimedia and Culture Instruction." *Journal of Imagination in Language Learning:* 36–40.

Gass, R., and C. Madden, eds. 1985. *Input in Second Language Acquisition.* Rowley, MA: Newbury House.

Gates, B. 1995. "The Road Ahead." *Newsweek* (Nov. 27): 59–68.

Gebhard, J. 1990. "Freeing the Teacher: A Supervisory Process." *FL Annals* 23 (Dec.): 517–525.

Genesee, F. 1987. *Learning through Two Languages.* Rowley, MA: Newbury House.

Genesee, F., ed. 1994. *Educating Second Language Children.* New York: Cambridge University Press.

Georgia Dept. of Education. 1988. *Georgia Guide for Elementary and Middle Grades.* Atlanta, GA: Georgia Dept. of Education.

Gifted Child Project. 1970. *French Achievement Test.* New York: Gifted Child Project, New York City Board of Education.

Glass, J. 1994. "Everyone Loves a Good Story: Take the Time." *Hispania* 71 (May): 295–297.

Goepper, J., and M. Murphy, eds. 1989. *The Teaching of French: A Syllabus of Competence.* Champaign, IL: Report of the Commission of Professional Standards of AATF.

Gookin, D., W. Wang, et al. 1993. *Illustrated Computer Dictionary for Dummies.* San Mateo, CA: IDG Books.

Gradisnik, A. 1966. "Television Can Be Effective in the FLES Program...If." *Hispania* 49 (Sept.): 485–489.

Gramer, V. 1988. "Cautions in FLES Program Planning and Implementation." In *So You Want to Have a FLES* Program!*, ed. G. Lipton et al., 75–78. Champaign, IL: Report of the National FLES* Commission of AATF.

————. 1990. "Working with Parents." In *Innovations in FLES* Programs*, ed G. Lipton, 67–70. Champaign, IL: Report of the National FLES* Commission of AATF.

————. 1998. "Differing Abilities in the Sequential FLES Class." In *A Celebration of FLES**, ed. G. Lipton. Lincolnwood, IL: NTC/Contemporary Publishing Company.

Green, J. 1979. "Hello World!" *Instructor* 89 (Oct.): 91–94.

Griffin, R. 1987. "Using Current Magazines as a Resource for Teaching Culture." *Hispania* 70 (May): 400–402.

Grittner, F. 1991. "Foreign Languages for Children: Let's Do It Right This Time." *Hispania* 74 (March): 40–44.

Grunstad, D. 1991. "The Integration of Language and Culture in the FLES Classroom: Process and Application." *Iowa FLES Newsletter* 6, 3 (Winter): 1, 4–6, 8–9.

Gunderson, B., and D. Johnson. 1980. "Building Positive Attitudes by Using Cooperative Learning Groups." *FL Annals* 13: 39–43.

Hadley, A. Omaggio. 1993. *Teaching Language in Context.* 2nd ed. Boston, MA: Heinle and Heinle.

Hallman, C. L., and A. Campbell. 1989. *Coordination of Foreign Language Teacher Training: Teaching Foreign Languages in the Elementary Schools.* Gainesville, FL: University of Florida.

Hammerly, H. 1989. *French Immersion: Myths and Reality.* Calgary, Alberta: Detselig Enterprises, Ltd.

Hancock, C., G. Lipton, et al. 1976. "A Study of FLES and non-FLES Pupils' Attitudes toward the French and Their Culture." *French Review* 49 (April): 717–722.

Hancock, V., and F. Betts. 1994. "From the Lagging to the Leading Edge." *Educational Leadership* 51, 7 (April): 24–29.

Harding, E., and P. Riley. 1986. *The Bilingual Family: A Handbook for Parents.* New York: Cambridge University Press.

Harmin, M. 1994. *Inspiring Active Learning.* Alexandria, VA: ASCD.

Hawley, D., and M. Oates. 1985. "FLES Certification for Secondary Teachers: An Idea Whose Time Has Come." *Iowa FLES Newsletter* 1, 2 (Spring): 4–5.

Hayden, R. 1983. "A Beginning: Building Global Competence." *State Education Leader* 2 (Fall): 1–3.

Heining-Boynton, A. 1990. "Using FLES History to Plan for the Present and Future." *FL Annals* 23 (Dec.): 503–509.

Heining-Boynton, D. 1991. "The Developing Child: What Every FLES Teacher Needs to Know." In *Focus on the Foreign Language Learner: Priorities and Strategies,* ed. W. Bartz and M. Nykos, 3–11. Lincolnwood, IL: National Textbook Co.

Hernández, N. S. 1994. *Elementary Foreign Language Programs.* Simsbury, CT: Simsbury, CT, Public Schools.

Herron, C., and J. Hanley. 1992. "Using Video to Introduce Children to a Foreign Culture." *FL Annals* 25, 5: 419–426.

Higgs, T., ed. 1984. *Teaching for Proficiency: The Organizing Principle.* Lincolnwood, IL: National Textbook Co.

Hines, M. 1991. "A Case for French." In *Implementing FLES* Programs,* ed. G. Lipton, 61–70. Champaign, IL.

Hirsch, E. D. 1994. *The Schools We Need and Why We Don't Have Them.* New York: Doubleday.

Hornby, P. 1980. "Achieving Second Language Fluency through Immersion Education." *FL Annals* 13 (April): 107–112.

Howe, E. 1983. "The Success of the Cherry Hill Spanish Immersion Program in Oren, Utah." *Hispania* 66 (Dec.): 592–597.

Huber, V. 1987. "Teaching for Oral Proficiency at the Elementary School Level." *Hispania* 70 (Sept.): 658–663.

Hughes, A. 1989. *Testing the Language Teachers.* New York: Cambridge University Press.

Hunter, M. 1969. *Teach More—Faster.* El Segundo, CA: TIP Publications.

———. 1974. "Individualizing FLES." *Hispania* 57 (Sept.): 494–497.

Hurst, D. 1996. "Teaching Spanish to Children with Different Learning Styles: Evolution of a Philosophy." *Hispania* (Mar.): 123–125.

Hyerle, D. 1996. *Visual Tools for Constructing Knowledge.* Alexandria, VA: Association for Supervision and Curriculum Development.

Jackson, C. 1996. "National Standards and the Challenge of Articulation." In *Foreign Language for All,* ed. B. Wing, 115–140. Lincolnwood, IL: National Textbook Co.

Jacobs, G. 1978. "An American FL Immersion Program: How To." *FL Annals* 11 (Sept.): 405–413.

James, K. 1990. "Why Not Technology for Children?" In *Innovations in **FLES*** Programs,* ed. G. Lipton, 51–58. Champaign, IL: AATF.

Jarvis, G., ed. 1984. *The Challenge for Excellence in Foreign Language Education.* Middlebury, VT: The Northeast Conference on the Teaching of Foreign Languages.

Johnson, S., and C. Johnson. 1986. *The One-Minute Teacher.* New York: William Morrow and Co.

Joiner, E. 1974. "Evaluating the Cultural Component of FL Tests." *Modern Language Journal* 58 (Sept.): 242–244.

Joint National Committee on Languages (JNCL). 1995. *The Impact of Education Reform: A Survey of State Activities.* Washington, DC: Joint National Committee on Languages.

Jones, K. 1982. *Simulations in Language Teaching.* New York: Cambridge University Press.

Kennedy, D., and P. Barr-Harrison. 1998. "ICAL: Variation on a FLEX Theme." In *A Celebration of **FLES***,* ed. G. Lipton. Lincolnwood, IL: NTC/Contemporary Publishing Company.

Kennedy, D., and W. DeLorenzo. 1985. *Complete Guide to Exploratory Foreign Language Programs.* Lincolnwood, IL: National Textbook Co.

Klein, R., and S. Slick. 1996. *Managing the High School Foreign Language Department.* Lincolnwood, IL: National Textbook Co.

Klippet, F. 1992. *Keep Talking.* 10th ed. NY: Cambridge University Press.

Korfe, P. 1992. "Portfolio Assessment of **FLES***." In *Evaluatinig **FLES*** Programs,* ed. G. Lipton, 38–51. Champaign, IL: AATF.

———. 1994. "Relating **FLES*** to the Regular Classroom." In ***FLES*** *Methodology I*, ed. G. Lipton, 33–36. Champaign, IL: AATF.

Koster, C. 1986. "English FLES in the Netherlands: How Good Must a Teacher Be?" *Modern Language Journal* 70 (Spring): 8–12.

Krashen, S. 1983. *Principles and Practices in Second Language Acquisition.* Oxford: Pergamon Press.

Krashen, S., M. Long, et al., eds. 1982. *Child-Adult Differences in Second Language Acqusition.* Rowley, MA: Newbury House.

Krashen, S., and T. Terrell. 1983. *The Natural Approach to Language Acquisition in the Classroom.* Oxford: Pergamon Press.

Kurk, K. 1993. *Un Calendrier Perpétuel.* A project of the National **FLES*** Commission of AATF. Champaign, IL: AATF.

Kurk, K., and H. Landwehr. 1993. "Reading the World: **FLES*** and Multicultural Teaching." In *Expanding **FLES*** Horizons,* ed. G. Lipton, 14–23. Champaign, IL: AATF.

Lafayette, R., ed. 1996. *National Standards: A Catalyst for Reform.* Lincolnwood, IL: National Textbook Co.

Landry, R. 1973. "The Enhancement of Figural Creativity Through Second Language Learning at the Elementary School Level." *FL Annals* (Oct.): 111–115.

———. 1974. "A Comparison of Second Language Learners and Monolinguals on Divergent Thinking Tasks at the Elementary School Level." *Modern Language Journal* 58 (Jan.): 10–15.

Larew, L. 1986. "The Teacher of FLES in 1986." *Hispania* (Sept.): 699–701.

Larson-Freeman. 1991. *An Introduction to Second Language Research.* New York: Longman.

Lenneberg, E. 1967. *Biological Foundations of Language.* New York: John Wiley.

Levenson, S., and W. Kendrick. 1967. *Readings in Foreign Languages for the Elementary Schools.* Waltham, MA: Blaisdell.

Lipton, G. 1964. "Welcome to FLES!" *French Review* 38 (Dec.): 229–232.

———. 1969. "The Effectiveness of Listening-Speaking-Only, as Compared with Listening-Speaking-Reading in Grade Four, the First Year of Study of French at the FLES Level, in the Acquisition of Auditory Comprehension." Doctoral dissertation, New York University, *Dissertation Abstracts International* 30/06-A, 2421.

———. 1971. "A Potpourri of Ideas for French FLES Classes." *Instructor* 80 (Jan.): 49–53.

———. 1988. "They Love Foreign Languages for Children." In *Children and Languages,* ed. K. Müller. New York: American Forum.

———. 1990a. "Enseigner la culture dans la classe de langue étrangère au niveau élémentaire." In *Culture et Enseignement du Français,* ed. R. Lafayette. Paris: Didier: 175–179.

———. 1990b. "**FLES*** Programs: Today and Tomorrow." *AATF National Bulletion* 16, 2 (Nov.): 7–10.

———. 1990c. "A Look Back...A Look Ahead." *Hispania* 73 (March): 255–258.

——. 1990d. "Successful **FLES***: How to..." *Northeast Conference Newsletter* (Sept.): 12–13, 31.

——. 1992. *Elementary Foreign Language Programs (**FLES***): An Administrator's Handbook.* Lincolnwood, IL: National Textbook Co.

——. 1994a. "The Basic Components of **FLES***: Communication and Culture." In *Dimension '94: Changing Images in Foreign Language,* ed. R. Terry. Valdosta, GA: SCOLT, 29–39.

——. 1994b. "**FLES*** Programs Today: Options and Opportunities." *French Review* 65, 1 (Oct.): 1–16.

——. 1994c. "What Is **FLES*** Methodology?" *Hispania* (Dec.): 878–887.

——. 1995. "We Can Teach All Students: **FLES*** Students Rarely Fail!" In *Reaching All **FLES*** Students,* ed. G. Lipton, 48–52. Champaign, IL: AATF.

——. 1996a. "Factors for Success in K–12 Foreign Language Programs: A Checklist." In *Managing the High School FL Department,* ed. R. Klein and S. Slick, 213–217. Lincolnwood, IL: National Textbook Co.

——. 1996b. "**FLES*** Research Packet." Baltimore, MD: National **FLES*** Institute, University of Maryland, Baltimore County, 21250.

——. 1996c. "**FLES*** Teacher Preparation: Competencies, Content and Complexities." In *Foreign Language Teacher Education,* ed. Z. Moore, 37–58. University Press of America.

——. 1996d. "The High School Chair's Relations with the Local **FLES*** Program." In *Managing the High School FL Department,* ed. R. Klein and S. Slick, 153–162. Lincolnwood, IL: National Textbook Co.

——. 1996e. "The Many Benefits of All Types of **FLES*** Programs." *Northeast Conference Newsletter* (Fall): 56–57.

——. 1996f. "Many **FLES*** Issues, Many Approaches in **FLES***." *ACTFL Newsletter* (Winter): 16–17.

——. 1996g. *Planning Effective **FLES*** Programs.* Baltimore, MD: National **FLES*** Institute, University of Maryland, Baltimore County, 21250.

——. 1996h. *Planning Effective Spanish **FLES*** Programs.* Greeley, CO: AATSP.

——. 1996i. "Suggestions for Attracting French **FLES*** Students." Carbondale, IL: AATF.

——. 1996j. "The Three C's of **FLES*** Teacher Preparation: Competencies, Content and Complexities." In *Foreign Language Teacher Education: International Perspectives,* ed. Z. Moore. Lanham, MD: University Press of America.

——. 1998. *Practical Handbook to Elementary Foreign Language Programs Including FLES, FLEX, and Immersion Programs.* 3rd ed. Lincolnwood, IL: NTC/Contemporary Publishing Company.

——. 1998. "A Retrosepctive on **FLES***: 1898–1998." *Hispania* (March).

Lipton, G., ed. 1987. *A **FLES*** Sampler: Learning Activities for FLES, FLEX, Immersion.* Champaign, IL: **FLES*** Commission Report to AATF.

——. 1988. *So You Want to Have a **FLES*** Program!* Champaign, IL: Report of the National **FLES*** Commission of AATF.

Lipton, G. ed. 1989. *The People Factor in **FLES*** Programs.* Champaign, IL: Report of the National **FLES*** Commission of AATF.

———. 1990. *Innovations in **FLES*** Programs*. Champaign, IL: Report of the National **FLES*** Commission of AATF.

———. 1991. *Implementing **FLES*** Programs*. Champaign, IL: Report of the National **FLES*** Commission of AATF.

———. 1992. *Evaluating **FLES*** Programs*. Champaign, IL: Report of the **FLES*** Commission of AATF.

———. 1993. *Expanding **FLES*** Programs*. Champaign, IL: Report of the **FLES*** Commission of AATF.

———. 1994. ***FLES*** Methodology I*. Champaign, IL: Report of the **FLES*** Commission of AATF.

———. 1995. *Reaching All **FLES*** Students*. Champaign, IL: Report of the **FLES*** Commission of AATF.

———. 1996. *Attracting French **FLES*** Students*. Champaign, IL: Report of the **FLES*** Commission of AATF.

———. 1998. *A Celebration of **FLES***. Lincolnwood, IL: NTC/Contemporary Publishing Company.

Lipton, G., and J. Mirsky. 1970. *Spanish for Elementary Schools*. Albany, NY: New York State Department of Education.

Lipton, G., R. Morgan, and M. Reed. 1996. "Does **FLES*** Help AP French Students Perform Better?" *AATF National Bulletin* 21: 4.

Lipton, G., and W. Teetor. 1972. *Why FLES?* Schenectady, NY: New York State Association of Foreign Language Teachers.

Lipton, G., and E. Bourque, eds. 1969. *The 3 R's of FLES*. FLES Report to AATF.

Lipton, G., N. Rhodes, and H. Curtain, eds. 1985. *The Many Faces of Foreign Language in the Elementary School: FLES, FLEX and Immersion*. Champaign, IL: FLES Commission Report to AATF.

Lipton, G., and V. Spaar-Rauch eds. 1970. *FLES: Patterns for Change*. FLES Report to AATF.

Lipton, G., and V. Spaar-Rauch, eds. 1971. *FLES Goals and Guides*. FLES Report to AATF.

Littlewood, W. 1981. *Communicative Language Teaching: An Introduction*. New York: Cambridge University Press.

———. 1984. *Foreign and Second Language Learning*. New York: Cambridge University Press.

Love, F., and L. Honig. 1973. Options and Perspectives: A Sourcebook of Innovative Foreign Language Programs in Action, K–12. New York: Modern Language Association.

Lucietto, L. 1994. "Linking Language and Content." In ***FLES*** Methodology I*, ed. G. Lipton, 7–21. Champaign, IL: AATF.

———. 1995. "Mon Parcours: Letting Them Tell Their Story." In *Reaching All Students*, ed. G. Lipton, 10–16. Champaign, IL: American Association of Teachers of French.

Macdonald, M., and S. Rogers-Gordon. 1984. *Action Plans*. Rowley, MA: Newbury House.

MacRae, M. 1957. *Teaching Spanish in the Grades.* Boston: Houghton Mifflin.

Makin, L., J. Campbell, et al. 1995. *One Childhood, Many Languages: Guidelines for Early Childhood Education in Australia.* Pymble, Australia: Harper Educational Publishers.

Maley, A., and A. Duff. 1975. *Sounds Interesting.* New York: Cambridge University Press.

———. 1978. *Variations on a Theme.* New York: Cambridge University Press.

———. 1979. *Sounds Intriguing.* New York: Cambridge University Press.

———. 1982. *Drama Techniques in Language Learning.* 2nd ed. New York: Cambridge University Press.

Marzano, R., D. Pickering, and J. McTighe. 1993. *Assessing Student Outcomes.* Alexandria, VA: Association for Supervision and Curriculum Development.

Masciantonio, R. 1977. "Tangible Benefits of the Study of Latin: A Review of Research." *FL Annals* 10 (Sept.): 375–382.

Mavrogenes, N. 1979. "Latin in Elementary School: A Help for Reading and Language Arts." *Phi Delta Kappan* 60 (May): 675–677.

Mazziotti, J. 1985. *Active Vocabulary Building.* Schenectady, NY: New York State Association of Foreign Language Teachers.

McKim, L. 1983. *Meeting the Foreign Language Crisis in the U.S.: Guidelines for Action.* Los Alamitos, CA: National Center for Bilingual Research.

McLaughlin, B. 1982. *Children's Second Language Learning.* Washington, DC: Center for Applied Linguistics.

———. 1994. "Are Immersion Programs the Answer for Bilingual Education in the U.S.?" *Bilingual Review* 11 (Jan./Apr.): 3–10.

Met, M. 1985. "Decisions! Decisions! Foreign Language in the Elementary School." *FL Annals* 18 (Dec.): 469–473.

———. 1988. "Cautions in Immersion Program Planning." In *So You Want to Have a **FLES*** Program!*, ed. G. Lipton, 79–81. Champaign, IL: Report of the National **FLES*** Commission of AATF.

Miller, E. 1994. "All the World's a Stage." In ***FLES*** *Methodology I,* ed. G. Lipton, 48–55. Champaign, IL: AATF.

———. 1995. "A Salad of Language Learners." In *Reaching All **FLES*** Students,* ed. G. Lipton, 1–8. Champaign, IL: AATF.

Miller, E., ed. 1995. *All the World's a Stage.* Project of the National **FLES*** Commission of AATF. Write 74 Tuscalusa, Atherton, CA 94025.

Montessori, M. 1966. *The Secret of Childhood.* New York: Ballatine Books.

Montgomery County Public Schools. 1994a. *Teaching Culture in the Grades K–8: Resource Manual for French; Resource Manual for Spanish.* Montgomery County Public Schools, MD.

———. 1994b. *Video Series on Training for Immersion Teachers.* Montgomery County Public Schools, MD.

Moore, Z. 1994. "The Portfolio and Testing Culture." In *Teaching, Testing, and Assessment: Making the Connection,* ed. C. Hancock, 163–183. Lincolnwood, IL: National Textbook Co.

Moore, Z., ed. 1996. *Foreign Language Teacher Education: International Perspectives.* Lanham, MD: University Press of America.

Moskowitz, G. 1976. "Competency Based Teacher Education: Before We Proceed." *Modern Language Journal* 60 (Jan.): 18–23.

———. 1978. *Caring and Sharing in the Foreign Language Class.* Rowley, MA: Newbury House.

Müller, K., ed. 1988. *Children and Languages,* R. Benya, compiler. New York: The American Forum.

Nadia, S. 1993. "Kids' Brainpower." *Oregonian* (Dec. 13): 8–9.

Nash, J. 1996. "Zooming in on Dyslexia." *Time* (Jan. 29): 62–64.

National **FLES*** Institute. 1991. **FLES*** *Programs in Action Video* and *Study Guide*. G. Lipton, project director. Baltimore, MD: National **FLES*** Institute, University of Maryland, Baltimore County, 21250.

National Governors' Association. 1989. *America in Transition: The International Frontier.* Report of the Task Force on International Education. Washington, DC: National Governors' Association.

National Standards in Foreign Language Education Project. 1996. *Standards for Foreign Language Learning: Preparing for the 21st Century.* Yonkers, NY: National Standards in Foreign Language Education Project.

NCSSFL/ACTFL. 1990. *Statement on the Study of Foreign Languages in Elementary Schools.* New York: ACTFL.

Negroni, P. 1998. "Public Education in America and the Implications of Foreign Language and Second Language Acquisition." In *A Celebration of FLES**, ed. G. Lipton. Lincolnwood, IL: NTC/Contemporary Publishing Company.

Nessel, D. 1987. "Reading Comprehension: Asking the Right Questions." *Phi Delta Kappan* 68 (Feb.): 442–445.

New York City Board of Education. 1963a. *French in the Elementary School.* New York: New York City Board of Education.

New York City Board of Education. 1963b. *Spanish in Elementary Schools.* New York: New York City Board of Education.

Nielsen, M., and E. Hoffman. 1996. "Technology, Reform, and Foreign Language Standards: A Vision for Change." In *National Standards: A Catalyst for Change,* ed. R. Lafayette, 119–138. Lincolnwood, IL: National Textbook Co.

North Carolina Teacher Handbook: Second Language Studies, K–12. Raleigh, NC: 1989.

Nunan, D. 1992. *Research Methods in Language Learning.* New York: Cambridge University Press.

Oates, M. 1980. "A Non-Intensive FLES Program in French." *French Review* 54 (Mar.): 507–513.

Obadia, A. 1995. "French Immersion." *Educational Excellence* (Mar.): 12–15.

Oller, J., and K. Perkins, eds. 1980. *Research in Language Testing.* Rowley, MA: Newbury House.

Omaggio, A. 1978. *Games and Simulations in the Foreign Language Classroom.* Arlington, VA: Center for Applied Linguistics.

————. 1993. *Teaching Language in Context*. Boston: Heinle and Heinle.

Otto, S., and J. Pusack. 1996. "Technological Choices to Meet the Challenges." In *Foreign Language for All: Challenges and Choices*, ed. B. Wing, 141–186. Lincolnwood, IL: National Textbook Co.

Paananen, D. 1981. "Why Your Youngster Should Learn a Foreign Language." *Better Homes and Gardens* (Oct.): 17–19.

Padilla, A., J. Anineo, et al. 1996. "Development and Implementation of Student Portfolios in FL Programs." *FL Annals* 29, 3: 429–438.

Papalia, A. 1986. "A Synthesis on What Research Says on Early Second Language Learning." *Language Association Bulletin* 37 (Jan.): 11–14.

Paquette, F., ed. 1968. *New Dimensions in the Teaching of FLES*. Bloomington, IN: Indiana Language Project.

Pawley, C. 1985. "How Bilingual Are French Immersion Students?" *Canadian Modern Language Review* 41: 865–876.

Peck, B. 1993. "The Language Explosion: Europe Starts It Early." *Phi Delta Kappan* (Sept.): 91–92.

Penfield, W. 1967. "The Learning of Languages." In *Foreign Language Teaching Today*, ed. J. Michel, 192–214. New York: Macmillan.

Penfield, W., and L. Roberts. 1959. *Speech and Brain Mechanisms*. New York: Atheneum Press.

Pesola, C. 1982. *A Source Book for Elementary and Middle School Language Programs*. Minneapolis: Minnesota State Department of Education.

Pfaff, C., ed. 1987. *First and Second Language Acquisition Process*. Cambridge, MA: Newbury House.

Postman, N. 1995. *The End of Education Beginning with the Value of School*. New York: Alfred A. Knopf.

Rafferty, E. 1986. *Second Language Study and Basic Skills in Louisiana*. Baton Rouge, LA: Louisiana Department of Education.

Ratté, E. 1968. "Foreign Languages and the Elementary School Language Arts Program." *French Review* 42: 80–85.

Rehorick, S., and V. Edwards. 1992. *French Immersion: Process, Product and Perspectives*. Welland, Ontario, Canada: Canadian Modern Language Review.

Rhodes, N., and R. Oxford. 1988. "Foreign Languages in Elementary and Secondary Schools: Results of a National Survey." *FL Annals* 21: 51–69.

Rhodes, N., and A. Schreibstein. 1983. *Foreign Language in the Elementary School: A Practical Guide*. Washington, DC: Center for Applied Linguistics.

Richards, J., and C. Lockhart. 1994. *Reflective Teaching in Second Language Classrooms*. New York: Cambridge University Press.

Rivers, W. 1983. *Communicating Naturally in a Second Language*. New York: Cambridge University Press.

Roberts, F. 1986. "Should Your Child Learn a Foreign Language?" *Parents* 61 (April): 58–62.

Robinson, D. W. 1998. "Celebrating the Success of **FLES*** Through Evaluation." In *A Celebration of **FLES***, ed. G. Lipton. Lincolnwood, IL: NTC/Contemporary Publishing Company.

Robinson, D. W., ed. 1995. *The OFLA FLES Guide*. Ohio State University, 13134 Wellesley Dr., Pickerington, OH 43147.

Robison, R. 1992. "Developing Practical Speaking Tests for the FL Classroom: A Small Group Approach." *FL Annals* 25, 6: 487–496.

Rosenbusch, M. 1985. "FLES: An Important Step in the Right Direction." *Hispania* 68 (Mar.): 174–176.

Sadow, S. 1982. *Idea Bank: Creative Activities for the Language Class*. Rowley, MA: Newbury House.

Savignon, S. 1983. *Communicative Competence: Theory and Classroom Practice*. Reading, MA: Addison-Wesley.

Savignon, S., and M. Berns, eds. 1984. *Initiatives in Communicative Language Teaching*. Reading, MA: Addison-Wesley.

Saxon, H. 1992. "A Kaleidoscope of Discovery." In *Evaluating **FLES*** Programs*, ed. G. Lipton, 21–31. Champaign, IL: AATF.

———. 1994. "La Francofolie." In ***FLES*** Methodology I*, ed. G. Lipton, 37–45. Champaign, IL: AATF.

Scarcella, R., and C. Higa. 1982. "Input and Age Differences in Second Language Acquisition." In *Child-Adult Differences in Second Language Acquisition*, ed. S. Krashen et al., 175–201. Rowley, MA: Newbury House.

Scheibel, A. 1997. "Thinking About Thinking." *American School Board Journal* (Feb.): 21–23.

Schinke-Llano, L. 1985. *Foreign Language in the Elementary School: State of the Art*. Washington, DC: Center for Applied Linguistics.

Schneider, J. 1984. "PTA and TPR: A Comprehension-Based Approach in a Public Elementary School." *Hispania* 67 (Dec.): 620–625.

———. 1990. "FLEX Goes to College: International Language Camp at UMBC." *Hispania* 73 (Sept.): 823–826.

Schrade, A. 1978. "Des Plaines FLES: Successful Language Arts and Social Studies Integration." *Hispania* 61 (Sept.): 504–507.

———. 1994. "Gameplay in Spanish Teaching." *Hispania* 77: 302–306.

Schrier, L. 1996. "A Prototype for Articulating Spanish as a Foreign Language in Elementary Schools." *Hispania* 79 (Sept.): 515–522.

Schrier, L., and M. Fast. 1992. "Foreign Language in the Elementary School and Computer Assisted Language Learning." *Hispania* 75: 1304–1312.

Schwartz, J. 1996. "The Site-Seer's Guide to Some Way-Out Internet Futures." *Washington Post* (July 3): 1, 18.

Seefeldt, C., and N. Barbour. 1994. *Early Childhood Education*. 3rd ed. Columbus, OH: Merrill.

Seelye, H. 1983. *Teaching Culture*. Lincolnwood, IL: National Textbook Co.

Segal, B. 1982. *Enseñando el espanol por medio de acción*. Brea, CA: Berty Segal, Inc.

Sheperd, G., and W. Ragan. 1982. *Modern Elementary Curriculum*. New York: Holt, Rinehart and Winston.

Shrum, J., and E. Glisan. 1994. *Teacher's Handbook: Contextualized Language Instruction*. Boston, MA: Heinle and Heinle.

Simon, P. 1980. *The Tongue-Tied American*. New York: Continuum.

Sims, W., and S. Hammond. 1981. *Award-Winning Foreign Language Programs: Prescriptions for Success*. Lincolnwood, IL: National Textbook Co.

Singer, M. 1992. "Louisiana Evaluation Project." In *Evaluating FLES* Programs*, ed. G. Lipton, 10–16. Champaign, IL: AATF.

Singerman, A., ed. 1996. *Acquiring Cross-Cultural Competence: Four Stages for Students of French*. Project of the Cultural Competence Commission of AATF. Lincolnwood, IL: National Textbook Co.

Slavin. R. 1991. *Student Team Learning: A Practical Guide to Cooperative Learning*. 3rd ed. Washington, DC: National Education Association.

Smith, S. 1984. *The Theatre Arts and the Teaching of Second Languages*. Reading, MA: Addison-Wesley.

Stanislawczyk, I., and S. Yavner. 1976. *Creativity in the Language Classroom*. Rowley, MA: Newbury House.

Stern, H. 1976. "Optimal Age: Myth or Reality?" *Canadian Modern Language Review* 32 (Feb.): 283–294.

———. 1982. *Issues in Early Core French*. Toronto: Ontario Institute for Studies in Education.

———. 1983. "Toward a Multidimensional Foreign Language Curriculum." In *Foreign Languages: Key Links in the Chain in Learning*, ed. R. Mead, 120–146. Middlebury, VT: Northeast Conference on the Teaching of Foreign Languages.

Sternberg, R. 1987. "Teaching Critical Thinking: Eight Easy Ways to Fail Before You Begin." *Phi Delta Kappan* 68 (Feb.): 45–49.

Stevens, F. 1984. *Strategies for Second Language Acquisition*. Montreal: Eden Press.

Stevick, E. 1976. *Memory, Meaning, Method: Some Psychological Perspectives in Language Learning*. Rowley, MA: Newbury House.

———. 1982. *Teaching and Learning Language*. New York: Cambridge University Press.

———. 1986. *Images and Options in the Language Classroom*. New York: Cambridge University Press.

Swain, M. 1985 "Communicative Competence: Some Roles of Comprehensible Input and Comprehensible Output in Its Development." In *Input in Second Language Acquisition*, ed. S. Gass and C. Madden, 251–271. Rowley, MA: Newbury House.

Swain, M., and S. Lapkin. 1989. "Canadian Immersion and Adult Second Language Teaching: What's the Connection?" *Modern Language Journal* 73: 150–159.

Sylwester, R.A. 1995. *A Celebration of Neurons*. Alexandria, VA: Association for Supervision and Curriculum Development.

Talbott, S. 1995. *The Future Does Not Compute.* Sebastopol, CA: O'Reilly and Associates.

Thomas, W., V. Collier, and M. Abbott. 1993. "Academic Achievement through Japanese, Spanish or French: The First Two Years of Partial Immersion." *Modern Language Journal* 77, ii: 170–179.

Thompson, L., compiler. 1995. *K–8 Foreign Language Assessment: A Bibliography.* Washington, DC: Center for Applied Linguistics and NFL Center K–12.

Trites, R. 1981. *Primary French Immersion: Disabilities and Prediction of Success.* Toronto: OISE Press.

Tucker, G. R., and R. Donato. 1996. "Documenting Growth in a Japanese FLES Program." *FL Annals* 29:539–550.

Tuttle, H. 1981. "Mnemonics in Spanish Classes." *Hispania* 64 (Dec.): 572–574.

Underhill, N. 1987. *Testing Spoken Language.* New York: Cambridge University Press.

Ur, P. 1984. *Teaching Listening Comprehension.* New York: Cambridge University Press.

U.S. Department of Education.1986. *What Works.* Washington, DC: U.S. Department of Education.

Valette, R. 1977. *Modern Language Testing.* 2nd ed. New York: Harcourt, Brace, Jovanovich.

———. 1992. "Using Class Quizzes to Promote Language Accuracy of Younger Learners." In *Evaluating **FLES*** Programs,* ed. G. Lipton, 1–9. Champaign, IL: AATF.

Vidrine, D. 1986. "The Fête Française: A Promotional Venture." *FL Annals* 19 (Sept.): 305–310.

Vigil, V. 1993. "Arizona's Elementary Foreign Language Mandate, Phase I: Now That We Have It, What Shall We Do?" *FL Annals* 26, 4: 535–541.

Vines, L. 1983. *A Guide to Language Camps in the U.S.* Washington, DC: ERIC Clearinghouse on Languages and Linguistics.

Vobejda, B. 1986. "U.S. Students Called Internationally Illiterate." *Washington Post* (Nov. 22): A-7.

Wallace, N. 1986. "The Early Second Language Experience." *Language Association Bulletin* 37 (Jan.): 1–4.

Wallace, N., and C. Wirth. 1985. *Vocabulary Building and Cultural Activities for Early Second Language Programs.* Schenectady, NY: New York State Association of Foreign Language Teachers.

Wasserman, S. 1987. "Teaching for Thinking: Louis E. Raths Revisited." *Phi Delta Kappan* 68 (Feb.): 460–465.

Watzke, J., and D. Grunstad. 1996. "Student Reasons for Studying Language: Implications for Program Planning and Develoment." *Learning Languages* 2, 1: 15–28.

Weeks, T. 1979. *Born to Talk.* Rowley, MA: Newbury House.

"Why **FLES***?" 1994. Brochure available from AATSP, University of Northern Colorado, Greeley, CO 80639, or AATF, Mail Code 4510, Dept. of Foreign Languages, Southern Illinois University, Carbondale, IL 62901-4510.

Wilde, S., ed. 1996. *Making a Difference: Selected Writings of Dorothy Watson.* Portsmouth, NH: Heinemann.

Williams, B. 1996. *The World Wide Web for Teachers.* Foster City, CA: IDG Books.

Wilson, J. A. 1988. "Foreign Language Program Articulation: Building Bridges from Elementary to Secondary Schools." *Eric Digest* (Nov.): 1–2.

Wilson, V., and B. Wattenmaker. 1980. *Real Communication in Foreign Languages.* Boston, MA: Allyn and Bacon.

Wing, B. 1984. "For Teachers: A Challenge for Competence." In *The Challenge of Excellence in Foreign Language Education,* ed. G. Jarvis, 11–46. Middlebury, VT: Northeast Conference on the Teaching of Foreign Languages.

———. 1996. "Starting Foreign Languages in the Elementary and Middle Schools." In *Foreign Languages for All: Challenges and Choices,* ed. B. Wing, 21–56. Lincolnwood, IL: National Textbook Co.

Wisconsin Public Radio Association. 1995. "Gray Matters…The Developing Brain." Transcript of Radio Broadcast. Madison, WI: Wisconsin Public Radio Association. Available from the Radio Store, 821 University Avenue, Madison, WI 53706.

Wolf, Kenneth. 1996. "Developing an Effective Teaching Portfolio." *Educational Leadership* 53, 6 (March): 34–37.

Wright, A. 1992. *Pictures for Language Learning.* New York: Cambridge University Press.

Wright, A., et al. 1984. *Games for Language Learning.* 2nd ed. New York: Cambridge University Press.